TREASURE

A Soul Journey with the Invisible

NEW EDITION II (REVISED VERSION)

KAREN WILLIAMS

Library of Congress Control Number: 2017903250
ISBN: Hardcover   978-1-5245-9817-4
                 Softcover   978-1-5245-9816-7
                 eBook   978-1-5245-9815-0

Print information available on the last page.

Rev. date: 04/12/2017

To order additional copies of this book, contact:
Xlibris
800-056-3182
www.Xlibrispublishing.co.uk
Orders@Xlibrispublishing.co.uk
748018

TREASURE

A free Gift
Dream On.
Karen ♡.

DEDICATION

Absolutely nothing in life is achieved in isolation. For this reason not a single part of my odyssey could have been lived out and then written about without the extraordinary love and support of two of the most exceptional human beings I have ever known. With incalculable love and gratitude
to:

my late beloved father

TOM WILLIAMS
(1925 – 2015)

and my beloved mother

ZOYA MENSHIKOVA WILLIAMS.

Also, the presence of some more than incredibly special people was indispensable in order for this odyssey to have ever happened in the first place. Fate brought them into my life, and each has shown me his/her greatness.

FOR
PAULO COELHO
WHO DARED TO DREAM

ALEJANDRO JODOROWSKY
my pilgrim brother and
Warrior of Light

my soul mate and treasure J
this is your legacy too

my Spanish prince Alberto

my late extraordinary soul sister
Vicky Urtecho Quezada

my magnificent, life-loving soul sister
Sila Escribano

and my 'Espana Magica'.

IN LOVING MEMORY
of the late

SIR LAURENS VAN DER POST

who inspired me to believe in my inner light,
and so dare to go it alone within the inner depths of my being.

ACKNOWLEDGEMENTS

WHERE to begin with my thanks to so many people who were vital to the success of my journey and also to its completion?

My father and mother have been the most important contributors to making my struggle possible. It has been 'on their extraordinary shoulders' where I have stood in my quest to reach spiritual light. They may not have understood me at times, or my 'peculiar' mission, but they gave me unconditional love throughout my long years of journeying. As parents, they also set me examples of courage, integrity, persistence, fidelity, compassion and so much more. I owe them both everything. Thank- you Daddy, Thank-you Mama.

My soul mate J has been fundamental to everything that happened on the English part of my journey. In fact, without him, this last part of the journey wouldn't have been possible. And so, dearest, beloved J, that is why this book is your legacy too. You really are one of the greatest souls I have everknown - more than you can imagine. I love you dearly.

My brother Sacha has also been an important person for me. Without him, and what we shared in our childhoods, I certainly wouldn't be who I am today. Thank you Sacha. You taught me, and your son to be daring - a better brother doesn't exist..

My sister-in-law Carolyn is a joy, and a bright shining light of a sister. Thank God you are so grounded Carolyn. I need that from you, and also the love you bring to our family.

My beloved nephew Harvey is an inspiration to me. He constantly surprises me with his maturity, and spiritual nature. He seems to have inherited the Williams' desire to create and explore, and I am in awe of his achievements thus far in his life.

To my friends. Thank-you Sila. You truly are my spiritual sister. You have always opened your heart to me. You have never judged me, and I know that in this life we are only meeting again because IT WAS WRITTEN that we should - before the beginning of time.

Thank-you Angela for being my 'warrior' sister, pulling me out of darkness so that we can share our spirits with each other - our inner child that never died as we embraced adulthood. You are irreplaceable.

Thank-you Graham for being a second brother to me, and for sharing all our deepest knowings together. You are a hero to me. Thank-you Vicky. I know you are no longer here on Earth, darling sister, but your example of courage and love lives with me forever.

My eternal gratitude to James, Mayka and Susanna. We met not by chance, and the connection between us made the first part of this odyssey possible. The word Thank you is simply not enough dear hearts.

Thanks to Connie, Imogen, Shirley, Dorothy, Carol, Marisela, and Marianna. You gave me love, when I needed it the most, and were central to my story.

Many thanks to my publishing house Xlibris, and particularly my assistant Jade Allen. Jade, you have been kind, attentive, and always willing to listen.

Finally, thank-you God, and anyone I have forgotten, and also all the anonymous people who showed me kindness and humanity as I stumbled along my path. Those smiles, gifts of money, food, compassion and, care made all the difference. They lifted me from despair to hope time and time again. The kindness of strangers can never be underestimated. - it's what makes our world go around.

CONTENTS

BOOK ONE: THE AWAKENING

BOOK TWO: THE QUEST

PART I: SHADOWLANDS (REDEMPTION ROAD)

PART II: 'COMING HOME'

PART III: THE SUMMIT

BOOK THREE: THE INITIATION (LABOUR PAINS)

POSTSCRIPT

AUTHOR'S NOTE

Dear Friend,

WHY should anyone contemplate reading a book by a completely unknown author? Why may you be drawn to reading THIS BOOK right now? In my own case I know that it is usually because my heart is searching for answers to the deepest questions buried within my soul. Essentially, I am looking for hope - and perhaps you are too.

The hope I am talking about is that which springs from our highest selves — our Spirits — and TREASURE is an account of my own 'audacity to hope'. This book is the true story of how Paulo Coelho's extraordinary fable THE ALCHEMIST was its author's unconscious psychic prediction of my personal spiritual odyssey. In other words:

THE ALCHEMIST HAPPENED TO ME IN REAL LIFE
long before I had ever heard of Coelho's work.

"How can that be so" I hear you mutter incredulously? Frankly, I realise that for many readers this may seem ridiculous - or even an utterly ludicrous thing to say. Nevertheless, as you read through TREASURE the truth of this claim will gradually reveal itself.

On August 10 2016 this year the universe suddenly gifted me a final, totally unexpected vindication of my claim, and like most real 'treasure' that seemingly comes into our lives as if by magic, I didn't go looking for it. It simply MANIFESTED for me at the right time, and in the right place. Whilst browsing on YouTube that August evening I came across a small section of an interview published there on September 7, 2014 in which Paulo Coelho was talking to Oprah Winfrey for her wonderful programme Soul Sunday.

In words infused with awe and humility Paulo said the following:
".............BUT OPRAH, YOU WANT TO KNOW, DID I WRITE THE

ALCHEMIST? (Pause) I'M NOT SURE (pause) I'M SURE THAT I WAS A GOOD INSTRUMENT...........''

Another great writer, the late Dr Wayne W. Dyer confessed to being intimately acquainted with this phenomenon, and wrote about it in his 2014 autobiography I CAN SEE CLEARLY NOW. In describing his experience of penning his fable **Gifts from Eykis,** Dr Dyer said: "Today I can see clearly that this was my introduction to the idea that all writing is really channelled from the world of the invisible. .... I know for sure that the creative process is something that I get from a higher realm."

However, above and beyond any of this - extraordinary as it is - my real-life spiritual quest is far more than 'just' the PHSYCIAL MANIFESTATION in our world of a hugely famous fable. It is actually about WHO WE ALL ARE AS A HUMAN RACE - as seen through the prism of my seemingly very unlikely, supernatural odyssey.

So, what hope can I offer you, dear friend, as you wonder whether or not to read my story? Well, this new 21st Century has brought our entire human species to a cosmic turning point in our evolution, and we are all in desperate need of some kind of road map for the future. My AUDACIITY to live out something highly intangible and seemingly crazy now means that I can provide that map for you.

"OK, that's fine" you may be thinking, "but WHERE is the hope you're promising when we are currently dealing with so much darkness in our midst – chiefly from the phenomena of horrific actions taken by lone-wolf terrorists, delusional psychotics, and the barbarous acts of Islamic State or Daesh?" Improbable as it may seem, 'my map' can provide answers as to why all of this horror is emerging at this moment in our human story, and how we can see it with new understanding and greater wisdom – both of which CAN and MUST inform and guide the responses we make to it.

TREASURE is an account of my search for my individual soul, and the sacred flame of my spirit within me. That search allowed me to face my individual darkness, and paradoxically in so doing I discovered that it wasn't as INDIVIDUAL as I had thought. And because of this, I began to see that even acts of utterly barbaric cruelty could be understood.

There is no doubt that as I sit writing to you dear friend in August 2016, with our whole human family living through very troubling and fast-changing times, understanding and awareness are both paramount. It is ever more urgent, and incumbent on all of us to unravel the human condition of our species:

THE WONDERFUL LIGHT AND TERRIBLE DARKNESS INSIDE EACH AND EVERY ONE OF US.

As I have just indicated, this book TREASURE has been my personal struggle to confront this reality inside myself.

Because what follows is a true story I have changed a few of the names of people and places to protect their privacy. I have also altered the content of some real-life events, again in order to ensure this privacy. The following places and individuals however retain their original identities.

London, The Royal Dorchester Hotel London, Madrid, Paris, the glass pyramids of the Louvre Museum, Place de la Republique, Hotel de Nemours, Musee d'Orsay and the Tuileries gardens in Paris, Granada, La Iglesia Santo Tomas de VillaNueva, Cafeteria Siglo 21, Malaga, Calle Puerta del Mar, Avenida de la Aurora, Santiago de Compostela, and The Hague.

Karen, Mayka, Susana, Marika, Harriet, Salvador, J, Sophie, Cecilia, Marta, Penny, Sila, Hansje, Connie, Rosa, Marisela, Marie, Fatima, Brian Weiss M.D, Bernie Siegel M.D, Paulo Coelho and Alejandro Jodorowsky.

I hope that my long journey will enable you to recognise yourself, and the turbulent times in which we are living, and at the same time provide you with real answers as to what it truly means to be a spirit occupying a human body on Planet Earth in the 21ˢᵗ Century.

Despite everything I have had to confront and endure on my quest over a period of nineteen years, I remain an eternal optimist, truly believing that Mankind really does possess the capacity to overcome its inner darkness and find its own inner Light — a light we can all start to consciously live from. So, thank you, dear friend if you have decided to read on; with I'm sure hope in your heart for self-discovery, insight and answers which will create a better future for us all.

With eternal gratitude and love,
Karen. Xxxxxxx

PAULO COELHO AND KAREN WILLIAMS

Santiago de Compostela, Spain. 2008.

**Your soul is a womb sheltering your greatest dreams; your destiny longing to be born.
ANON.**

All human beings are also dream beings.
Dreaming ties all mankind together.

Jack Kerouac

PREFACE TO NEW EDITION II (REVISED VERSION) BORN TO DREAM

Dream manfully and nobly, and thy dreams shall
be prophets.

Edward G. Bulwer-Lytton

TREASURE – **what an alluring and magical word!** Can there be anyone in the world, whether young or old, who hasn't at one time or another dreamt of finding just that? Treasure certainly isn't a word which any writer would think of using gratuitously for the title of a book, and so if I have done this with my own work, dear friend, it must be for a very special reason.

Contained within it is the promise of being able to offer you either your own personal treasure, or a glimpse of some kind of treasure which 'shines' for all of us. Surprisingly, the latter is exactly what I am able to deliver in this real-life testimony: a UNIVERSAL TREASURE which belongs to each and every one of us.

It is the eternal light of SPIRIT within every human soul.

THE INVISIBLE SPARK OF THE DIVINE.

I discovered that Divine spark only because I was willing to follow my personal destiny, and in so doing fulfil the dream I was BORN TO DREAM here on planet Earth.

LIFE IS A JOURNEY – A CLICHE OF COURSE BUT TRUE.

Life is a journey and we its 'pilgrims' carrying our souls with all their longings, frustrations, desires, and pain in search of that universal treasure I have just mentioned.

This book is an account of my own personal quest for this 'spiritual gold', and astonishingly mysterious forces of fate seemed to know EXACTLY WHAT FORM THAT JOURNEY WOULD TAKE. As I have just recounted in my Author's Note, as bizarre as it may sound, those forces decided to 'arrange' for a famous 'fictional' fable to happen to me in real life. That fable is known to millions of readers as:

THE ALCHEMIST BY PAULO COELHO.*

Now, I know that it has never been said before in print but, as I hinted in my Author's Note, and as Paulo Coelho himself speculated in his interview with Oprah Winfrey in 2014, the truth is that his iconic best-seller THE ALCHEMIST is *not strictly-speaking completely a work of fiction.* Within the pages of TREASURE I shall be able to reveal something truly miraculous, and give many new answers — or perhaps old 'forgotten' answers - to questions regarding the meaning and purpose of the 'apparently' invisible aspect of our lives we call SPIRIT. However, nothing was uncovered without an enormous amount of blood, sweat and tears.

Like most journeys worth making, the content of my odyssey was far from easy, and to believe it you will need to trust me. You will also need an enormous amount of patience and perseverance as well as a passionate desire to know. But, the reward for your open-mindedness and commitment will be REAL TREASURE — THE ONLY KIND THAT TRULY MATTERS. Now, in the tradition of all great dreams and adventures, let us begin at the beginning!

ONCE UPON A TIME.................As children, when those magical words are spoken to us, we begin to REMEMBER and unknowingly reconnect with the truth about ourselves deep within our souls. This truth is that here on Earth EACH OF US IS A DREAM; A DREAM WAITING TO BECOME A REALITY.

(For my summary of Coelho's The Alchemist, go to the appendix at the end of this book.)

Every child has some kind of unconscious sense of this mystery buried within his/her own heart. The fact is that, whether we know it or not, none of us can live without our own highly individual Once Upon a Time.

ONCE UPON A TIME in 1987 a little-known Brazilian writer and dreamer called Paulo Coelho decided to honour his inner child, and so began to write his own personal fairy tale. It became the fable known to millions as THE ALCHEMIST. Paulo based his story on an ancient allegorical tale he had read in the centuries-old book The Arabian Nights.* Decades earlier, the famous Argentine writer Jorge Luis Borges, whom Coelho had read avidly as a young man, also found inspiration in the same story and created his own version called A TALE OF TWO DREAMERS.

THE ALCHEMIST made its first appearance in Brazil in June 1988, and after a somewhat unsuccessful start, its sales began to 'take off' in a completely unexpected and spectacular way. Within a few years its author suddenly found himself catapulted to international literary stardom and worldwide acclaim. As those initial years turned into decades, the book's success proved to be no mere fad or fluke, and Paulo Coelho became the author of one of the most iconic works of the late twentieth and early twenty first centuries.

Millions of people around the world are devoted and unconditional fans of the fable, and one unintended consequence of that overwhelming love for the story is that its author has unwittingly been cast in the role of a new-age 'guru' and spiritual sage. However, after twenty nine years in print, and with more than 65 million copies of THE ALCHEMIST sold - giving it an almost mythical status in world literature - over a period of nineteen long years I discovered that no one, and I suspect NOT EVEN PAULO COELHO HIMSELF, could understand or explain the extraordinary success and appeal of his book.

In an interview published in the Metro Newspaper on April 19, 2012 Paulo Coelho was posed a familiar question; one which he has repeatedly been asked in countless interviews over the years: **"Why has The Alchemist done so well?"** With total sincerity and honesty, he gave the following answer:

(This tale is: The Ruined Man Who Became Rich Again Through a Dream)

> **"That's the one-million-dollar question.**
> **I honestly don't know.**
> **It's a metaphor for my own life and by writing about**
> **it I touched a nerve with other people............"**

From the outset I want to say that I consider THE ALCHEMIST to be a true work of genius — a story-telling gem from start to finish. Nevertheless, is there really such an enigma and mystery associated with the popularity of the book? And what exactly was the 'nerve' Paulo Coelho touched in so very many people?

Just like the book's author, and along with the majority of all the readers of the fable, over a period of many years I discovered that the story was also a metaphor for my own life. But, beyond this reality, I also discovered SOMETHING FAR, FAR DEEPER. That illusive *something* turned out to be the answer to the apparent enigma of the book's astonishing success, and it can be summed up in three very short words:

THE BIG DREAM.

So, whether or not you are one of the millions of people who has read Paulo Coelho's book, in these pages you will find the story of our times, and engage in your very own *Soul Journey with his fable* *THE ALCHEMIST.*

***

WHAT EXACTLY IS THE BIG DREAM?

Through my personal odyssey I discovered that it is a transcendental goal for which Mankind is constantly striving. The MEANS by which we have all been attempting to achieve that goal is:

an archetypal pattern contained within
THE ALCHEMIST,
and also the original fable on which it is based.

Paulo Coelho knew that what I have called THE BIG DREAM was Divine Love — the light of our spirits, or that eternal flame of Love within our souls — but had no conscious or explicit awareness of the hidden archetype inside his own work. It is that HIDDEN process which I uncovered over nineteen long years.

Even though every single person on Planet Earth is the physical manifestation of a very specific dream, each one carrying its own highly individual stamp of personal ownership, my odyssey taught me that no matter how different those dreams may seem, they are all intimately connected. They are in fact the billions of pieces of THE BIG DREAM inside the collective soul of the human race.

Paulo named this soul **The Soul of the World**, and one of the central themes of his fable is our individual 'membership' of this unified whole. The apparent 'magic' of THE ALCHEMIST is that it triggers in each of its readers a deep 'memory' of our shared BIG DREAM, and unconsciously we sense that the story is a core part of both our individual and collective spiritual DNA.

IT IS THIS SPIRITUAL 'MEMORY' OF OUR SELVES WHICH
IS THE 'NERVE' PAULO MENTIONS IN HIS INTERVIEW.

In August 2009, when I sat down to write my book TREASURE I knew nothing of Jorge Luis Borges' version of the original Persian allegory from The Arabian Nights, but was more than intimately acquainted with THE ALCHEMIST. I was about to claim that Paulo Coelho's story wasn't a so-called inspired work of fiction, as everyone supposed, but was actually A PSYCHIC PREDICTION OF MY OWN SPIRITUAL QUEST.

My book **TREASURE: A Soul Journey with The Invisible**
would therefore be the account of this extraordinary,
supernatural odyssey, and how it came about.

If you are one of the many people who has read Paulo Coelho's story dear friend, you may be struggling to take my claim seriously, despite what I have told you earlier. Am I part of a small, new-age lunatic fringe convinced of the truth of its own self-deluded ideas? Well, I can categorically assure you that I am not. I know that for our rational minds my claim most certainly seems more than a little 'borderline crazy'. However, for the human soul an altogether different 'irrational' reality exists.

It is that reality — OUR DREAMING SELVES - which is the mystery and magic running throughout the fabric of our existences. Subconsciously it motivates all of our actions, and in so doing good old logic then becomes something which we can no longer rely on in order to understand the true meaning of our own individual lives and life itself.

If you think that I say any of this lightly, dear friend, then I would ask you to think again. By choosing to journey in search of my own inner dream and truth, one unforeseen consequence of that choice was that over many years my mind 'tortured' me with constant and sometimes agonizing self-doubt. During those long and sometimes deeply confusing years, believing or rather KNOWING that a worldwide best-selling book had been a prediction of my own life story wasn't something I ever allowed myself to accept without an enormous amount of soul searching.

Nevertheless, my passion to dive into my DREAMING SELF, and be willing to trust the irrational, meant that the supernatural and seemingly impossible constantly *popped up* to guide me as I went on a quest in search of my portion of humanity's BIG DREAM hidden inside me.

LIFE IMITATING ART

**In The Alchemist its author weaves a mysterious
dance between his hero Santiago, an Andalusian
shepherd boy, and the invisible realm
of**

THE SOUL OF THE WORLD.

Through the appearance of 'omens' or signs Santiago is given access to this universal space both inside and outside Mankind, where all of humanity's past, present and future coexist.

After nineteen years of questing, I have now come to realise that when Paulo began to write his iconic fable, just like his hero Santiago, his own subconscious mind had also inadvertently accessed our collective **Soul of the World.** Some people call this process CHANNELLING, and I know from my own life experience that each and every one of us 'channels' from this universal reality to which we are all connected – but usually completely unconsciously,

When referring to this process I prefer Paulo Coelho's use of the word *'immersion'* to describe our unexpected contacts with **The Soul of the World.** In THE ALCHEMIST he speaks of it as follows:

"........intuition is really a sudden immersion of the soul into the universal current of life .... and we are able to know everything, because it's all written there."

I believe that this is exactly what took place inside Paulo Coelho's mind. Without any conscious awareness on his part, Paulo experienced a *sudden immersion* of his soul into the universal current of life, and his imagination then PREDICTED or FORESAW places and events which would later begin to manifest in my own life. This phenomenon whereby future real-life events are uncannily predicted by a work of fiction is commonly known as 'LIFE IMITATING ART' and THE ALCHEMIST is by no means the first case in the history of world literature where you will find this happening,

By way of a slight, but very important digression, and also to illustrate this point, I can turn to one of the most famous instances of this process of IMITATION. It was the publication of a novel called TITAN in 1898. Its author Morgan Robertson created a fictional story about a huge ship named TITAN which was the largest of its kind afloat at the time. In the novel TITAN sinks one fateful night in April on a voyage in the North Atlantic when it tragically hits an iceberg.

Fourteen years after Robertson penned his fictional story, the world received the shocking news in April 1912 that the newly-built ship THE TITANIC, the largest of its kind at that time, had just met the same fate as the imaginary ship in his book. Now, the question is how could the writer possibly have known with such accuracy and precision what lay ahead in the future? Of course the only credible answer is that he experienced a 'sudden immersion' of his own intuition into our collective **Soul of the World.**

There are many more examples such as this where writers seem to have unknowingly 'foreseen' future events, and all point to one inevitable conclusion: THERE ARE ABSOLUTELY NO 'ACCIDENTS' IN LIFE. The universal intelligence which is at the heart of our collective soul seems to have a supremely metaphysical plan for all of our lives.

Back in 1987, through this mysterious process of channelling, its plan had been to use Paulo Coelho as a MESSENGER – or in his own words, as AN INSTRUMENT. But, because that message was quintessentially spiritual and transcendental, it needed more than just a fable which would sell millions of copies for its dissemination and unravelling. And, so it was that seven years after the publication of THE ALCHEMIST, I too found myself 'channelling' from the very same source as Paulo Coelho. Unconscious forces of fate would mean that I began to experience 'immersions' into the very same **Soul of the World,** and the key elements of The Alchemist would unknowingly become the central events of my life.

In a sense, my dreaming spirit was quite unwittingly being 'handed' the baton in a cosmic relay as I found myself chosen to be the NEXT OF LIFE'S COSMIC MESSENGERS in a truly extraordinary real-life 'miracle'. However, as I pushed forward on my seemingly never-ending quest, I also discovered that I wasn't someone special. Although the **Soul of the World** is highly specific in its choice of what each of us is 'selected' to do in our present incarnations here on planet Earth, the truth is that:

IN THIS LIFE WE ARE ALL 'COSMIC MESSENGERS' FOR
EACH OTHER.

***

TREASURE - New Edition II (Revised Version) is now the fifth incarnation of my story in print, and that is only because this journey was so unpredictable, unfathomable and mysterious.

There were quite literally several moments during my nineteen year quest when I erroneously concluded that everything was over.

One final epiphany seemed to come when I brought out TREASURE as an e-Book with the publisher Author House in June 2013. But no, life is never so simple, and in my case most certainly wasn't. Thus it was that my odyssey continued for many months after that publication, and it was only in June 2014 that I was finally able to complete this extraordinary supernatural quest.

I published my account of it as an e-Book in December 2014 with Honey Bee Books on Amazon Kindle. At that time it had the original title I had chosen for my book: TREASURE: A Soul Journey with *The Alchemist,* and I further amended the original title to: NEW EDITION II. This version was organized into two main sections I called BOOK ONE and BOOK TWO, however for this final definitive publication of TREASURE: NEW EDITION II (Revised Version) I have decided to turn Section III of BOOK TWO into BOOK THREE. I do this specifically in order to give greater clarity to the recounting of my quest.

The first two books in TREASURE can in fact be treated as just that — two separate pieces of writing. This means that they can be read individually and it would even be possible to start my odyssey at BOOK TWO, without losing out on the adventure. However, I recommend that TREASURE be read chronologically from start to finish in order to understand and also to appreciate its full meaning.

In this final version of my work, with the new subtitle: A Soul Journey with the Invisible, I have written some new material, and made several changes to the text in order to improve the quality of the reading experience. In addition I have eliminated some quotations from Paulo Coelho's THE ALCHEMIST and added new ones from other sources. I have also replaced many illustrations with new ones, and omitted some which seemed to clutter the e-Book published in December 2014.

I have also added a prologue to the beginning of BOOK TWO, and divided this book into two parts, but otherwise the content of the TREASURE you have here is essentially almost the same as that of the 2014 New Edition II on Amazon.

***

BOOK ONE of this quest contains most of the premonitory elements of Paulo's fable, and is an account of how THE ALCHEMIST happened to me as a spiritual initiation or awakening over a short period of time. BOOK TWO is the story of how, after that 'cosmic initiation', I journeyed for another sixteen years, living out the central archetypal pattern of Paulo's fable in an attempt to decipher the book's meaning, and ultimately experience the REBIRTH OF MY SOUL.

However, just as I thought my quest had ended, I was surprised by another 28 months of unexpected 'tests and trials'. These proved to be a SECOND BIRTH of my soul, and a brand new rite of initiation for me at the very end of my odyssey. The initiation was a final rite of passage into the next phase of my life, and it is this section of my quest I have decided to call BOOK THREE.

I have deliberately placed the account of those last 28 months into BOOK THREE in order distinguish between two separate processes I have just alluded to:

those of SOUL REBIRTH and SOUL BIRTH.

BOOK ONE AND TWO are the accounts of my SOUL REBIRTH, and BOOK THREE the account of *a second, but slightly different birthing of my soul.* Confusing as this may appear at the moment, all will become clear to you, dear friend, as you read through this book.

These last unexpected months of my journey were something I had never anticipated, and meant that my odyssey actually lasted nineteen years in all. They revealed a quite astonishing reality for me — one which had been 'following' me throughout my quest, but which I had never been able to see with any clarity. That REALITY was that there is an intimate cosmic connection between THE ALCHEMIST AND THE ARCHAIC SYSTEM OF DIVINATION KNOWN AS THE TAROT.

The Tarot had quite spontaneously appeared to me very early on in my journeying, and I had superficially made a connection between it and my odyssey. But, despite this fact, the truth was that from the very start of my epic search my obsessive focus had always been the deciphering of the meaning of THE ALCHEMIST, and this meant that subconsciously I had set aside any serious exploration of The Tarot. So it was that I had to wait seventeen long years, and right up until the very end of my quest, before the metaphysical connection between Paulo's fable and the Tarot was revealed to me in all its glory.

Because of this, as an act of hindsight, I have placed many of the 22 major Tarot Arcanas in strategic positions throughout the text. As I journeyed over nineteen long years, I had very little idea that they were there, accompanying me all along. They followed me, sometimes visibly and sometimes invisibly, as year after year I ploughed forward on a path I COULD BARELY UNDERSTAND OR DEFINE. And so it is fitting that they now appear inside this book — bearing witness to the truly 'cosmic' nature of my endeavour.

THE FIRST MAJOR ARCANA OF THE TAROT

What you will find in the pages of TREASURE, dear friend, is a quite extraordinary adventure: the passionate and obsessive search of one woman for spiritual meaning and truth - and that is no small enterprise for any one person to undertake in this life.

It meant that I needed to be a complete and utter FOOL to embark on and finally finish this odyssey. But, then again, my foolishness was not that of the so-called 'normal' kind. The Danish philosopher Soren Kierkegaard encapsulates 'normal' foolishness in this quotation:

There are two ways to be fooled. One is to believe WHAT ISN'T TRUE; the other is to refuse to believe WHAT IS TRUE.

These, my friend, are the two traps of our ordinary, thinking ego-minds. However, I have just hinted at another type of foolishness in this preface by mentioning The Tarot, and its 22 major Arcanas – the first of which is THE FOOL ARCANA. This odyssey was my personal *'act of foolishness'* or perhaps even *'madness'* as I embraced THE FOOLISHNESS OF THE SPIRIT.

The challenge of my account is a sort of metaphorical gauntlet I throw down before you, dear friend. In that challenge I ask you to leave behind the apparent 'certainties' of the ego-mind, and believe what IT would normally REFUSE TO BELIEVE. In other words, I am appealing directly to your irrational dreaming spirit. Through the pages of TREASURE I promise that I will not lead you anywhere you cannot go, and besides, the reality is that if you have chosen to read this book, it is only because a supremely divine timing has led you here.

In the end, the universe, or whatever name belongs to that force which created us, knows exactly who we really are, and that is something so very simple and yet simultaneously so deeply complicated. Yes, with our pilgrim souls each and every one of us is a FOOL FOR LOVE – DIVINE LOVE. So, thanks for reading this far, and welcome aboard, dear friend for: A Soul Journey with The Invisible.

BOOK ONE:
THE AWAKENING

(Once Upon a Time in Andalusia)

**When you want something,
all the universe conspires
in helping you to achieve it.**

**The Alchemist:
Paulo Coelho**

Do not follow where

the path may lead,

go instead where

there is no path

and leave a trail.

Ralph Waldo Emerson.

1

THE RUIN: ANDALUSIA – SPAIN

**The process of life should be the birth of a soul.
This is the highest alchemy, and this justifies our
presence on Earth. This is our calling and our virtue.**

HENRI FREDERIC AMIEL.

WHERE does a treasure hunt begin? Well, mine began in my parents' house on a hill in Andalusia, southern Spain, overlooking the Mediterranean Sea. 'Coincidentally' seven years earlier a 'fictional' treasure hunt had also started amongst these very same hills of Andalusia – ONLY I DIDN'T KNOW IT.

This is the first of countless amazing coincidences you will discover in my story, and if you ask me on the deepest of levels how they actually happen, I honestly can't say. Bernie Siegel MD in his book Love, Medicine and Miracles tells of how he was once handed a card after one of his talks and on it was written, 'Coincidence is God's way of remaining anonymous'. After nineteen long years of journeying, I don't believe this to be true, I KNOW IT IS TRUE, and I know it only because my journey became possible when I started to believe that these kinds of coincidences contained real messages from AN INVISIBLE SPIRITUAL REALM.

**I had come to live in this southern region of Spain
in 1984.**

In the spring of that year I had been fired from my low-grade clerical job in London and was looking for adventure. I was only twenty-six years old and felt that I was far too young to commit myself to a career and what I perceived as the monotony and meaninglessness of ordinary life. Frustrated, unsettled and lonely, I quickly booked myself a cheap flight to the Andalusian city of Malaga. However, I didn't intend to do anything in a normal or apparently conventional way.

Instead, I had a small two-man ridge tent with me, and on my arrival headed off to a campsite on the outskirts of a local seaside town. I was more than ready to begin my 'adventure'. Completely naive and innocent as I was back then, I had no idea that destiny was keeping its beady eye on me, and had decided that within a few days I would meet and begin a romance with a young Belgian man I had seemingly encountered *quite by accident*. Weeks later this culminated in the young man inviting me to live with him in his small apartment in this Spanish coastal resort - again seemingly *quite by accident*. Yes, I had wanted adventure, but never suspected in any way that it would take this form.

Five years later, after visiting me many times in my new Spanish life, my parents decided to sell their house in London and retire to Andalusia. And so it was that they came to buy their villa in the hills. The relationship with my young man ended after two incredibly enriching years, and although I lived alone for several years after the break-up, working in different jobs, and even returned to London for a while, here I was eight-and-a-half years later, at the age of thirty-six, living with my parents amongst the idyllically picturesque olive groves of Andalusia.

***

It was the beginning of 1995 and I had been noticing coincidences, which I referred to as signs, for at least six years. The first time a really remarkable coincidence happened to me was in some ways an extraordinary awakening. The year was 1989 and I had been with my then boyfriend inside the Houses of Parliament in the centre of London. We had stood in front of a life-size statue of the Victorian Prime Minister William Gladstone and were reading the inscription giving Gladstone's dates of birth and death.

In an instant each of us had become transfixed by what we saw. The statesman had been born on my boyfriend's birthday, and had died on mine! At that moment, both of us had felt as if we had been handed some kind of cryptic message from an invisible realm we had always suspected existed. In a sense, this experience in front of the statue marked a major turning point in my life. Somehow, I had been introduced to something *way beyond* the material or physical world in which I lived, and my intuition seemed to know that it was the place where TRUE REALITY LAY.

Over the next few years as well as receiving 'signs', once in a while I would experience a very deep dream, and one such dream in April 1993 changed the direction of my life completely. I never wrote it down, but I do remember that in it I had clearly experienced my soul. On waking I understood that the dream had revealed to me that there were two very separate and distinct Karens in the world. There was my personality, which seemed to dominate my waking hours, and then there was my soul - for me the real Karen - which had appeared so vividly in the dream. Not only that, but I was shocked to see that the dream had revealed to me that during most of my daily life I was operating from my superficial personality, and not from this deepest part of me.

This insight left me feeling as though I was standing at a vital crossroads in my life, and so I vowed that from that day on my mission was to go in search of my soul. Only living from this truest part of me would give my life the meaning I so desperately needed – NOTHING ELSE WOULD DO!

So it was that at the beginning of 1995 I had already been on a sort of quest for nearly two years, and in that time had been surprised to discover a lot of confusion and emotional pain inside me. Normal life had somehow become sabotaged by inner angst which I had never known was deep within me. At the time this both alarmed and shocked me, and made living decidedly difficult and stressful.

Nevertheless, I was young, idealistic and naïve, and assumed that none of this pain I had been experiencing would last for very long. Besides, I reasoned that this was probably the price I needed to pay in order to be engaged in the most important task of my life: THE FINDING OF MY SOUL.

***

The invisible realm I had discovered back in 1989 decided to give me a huge helping hand in my endeavour, and only a month earlier in December 1994 gifted me the deepest dream of my entire life. In the first week of December I innocently and unsuspectingly went to sleep and experienced the most horrific nightmare possible. The word horrific doesn't even come close to what happened. In that dream state I found myself descending into Hell.

When I awoke I had the taste of Hell in my mouth and the smell of it in my nostrils, and I instantly felt suicidal. The taste and smell persisted for some minutes and I immediately knew that this dream hadn't been some kind of psychotic aberration, or just an invention of my overactive imagination. At that moment I sensed that a very real, deep and horrible truth had been communicated to me about my own soul, and Hell was far from being a mere religious invention.

Over the following weeks the consequences of this nightmare were that it left me feeling even worse off than before. Although there were times when I completely forgot about it and felt able to be quite normal, equally there were other moments − and they were many − when the dream returned to me with full force, and I experienced myself plunging into those suicidal feelings all over again. I had thought that the last two years had been painful and confusing, but now everything had become several degrees more so.

It was in this jittery and haunted state that I left my parents' house one morning in early February 1995 and took the bus down the mountain road into the seaside town of Salveira to go to the local bookshop. I was in desperate need of explanations for my emotional angst and turmoil, and it seemed that only a book would provide me with what I needed.

On my arrival at the shop I headed for the basement area, and to the esoteric section which was my usual haunt. I scanned the shelves in front of me at lightning speed, looking for a title which would speak to me in some way. Suddenly, I saw something. The title 'peeking' out from a group of books MOST DEFINETELY DID JUST THAT:

Psicomagia - Una Terapia Panica.

It was the word 'panica' which first caught my attention. Since the December 1994 dream of Hell I was almost constantly in a panic about my emotions and the state of my soul. I wasn't sure if the word 'panica' in the title of the book was figurative or not, but for me the association with my own feelings was instant. The word 'magia' in the title also gripped me, and seemed to reinforce my sense of having seen something very, very special. I slid the book out from its place on the shelf and started to read the inside cover where the biography of the author appeared.

The writer's name was Alejandro Jodorowsky, and he was Chilean, but of Russian parents, hence the surname. He had been a theatre director and was a film director as well. To add to his multifaceted personality, he had also elaborated his own emotional therapy, which he called PSYCHOMAGIC.

The book was about this therapy and contained many case studies of people he had managed to 'cure' of various subconscious malaises through his highly intuitive technique. Psychomagic involved the prescription of a so-called PSYCHOMAGICAL ACT which used the language of symbols to work directly on the subconscious mind of the suffering person. My God! Standing alone in the basement of the bookshop, I felt myself to be in the midst of a Eureka moment. I didn't actually shout out the word 'eureka', but I felt very much like doing just that.

As I read through Alejandro Jodorowsky's biography inside the book, there seemed to be so many strange 'coincidences' between this man and myself. His parents were Russian - my mother was Russian. He had been involved in theatre as a young man - I had done quite a bit of amateur theatricals as a youngster. He had gone into film making – well, here we didn't have this in common. But, good God, his therapy worked directly on the subconscious mind, and all my adult life I had been convinced that this was the Holy Grail of emotional happiness.

Ever since my days of studying psychology at university I had thought of the subconscious as the place where most people's problems lay, and this of course included my own. It was only logical therefore that once these problems were HEALED in some way, the subconscious would then become the inner seat of each person's wellbeing and happiness. The feeling of having discovered something truly and utterly amazing overwhelmed me completely. It seemed that I had quite 'accidentally' stumbled upon a soul mate or kindred spirit in this complete stranger, and little did I know just how true this would prove to be over the coming years.

The other extraordinary aspect of all of this was that I had only scanned the books in this section of the shop superficially. I hadn't in any way gone through a detailed search of pulling out book after book. Uncannily, and almost mysteriously, it was as if I had somehow turned up for a divine appointment in the basement of the shop, and the treasure I had so desperately been hoping for was there just waiting for me to notice it.

And it seemed that only I would have been drawn to the words 'panica' and 'magia': THEY FITTED ME LIKE A GLOVE.

***

MYSTICAL BEGINNINGS

So, who was I, this thirty six year old person who went by the name of Karen Williams?

Well, the adult me's existence up until this life-changing instance in February 1995 had been more than a little unconventional in the eyes of the world. Since leaving university in 1981 I hadn't chosen to establish myself in any kind of profession, or build a career path.

My 'escape' to Andalusia at the age of 26 had been exactly that — an escape — and the subsequent time I had spent in Spain had been a case of eking out a living teaching English to Spanish children in the local town and surrounding area. I had briefly had the 'exalted' position of a lecturer in public speaking and psychology at an American college for the expatriate community, but that had only been a part-time job and hadn't in any way been enough to pay the bills.

The truth was that my apparent lack of drive and direction - something very obvious to everyone I have to say - was due to the fact that I had never been able to fully embrace what most people called 'REAL LIFE' and commit to it whole heartedly. The simple reason for this was because for me 'real life', as I saw and experienced it WAS NOT WHAT I WOULD CALL LIFE AT ALL.

From childhood I had always been an observer of everything around me. At the tender ages of six and seven I had been worried about the population explosion, and couldn't accept the inequalities in our society. I hadn't for example been able to understand why my family lived in quite a big house, and most of my primary school classmates lived in much smaller houses.

Martin Luther King Jr. and Robert Kennedy were both assassinated in the sixties when I was still worrying about all of these issues at the age of ten, and this just seemed to fuel my inherent tendency to observe and look at life from the outside. At that stage in my childhood I didn't have any access to the sophisticated thinking of an adult, and so never knew that I was by nature a contemplative; a person who watches and reflects on life rather than plunging into it. However, this was what I was as a child, and what I continued to be in adulthood.

Fate is truly miraculous because when I finally left school at the age of eighteen, and found myself becoming *almost* an adult, I went to university to study psychology. My mother had wanted to help me, and so had consulted a friend who recommended psychology as a good professional field for women. The idea was that I could mix a professional life with that of bringing up a family. Of course this was back in the 1970s when the world and we were all much more innocent and naive than we are now, and so that meant that when I applied to study psychology, incredible as it may seem now, I didn't really have much of an idea as to what it actually was.

In a pre-digital era, where experiences only used to come through the family or the television set, countless 'worlds' were unknown to many of us back then. Nevertheless, psychology proved to be the perfect introduction to life as a contemplative for here was my initiation into the world of emotions, the unconscious, and models of the human mind.

However, by the second year of my university studies my contemplative self had well and truly taken charge of me, and come to dominate every aspect of my thinking. It had outstripped the

boundaries of modern day psychology, and the result of this was
that I began to discover that I somehow couldn't believe in a lot of
what I was being taught. This wasn't because there was anything
inherently WRONG with psychology, but because I was always on
a far deeper search - hunting for something much more meaningful,
and yes – INVISIBLE.

Now, looking back at that time at university, I can see that the
young student Karen's point of view was invariably mystical, although
I certainly wouldn't have possessed that word in my vocabulary at
the end of the 1970s. I was constantly the outsider, asking my tutors
existential questions, and then finding myself *walking away* from the
theories I was being taught.

And, so it was that eighteen years later, living in another country,
I had made absolutely no further progress as far as entering into life
was concerned, and becoming something or somebody society could

recognise. Although I had experienced a lot of different situations and people in those years, and had observed others and myself very intensely, I was still hunting for the illusive MEANING OF LIFE, and ultimately: that prized connection with my soul.

Whilst tourists frolicked on the nearby beach or bought souvenirs from the countless shops along Salveira's promenade, there I stood, in the basement of the bookshop, heading into middle age – even though I didn't realise it - and traumatised by a dream about Hell which I knew had come from the COSMIC DEPTHS.

This, I knew instinctively, was the type of dream only experienced by a very small minority of people on our planet, and I was still in need of answers and healing. My overwhelming excitement as I held Alejandro's book in my hands told me that perhaps I had finally found what I was looking for. With that tantalizing and intoxicating hope in my heart, I paid for the book and made my way back to my parents' house.

***

Their villa formed part of a cluster of houses situated on a hill.

It was exactly midway up the mountainside, with the seaside town of Salveira on the coast in the downward direction, and the small, quaint Andalusian village of Campana, with the ruins of its old Moorish fortress, at the top of the mountain road. There was quite a lot of 'campo' or countryside around the house consisting of olive trees on dusty hillsides, and terraces which were now abandoned to the elements because tourism had taken over as the major economy.

Less than a minute's walk from the house stood an adjacent hill which was crowned by a beautifully romantic-looking ruin on its summit. The ruin's shape and rough stone walls spoke of an Andalusia that was now fast disappearing, but still a part of the star-studded skies at night and the searing, sometimes blistering heat of the summer days. It was an evocation of the mystery embedded in the earth of this land which over millenia had seen so many conquests and so many civilisations.

When I had the time, one of my favourite things to do was to climb this hill, picking my way through the crumbling terraces which were covered with wild herbs and grasses. On my arrival at the top where the ruin stood, I would sit at the foot of the ruin, leaning against one of the broken walls and stare out at the Mediterranean Sea below. This spot was my sanctuary and the place which CALLED TO ME whenever I wanted to be alone. Strangely, although it was only a three-to-four-minute climb to the top of the hill, and overlooked the cluster of villas where my parents' house stood, no one ever seemed to come here.

This was the magical old Andalusia the romantic mystic in me longed to experience. The ruin was timeless and primal - local stones and rocks from the earth formed the broken walls and were held together with an equally primitive mortar. The surrounding terraced ground gave off the idyllic aromas of oregano, fennel and rosemary which had grown on these hills forever and a day. As the ruin was at the very summit of the hill, the views from here were breathtakingly spectacular.

In front of me, looking due south was the azure Mediterranean Sea stretching to the horizon. On certain days in the winter, when the visibility was good, you could see the faint outline of the African coast - the coast of Morocco. Gazing west, I saw other hills merging with mountain ridges in the distance. The sunsets from here were often of great poetic beauty. To the east were more hills rising up to the local sierra, which curved round and then dropped down into the sea.

And finally, behind me to the north, I could see the traditional white houses of Campana built into the mountainside, and then the peak of the sierra looming above the village. This was the perfect place for me to come to and be my weird, mystical, contemplative self. It was where I could sit all alone and somehow connect with that part of me which I felt was as deep and as old as this abandoned hill with its ruin. Leaning against *'my ruin'*, as I liked to call it, my soul came home, and I could talk to God and pray.

Whoops! I have just mentioned two somewhat 'dangerous' and controversial words: God and pray, so I better clarify my religious or spiritual beliefs before we go any further with this story.

THE RUIN, ANDALUSIA.

ILLUSTRATION BY KAREN WILLIAMS

Over the years, I have developed my own private relationship with God, based on passionate feelings I had as a child. This means that for me He is the creator of all the world's great religious faiths. Just as He gave us different coloured skins and different languages to speak, He also gave us different ways of expressing the transcendent. My particular faith is Christianity, but only because

I was born in England, learned to speak English, and taught this religious faith at school.

It is the spiritual language of my culture, and just like the English language, it is my language of communication. English allows me to communicate with people, and Christianity allows me to communicate with God. Nevertheless, although I declare myself to be a Christian, I also need to say that I can't seem to find a home in any of the Christian denominations I have tried. This is because life has shown me that with my questioning, contemplative nature, I am driven to seek out truth, and so I have always needed real answers to my spiritual hunger - not rules or religious dogma.

Essentially, this has made me a spiritual explorer; born to discover a living, breathing spirituality, and so, despite my very best intentions, whenever I have tried to put myself into an established form of worship my heart has always told me that my purpose lies somewhere else.

And so it was that with this solitary and private relationship with the divine I used to go to *'my ruin'* to pray and to be with God. For me, the omnipotent He, She or It couldn't be corralled into any kind of manmade structure; He simply was the One who had created everybody and everything, and so belonged to all of us - IRRESPECTIVE OF CREED OR CULTURE.

***

'My beloved ruin' was the obvious place to head for with Alejandro Jodorowsky's book when I returned from Salveira's bookshop. For the next three or four days I devoured its pages, mostly reading in the house, and then going up to *'my ruin'* to think about what I had read. The book didn't disappoint me in the least. Alejandro's case studies were absolutely fascinating, and everything he wrote about his 'cures' for the people who came to see him rang completely true for me.

The excitement I felt grew as I realised that his book confirmed exactly what it had promised: that this man had actually found a unique way into the subconscious mind, and had formulated a revolutionary technique for healing traumas embedded there.

Around the fourth day of my reading, I went up to the ruin in the early evening to watch the sun go down in the west. I had only a few more pages to read, and then the book would be finished.

I found that I WAS the book, and the book WAS me!!!!

Destiny seemed to have found me, for I had never read anything in my entire life which spoke to me so very personally, Lonely, 'peculiar' and isolated Karen, who had stood on the side-lines for years 'watching' other people live life had suddenly discovered her path and purpose. Finally, I was being shown that I was not completely and utterly alone in this world, and I was already convinced that I would have to see Alejandro for a healing – THE HEALING OF MY SOUL. After so long in an emotional and spiritual wilderness, there are simply no words to describe the existential relief I felt.

With these amazing thoughts running around in my mind, I left *'my ruin'* and clambered down the terraces to return to my parents' house. Once inside, I joined them for dinner, then watched a little T.V. and finally went to bed rather earlier than usual. And yes, the universe seemed to have set its *invisible sights* on me, because that night I was visited by yet another one of its truly incredible COSMIC DREAMS!

**Life begins as the quest of the child for the man
and ends as a journey by the man
to rediscover the child.**

Laurens Van der Post

2

TARIFA AND TANGIERS: THE JOURNEY BEGINS

WHEN I woke up the next morning I wrote it down. I had dreamt that I was a woman who had just given birth to a baby girl.

In the dream I was BOTH the mother AND the baby.

The mother — ME — had the new-born baby — ME - in her arms, and was just about to kiss the infant on the cheek, when she felt repulsed by what she saw. The baby's cheek and face were covered with the blood from her placenta. The mother found herself completely incapable of giving her own child a loving, unconditional kiss because this act would have meant making contact with the putrid, drying blood. Suddenly, a voice from above spoke to the woman:

**"Babies are not all sweetness and light.
They are also this blood."**

As I sat in bed writing the details of the dream down, something inside me galvanized. I knew instantly that this was yet another dream from a much deeper realm than our ordinary everyday dreaming. I also had enough insight and intelligence to be able to understand its meaning — even if only superficially. For me, the baby was clearly a symbol of life, and the voice was telling me that life in general was not 'ALL SWEETNESS AND LIGHT.' There seemed to be a very real negative or downside to everything, and I needed to be willing to embrace the totality of both the good and the bad.

Momentary relief flooded my heart. I felt really pleased to have had this deep dream with an apparently 'new message' for me, and one which it seemed I was able to decipher. It instantly created some distance between me and the terrible nightmare of Hell I had experienced only three months earlier. I was also glad that there had been a baby in the dream. This fact alone made me sense that perhaps my soul wasn't condemned after all, and that there was the possibility of new life coming my way.

That day I quickly finished Alejandro's book and now knew with total certainty that I wanted to see him in order to undergo the healing he could give me. I had found my own personal Holy Grail:

AND NOTHING, BUT NOTHING COULD
STOP ME FROM REACHING IT!!!

***

Nevertheless, there was just one slight problem my emotions hadn't factored in - Alejandro lived in Paris and I was here in southern Spain. Not only that, but I had very little money because I had stopped teaching English for a while, and had no savings worth mentioning. How on earth was I going to get to Paris, given that my whole being seemed to be pushing me to be there within a matter of a few days?

Such was my all-consuming zeal for Alejandro's therapy that I even told my parents that I had just read the most amazing book, and felt I needed to see the author in Paris to undergo his therapy. They were both stoically patient as they listened to me, and my father even went so far as to agree to read the book himself. However, after a week of waiting for his verdict, I was disappointed when he proclaimed that he wasn't particularly impressed by what he had read. As far as he was concerned, there didn't seem to be anything particularly remarkable about Mr Jodorowsky's work.

Despite this setback, February began to pass and my conviction that I simply had to travel to Paris became my one and only focus. I didn't speak about it to anyone, but this morphed into the *be all and end all* of my entire existence! Now, dear friend, you may be starting to ask yourself what on earth Paris has to do with the story of The

Alchemist? Didn't that fictional shepherd boy in Paulo Coelho's fable go to Egypt? The simple answer to this is:

EVERYTHING.

The Alchemist is a symbolic book,
but also
A PREMONITORY TALE:
a prediction of a real-life future.

As I hinted in the preface to TREASURE, the unknown premonitory aspect of Paulo Coelho's story is in all the strange, apparent 'coincidences' between what happened to his hero, the shepherd boy Santiago, and the real-life me – Karen.

Paulo tells how young Santiago dreamed of finding treasure near the Pyramids of Egypt. At the time the shepherd was living in Andalusia, southern Spain and his dream came to him one night for a second time whilst he slept in an old ruined church. Here I was, also living in Andalusia in southern Spain, and experiencing a powerful dream after having come down from *'my ruin'* in order to sleep in my bed. And, although I wasn't planning to go to Egypt as Santiago had in The Alchemist, I was dreaming of going to somewhere which has exactly THE SAME SYMBOLIC MEANING as Egypt in Paulo Coelho's book.

Unknown to me in 1995 Paris was, and still remains along with many other places around the world, a modern symbolic equivalent of Egypt. How so, you may be wondering? Well, the invisible realm, ever specific in its use of SIGNS, did more than just CHOOSE Paris out of many possible destinations for me. On a metaphysical level, this city was the one and only contender for what I was about to do because, surprise, surprise:

it is home to its very own pyramids.
YES PARIS JUST LIKE EGYPT HAS PYRAMIDS!!!

One of the most emblematic structures of modern Paris is the giant pyramid which stands in the courtyard of the Louvre Museum, surrounded by three smaller pyramids. It was completed in 1989 and serves as the entrance to the museum. Not only are there pyramids in Paris, but significantly, THEY ARE MADE OF GLASS. This is no 'accident' for it allows light to pass straight through into their interiors and also to pass out again into the outside world when it is reflected off any objects or surfaces inside.

The transmission and transparency to
LIGHT
is a central metaphor describing the true symbolic meaning
of these Parisian pyramids.

As if this were not enough, Paris is also known around the world as the CITY OF LIGHT. The name was given to it in the nineteenth century because of its reputation as a centre of culture and learning and also because it was the first city in Europe in 1828 to use gas lights to illuminate part of its centre.

In Paulo Coelho's The Alchemist, the shepherd Santiago travelled to the Pyramids of Egypt in search of an enigmatic treasure, and because the fable is an allegory, it never actually explains to the reader what this treasure is. Instead it relies on the language of symbols and metaphor to weave its magic. Nevertheless, allegory or fable, what the story is really all about is Santiago's search for the treasure of HIS OWN INNER LIGHT:

THE LIGHT OF HIS SPIRIT WITHIN HIS SOUL.

Seven years after the publication of The Alchemist, here I was, hoping to leave Andalusia to unconsciously do the very same thing, but finding that ancient Egypt had now moved to the centre of Paris!

***

At the end of February 1995, - because these were the days before mobile phones and the internet — in my semi-rural, backwater existence in southern Spain I had never heard of a book called The Alchemist, and nor for that matter any glass pyramids in Paris. But despite all of this, as the end of the month approached I did know one thing for certain and it was that, money or no money, I had already made the firm decision to see Alejandro Jodorowsky.

Inevitably, this would mean leaving my beloved Andalusia for a journey into an unknown and unknowable future. Would I return to this magical place? Would Alejandro prescribe me a cathartic psychomagical act which would heal my soul, and then lead me into a brand new life? The truth was that I had absolutely no idea. Although I continually posed myself these unanswerable questions, no answers came, either in the form of dreams or sudden, unexpected flashes of insight. All I knew was that something deep within me had ignited a passion I simply couldn't leave alone.

Despite all of this, I didn't find myself completely without guidance. My intuition quickly came to my rescue, and gave me a clear sense that somehow I would be embarking on a new phase of my life, and a thought suddenly popped into my head that here I was on the edge of the Mediterranean, within hours of the great continent of Africa, and I had never once made an attempt to set foot on that mysterious land.

It felt almost sacrilegious on my part to leave Andalusia and not make this journey as a sort of salutation and recognition that this ancient and enormous continent was only a few hours away by bus and boat. And so, that is exactly what I did. At the beginning of March I walked into a travel agency in town and booked myself on a day trip to Tangiers on the North African coast; the nearest African destination to Spain.

I had been enormously privileged to experience a foreign culture during my many years in Andalusia, and so the trip to this vast neighbouring continent would be my final farewell to this part of the world. Nonsensical and illogical as it may have seemed to my rational mind, my intuition instinctively knew that no departure was possible until I made the effort to touch African soil.

***

I boarded a tour bus in the first week of March and it took a group of us down to the small seaside town of Tarifa from where the boats to Tangiers left. A few miles before Tarifa, the bus climbed away from the large Spanish port of Algeciras and then ran along the top of a hill overlooking the straits of Gibraltar. It was quite extraordinary to see how narrow the straits actually were - only eight miles wide – and gazing from the window of the bus it felt as if I could quite easily just swim across to the African landmass on the other side.

When we finally arrived in Tarifa, it turned out to be a tranquil town with a much slower feel to it than the tourist coast where I lived. The bus drove through the quiet, white-washed streets and deposited us at the small harbour where the Tangier ferry was waiting. This craft was definitely not what I had expected. It certainly wasn't what one could call an 'ocean going' affair, but more like a very large river boat. It took a few cars and small trucks, and the rest of us were all foot passengers.

At the highest point in Tarifa there is an old fort, ...Melchizedek watched a small ship that was plowing its way out of the port."

THE ALCHEMIST: PAULO COELHO

The day was beautifully sunny as we chugged slowly out of Tarifa's small port with a view of the old Moorish fortress standing on a hill overlooking the town. We were no longer in the Mediterranean Sea, but at the edge of the much larger Atlantic Ocean. The sea was a sparkling blue, wonderfully calm, and almost waveless. The journey from Tarifa to Tangiers lasted about an hour, and when we were roughly half way across, I vividly remember seeing the faint outline of a minaret on the horizon in the direction of Tangiers. Turning my head back towards Tarifa I could also still see faint specks of white which were the houses in the town.

This moment was magical and mystical for me. Here were two worlds and two continents, and I could see something of both of them from this small ferry crossing an ancient sea route.

Now, here is a question I have for you dear reader. Why did Santiago the shepherd in The Alchemist go to Tarifa, and then from there take a boat to Tangiers? And, why did I, seven years later, DO EXACTLY THE SAME THING? Were these small, inconsequential details; unimportant coincidences? Oh no, dear friend, NOT AT ALL! Something truly mysterious was at work, and if you wish to know the reason for this coincidence, you will find it by going to the POSTSCRIPT at the end of this book.

***

Arriving at Tangiers turned out to be a very peculiar experience — if not a little surreal. Standing on one of the outer decks of the ferry as we entered the port, I felt as though I had just entered a Pink Panther movie set. A lot of old white Mercedes taxis were lined up on the quay, and there were quite a few men dressed in white caftans, waiting for the ferry. The group of us who had come on the bus were ushered together to meet our guide; a very tall, handsome Moroccan man - also wearing a white caftan. He spoke perfect English and was obviously a cultured and educated man. And so began our visit and tour of this famous North African town.

It was astonishing, but also disturbing to me to find what a difference a small gap of water between two landmasses could make. This was most definitely the Third World. There was no hiding the fact that Tangiers was poor - and I mean very poor. If travelling can do anything for anybody, it must open our eyes and our hearts to the reality of our world. The truth is that the majority of our planet's citizens live in abject poverty. However, we who live in the First World are largely unaware that we too are poor - BUT SUFFERERS OF A DIFFERENT KIND OF POVERTY.

As our lives become more and more cluttered with things, our souls lose contact with everything that is infused with divine energy and life. If you are materially poor, it would seem only natural to me that you would look to the way of life in the First World and think that it is probably the solution to your own plight. But sadly, more TVs, I-Pads, mobile phones and computers will just make our world an uglier and more soulless place.

I feel deeply in my heart that the answer lies not in the acquisition of more technologies, but for all of us, rich and poor, to live in a different way. And that way must be to live:

NOT FOR
WHAT WE CAN HAVE AND OWN,

BUT FOR WHAT WE CAN BE AND SHARE.

Tangiers had long ago been abandoned by the artists and hippies who came to revel in and savour its exoticism in the 1960s. It was now just forgotten and poor. Our small group walked the streets and alleys of the town seeing women squatting on the ground, selling their vegetables. We ate like royalty in a beautiful Moroccan restaurant, but then had to endure the relentless bargaining of the traders in a carpet market.

For me, this turned into a very sad and salutary day. Perhaps what I was seeing was just a more naked expression of twentieth century capitalism. Deep down, I knew that things were really the same where I lived in southern Spain. Of course, the material and spiritual poverty was not as obvious as it was here in Tangiers, but that was only because the economic margins were more generous. At the end of the day I was relieved to find myself back on the ferry and returning to Tarifa on the Spanish mainland. However, I was also glad that I had not been so crass and stupid as to ignore this great African continent, which had literally been on my doorstep for all the years I had lived in Andalusia.

It made me understand more deeply than ever that all of us are intimately connected, and that I cannot turn away from my brother on our shared planet. As the bus drove us back to a more apparently 'comfortable' European reality, we passed endless new developments of half-finished apartments and villas which were beginning to literally litter and scar the landscape. I felt deeply depressed. Money - and its complete dominance as a value in our culture - was destroying this beautiful part of Spain. It produced poverty in Tangiers and another type of destruction here. What to do I asked myself despondently?

At least I could console myself with the fact that I had eyes to see, and was aware and conscious. But, much as I felt myself drawn at that moment to my insights and feelings concerning the state of our world, I knew in my heart that a different agenda awaited me. Subtly, my spirit was showing me that if any radical change were to be possible on our planet, then my first task would be TO CHANGE

MYSELF! Inner and not outer work was calling me, and I was now free to move forward and pursue the burning passion in my heart:

a meeting with Alejandro Jodorowsky.

***

On my return from Tangiers I sent a letter to the publisher of Alejandro's book, together with a photograph of myself, almost PLEADING with the poor man to consider helping me. I then spent about a month waiting for a reply which finally arrived with details of Alejandro's therapy, telephone numbers and the cost. I breathed a huge sigh of relief when I saw that it was not prohibitively expensive, but still had the problem of finding money to get me to Paris, paying for a hotel, and then paying for the therapeutic session.

I considered the option of staying in Spain, returning to my English teaching and saving the money for the trip. However, my earning capacity was so meagre that it seemed to me that I would need an awful long time of working and saving before I could even contemplate making the journey. By the end of April I became almost frantic to put my desires in motion. My thirty-seventh birthday came and went in the middle of May, and my frustration mounted. I had virtually nothing in the bank and the summer was looming when it became harder to make a living teaching English as all the school children would be on their summer holidays.

One morning at the end of May I woke up unable to contain my frenzy any longer. That was it. I would just take whatever money I had in the bank and go to England. My homeland was so much closer to Paris than Andalusia, and that very closeness would make me feel that I was one step nearer to my prized goal. Once this decision was taken, the following day, with next to no clothing stuffed into my small backpack, I caught the bus down to town, went to the bank and took out the two hundred pounds that I had there. I then boarded the local bus to the airport.

I was hoping to get the cheapest possible plane ticket and my thinking told me to go to the airport and see if I could find myself a last-minute standby flight. When I arrived at the terminal I was told that the standby flights started to come on sale in the late afternoon, and that I could queue for a ticket by waiting in a small room at the far end of the airport. This meant having several hours on my hands, and so I sat on a chair and collected my thoughts.

Logically I needed to think about where I was going to stay in England. Adrenalin and sheer passion had prompted me to leave the house in the morning and decide to find a flight to England, but it was not adrenalin and passion that would get me somewhere to stay.

I considered phoning my brother but quickly realised that he would not appreciate being lumbered with me with just a few hours' notice, only because I was in the grip of a passion to see a bohemian film director who specialised in psychomagical acts. How on earth would I explain that! I soberly realised that I had been here in Spain now for nearly a decade, and had lost touch with all my old friends back in my homeland, so there was no one I could ring. However, just as a twinge of desperation was beginning to knock on the door of my heart, a brainwave suddenly hit me.

Over the Christmas period I had made friends with a young English man, and he had warmly given me his phone number in England, saying that I was welcome to come and visit him *whenever I felt like it!* So it was this relatively new 'friend' whom I rang from the airport. He was SURPRISED to say the least to hear my voice - perhaps 'shocked' is more accurate - and even more surprised to know that I would probably be sitting on a plane within the next twenty-four hours, winging my way in the direction of his hometown.

Luckily, he felt disposed to offer me free lodgings at such short notice. After receiving a 'yes' to my frantic request, I put the phone down and felt a wave of euphoria flood through me as only it can when one is relatively young in life and full of dreams. With the relief of having successfully negotiated my first major challenge, and now knowing I had somewhere to stay I wasted no time in setting about the business of enjoying the airport — but it seemed that unconsciously my body was still running on adrenalin.

***

For me airports are exciting domains, even though I fear flying. In those magical buildings you find yourself right on the edge of new experiences, and once inside the terminal, you are no longer connected to your old life, but in a place of unknown and incredible possibilities.

IT IS A SACRED SPACE CALLED JOURNEYING.

In this magical KINGDOM OUTSIDE ALL KINGDOMS you become much more aware that you are engaged in co-creating your destiny with the universe. Here we are connected to and interacting with the invisible forces which shape our lives and world. At this moment in my life, the excitement I felt far outweighed my fear. Right there and then I was grabbing hold of my destiny in an incredibly dramatic and forceful way, and I felt awesomely powerful – if not OMNIPOTENT.

I walked around the airport shops and cafeterias, enjoying this 'limbo land' before the new beginning. Then several hours later, tired but still enthralled by the prospect of what I was doing, I made my way to the room where people were queuing for standby tickets. There I sat through the whole of the evening, and a good part of the night, until finally I was told that I had a seat on a flight leaving about an hour after midnight. Bleary eyed, but satisfied, a mere half an hour later I boarded the plane and took my seat at the very back of the craft, right next to the toilet.

As the plane juddered and accelerated down the runway on its kamikaze trajectory into the inky black night sky, I prayed for God to bring me luck. With all my youthful exuberance, and naivety, I felt that life couldn't get more thrilling than this:

I WAS WELL AND TRULY ON MY WAY!

3

ENTERING THE DESERT: THE SOUTH COAST OF ENGLAND

MY new FRIEND met me enthusiastically on the pier of the seaside town of Ambleton, on the south coast of England. Was the effusive and very tight hug he gave me because he was seeing me as a potential girlfriend I nervously wondered? With great pride Daniel took me on a whirlwind tour of the town before I duly invaded his privacy by sleeping on the floor in the lounge of his small one-bedroom apartment. However, after a few days of tension and awkward silences, we both realised that this was not what either of us had bargained for when I had made my frantic call from the airport in Spain.

Hurriedly I bought a local paper and began to dissect the advertisements for accommodation in the area. I was now no longer planning my dream, but being given a harsh initiation into LIVING IT! I had already spent a sizeable amount of my original two hundred pounds on the flight, food, and a train ticket down to my friend's town, and now there was very little money left. I certainly had no funds for deposits and paying rent in advance. As the reality of my situation began to sink in, I could feel fear spreading through my body like a white heat and my heart racing.

It was starting to dawn on me that the only accommodation advertisements I would be able to consider would be those where the landlord was offering rooms to people on government benefits. Sitting on some grass in the housing estate where my friend lived, I underlined the telephone numbers where landlords stated that they took benefits, and then went to a nearby callbox to begin ringing. As I mentioned earlier, this was a pre-mobile phone age and youngsters today can have absolutely no idea of just how much slower, and difficult communication was back in the 1990s.

After a few calls where I repeated a quick explanation of how I had no money but would go down to the town's benefits office immediately to set in motion the wheels of rental payment, I hit on a landlord who didn't seem in a hurry when I spoke to him. As I explained my inability to provide a deposit, I knew that he had grasped the fact that I was desperate.

"Well, I have a room," he said, "but it's not much, you know, and it's also in the red light area of town. I don't know how you feel about that?"

Fully aware that my finances didn't give me the luxury of FEELING ANYTHING ABOUT ANYTHING, I adjusted myself to this new reality in an instant and swallowed the bad news telling the man that this really wasn't a problem. With my phoney, but convincingly self-assured tone on the phone, the landlord told me to meet him that evening for a viewing of the room.

***

Even before seeing the accommodation I had already decided I would take it - red lights or no red lights. In the early summer evening light, the street didn't actually seem as bad as I had imagined. True, the property itself was extremely dilapidated with no lock on the front door, and the room he showed me was tiny and very basic, however, he was willing to wait for his money and didn't need a deposit. I said yes immediately and the next day moved in with my small backpack to sleep on the grubby floor.

How we all yearn for adventures in life:
sweat on our bodies, mountains in front of us, food
running out, and a hole in our water bottle. Yes:

LIVING!!!
FEELING ONE HUNDRED PERCENT ALIVE
AND CHALLENGED

This is what we dream of when we sit at a desk in an air-conditioned office, watching the hands on the clock drag themselves in slow motion through the hours. But adventures, when we chase them into our lives, are never the romantic pictures we idly fantasise about. They always, but always, take us by surprise. Such was my situation now. I simply hadn't thought further than my desire to board a plane in Malaga and get to England as fast as I could.

The landlord had in fact shown me two rooms in the house, but I had decided to take the smaller room because I was just beginning to understand how vulnerable I was with so little money in my pocket. Also I realised that the smaller room was a space I could wrap around me like a warm duvet, or crawl back into for safety and comfort, much like a welcoming mother's womb. Little did I know right then that the womb-like feeling of my shabby room would be both prophetic and highly symbolic of this entire journey.

The next three weeks were filled with tremendous anxiety and strain for me. I spent my first day rushing around the local town applying for benefits. I estimated that the housing benefit would take several weeks to be authorised and I wanted my landlord to see that I was a person of my word. The government benefit for my living expenses would also take some weeks to come through, so given the very meagre amount of money I had left, this had to be applied for immediately.

Although the landlord provided me with a bed the day after my arrival, I had no sheets, pillow or blankets, and so was forced to go out to the local charity shops to purchase some cheap bedding. My kitchen was not in the room, but on the landing outside, and was a narrow slit - about a metre and a half wide and three and half metres long - with a very greasy old cooker inside it. I don't remember seeing a fridge.

I was now down to a few pounds of the two hundred I had started with, and real adrenalin-fuelled anxiety began. I knew I was on track with my calculations regarding the timing of the arrival of my benefits, but knowing something with your logical mind is not the same as knowing this with your being. Naked terror took up residence in my heart and soul. In desperation, I managed to find some regular soup kitchens for the homeless in town and went to them for my lunch, mingling with people in a real state of destitution. In the mornings, however, my routine was to get up and walk about three hundred metres to a local bakery. There, I would buy a pint of milk and a large, sticky bun-come-loaf, which served as my breakfast.

Seated on a bench near the bakery, with the noise of traffic competing with the noise of the fear inside me, I would work my way through the bun and the pint of milk. The food kitchens for the homeless were not always available at lunch time. Sometimes they were scheduled for the evening, and so I needed enough calories inside me to keep me going for at least eight hours. This period of *survival* before I received any money was something which tested me to my very limit.

After the first week the stress of it all proved too much for me, and I began to experience panic attacks which I hadn't had for quite some time. Two years earlier I had been to a dentist who had injected a dental anaesthetic incorrectly into my gums. The anaesthetic had been an old type which used cocaine as part of its formula, and about an hour after leaving the dental surgery, and the consumption of a small alcoholic drink, I had experienced absolute terror as I felt myself teetering on the edge of violent convulsions and a total loss of consciousness.

Luckily, this terrifying incident had been a one-off and never recurred, but had subsequently precipitated horrible panic attacks in me which had eventually subsided six weeks after my visit to the dentist. However, in the two years that followed, whenever I had a period of great stress, the panic attacks would return, and I would feel as though I were about to convulse or harm myself in some way.

In my new situation of extreme stress, as I walked to the food kitchens each day along busy roads, I could feel panic rising inside me and the impulse to throw myself out in front of any oncoming car flooding the veins inside my head. This most certainly wasn't what I had bargained for in Andalusia when I had joyfully stepped onto the plane full of the emotional high of knowing I was on my way to see Alejandro Jodorowsky.

***

Eventually, the money for my room rental and living expenses came through and I was able to tentatively let go of all the tension this three-week period had caused me. It was then in my little womb-like room that I simply lay on my bed for several days in a state of complete and utter exhaustion.

The road I lived on, despite being the red light district of the town at night, was a tranquil residential area by day with very little traffic. Nevertheless, even in this environment I still felt panicky as I walked to the hypermarket each day to shop. This was a very worrying turn of events for me, and so I decided to go and visit a doctor I had only just registered with. My idea was to ask if it would be possible to have a few days rest in a local hospital, and some routine medical tests. This request of mine, which I had formulated whilst lying on my bed in my womb-like room, was extremely revealing to say the least. It showed just how incredibly naïve I was, even at this advanced age of thirty-seven.

The doctor greeted me, his new patient, with the customary lack of interest that seemed to characterise modern life. He listened with as much patience as he could muster to my description of my panic attacks, and my request for a few days' rest in a hospital. He then made some notes and told me that a taxi would pick me up the next morning to take me to the hospital. The relief I felt was enormous. I left the surgery almost *hopping and skipping,* with my blood pressure returning to normal levels, and the feeling that I did live in a benevolent and caring world after all.

The next morning the taxi duly arrived and I clambered in to it with a few things in my basic rucksack. The driver and I made small talk as he drove us through leafy suburbs in the direction of the hospital. After about ten minutes in the car, I confessed that I had been having some panic attacks and that the doctor had kindly made it possible for me to have a few days rest in the local hospital. The driver did not reply to this, but became very quiet.

"It is the hospital where we're going?" I suddenly asked, feeling very nervous.

"Yes," he replied," but I'm taking you to the local psychiatric hospital, not the general hospital."

A shockwave passed through me and before I had time to take in what he had said, he swung the taxi into a large gravel drive, and announced, "Here we are."

Oh, my God, I thought to myself, as panic began to take hold of me. Oh, no, the world was not that benign, fairy-tale place I had lulled myself into believing it to be. The doctor had effectively tricked me, and I started to feel very disorientated indeed! But this was not the first crisis I had had in my thirty-seven years on this planet, and so putting myself into emergency mode, I programmed myself to 'survive'. I stepped out of the taxi, paid the driver, and was greeted by an employee of the hospital who had been expecting me.

She let me into the old Victorian building, and asked me to wait in a corridor, AND IT WAS HERE THAT MY FIRST TEST MANIFESTED. As I sat waiting to be seen by someone, a very large woman in her thirties approached me. She had spotted me sitting alone from some distance, and I saw her make a beeline for me. Her eyes were utterly manic and she exuded an energy of total madness. She moved towards me much like a shark would as it zoomed in on its prey - convinced that I was about to become her lunch!

A horrific fear welled up inside me as she came closer. I felt completely naked and unable to defend myself from whatever this malevolent energy was that she was projecting towards me. Nevertheless, I knew that I had survived worse in the past, and so summoning up every ounce of willpower I possessed, I repelled her with some curt and dismissive words as she pretended to offer me a friendly greeting. Even though I was terrified, my tactic worked, and the attack I felt she had been about to launch on me was somehow defused by my 'apparent' wall of indifference.

As this very ill lady turned and walked away, a member of staff from the hospital greeted me and showed me to a room with four beds in it. She led me to my bed and told me that although I would be the only occupant that night I was sure to have company pretty soon. And she was right because that company was in the bed next to mine the following morning. It was the slight body of a heavily sedated lady who slept well into the afternoon. When she finally awoke just before teatime, Barbara and I began to talk.

The most striking thing about my new roommate was just how very normal she seemed to be. In the last few days preceding her admission Barbara had been through a terrible experience. This had tipped her over her own personal edge, and she had tried to commit suicide the previous day. Why was my journey to see Alejandro beginning in this most peculiar way, I asked myself? BEING IN A PSYCHIATRIC HOSPITAL WAS SOMETHING I HAD NEVER IMAGINED BACK IN SPAIN. However, understanding and answering this question would have to wait until a few years further on.

***

During the first two days in the hospital I made good friends with my roommate, and came into contact with the other patients as we congregated in the dining room and also a communal lounge. The extremely ill patients, like the shark lady who had homed in on me when I arrived, were kept in another area of the hospital, but my companions in this section of the hospital all seemed to be very normal people.

My memory of my time there is somewhat blurred now, but I do remember telling the nursing staff who came around with their pills every morning and evening that I was in no need of any kind of medication. I had a terrible fear of being labelled and losing control of my life, and my contact with some of the other patients showed me that my fears were not unfounded.

These souls only needed some compassion, a listening ear, and perhaps a little medication over a short period of time. Instead they had been given electroconvulsive therapy - electric shock treatment. This left them worse off than when they had arrived, and many of my companions walked around the corridors with terrible headaches, memory loss and a feeling of exhaustion and mental fuzziness.

After the first week of determined refusal on my part to swallow any kind of pill that was placed in front of me, I was given the dubious privilege of being interviewed by the hospital psychiatrists. A group of us waited nervously in the corridor as if we were about to have an audience with the Queen of England. When it finally came to my turn, I entered the room and saw about five health professionals seated in a row, rather like a firing squad, ready to ask me awkward questions as I sat in a lone chair in front of them. This was one thing and one thing only:

a concentrated encounter of the powerless with the powerful.

I don't remember any of the people there sounding or looking remotely compassionate. They projected a clear subliminal message of seeing me as one of society's misfits. I answered questions designed to make me confess that I was, in fact, a maladjusted, psychologically ill person PRETENDING to be normal, but I resolutely refused to tow the line. I kept hold of my dignity and self-esteem as they tried to pick holes in both, and generally refused to place myself into the mould they had clearly decided upon, even before I had come into the room.

It was a nerve-wracking and humiliating experience, but eventually I left the room feeling as if I had probably won this particular battle. However, the next morning shattered this illusion when one of the senior nurses came to my bed and poured out a concoction of pills that the psychiatrist had decided I needed to take. Saying that I felt like a caged animal doesn't really describe just how vulnerable I felt. I had unwittingly entered some kind of existential 'battlefield', the nature of which I couldn't quite grasp, and my sense of powerlessness was total.

Instantly, the 'warrior spirit' within me told the nurse that I wouldn't take any of the pills and that I was discharging myself from the hospital there and then. From the look on the nurse's face, I could clearly see that he hadn't been expecting this reaction from me. A lengthy conversation between the two of us then ensued, and I was lucky to find that I was talking to the human face of this establishment. The nurse was sanity and reasonableness itself. He quickly made a pact with me behind the drawn curtain of my cubicle. I should stay a few more days and he would see to it that I wasn't given any medication.

With a nod of complicity and a very humane smile, he left me alone, and my completely stunned self could do nothing more than gaze in the direction of his departure. My God, I thought, this was victory at last!

***

After this encounter with the nurse, I spent another three days in the hospital, but was still feeling a little panicky. None of this boded well for me, but as fate would have it my confidence was boosted when I left on an unexpectedly high and rebellious note. That note began a day or so before my departure when I went into the communal lounge where all the patients met up in order to flick through magazines and listen to the radio. On this particular day, as I walked in, someone had tuned the radio to a music station with some lively dance music.

I sat down in an armchair for a while and then couldn't contain myself any longer. I stood up and started to dance, noticing smiles suddenly appearing on the faces of my depressed and bored companions. These smiles had only one effect on me - they made me want to give a little more joy with my dancing. After about a minute I decided to invite a few of my friends to join me on the floor.

They were all very shy and self-conscious at first, but I managed to inspire one or two of them up from their chairs as I started to execute some simple steps. Within less than twenty seconds I had about four people in the middle of the lounge floor, all copying my movements, and with this the atmosphere in the room changed radically. Where a minute earlier there had been an air of hopelessness and depression, now there was a feeling of fun and normality all around us.

To my surprise more people joined in this impromptu dance class, and as I led my companions in dance moves, I could see the nursing staff peering at this amazing spectacle through the glass window in the lounge door.

The dancing continued for about twenty minutes, with the help of the radio, and then suddenly I just ran out of energy and we all stopped, flopping back into the empty armchairs and sofa. As we lay back in a semi-state of exhaustion and caught our breaths there was such an exhilarating glow of happiness inside us all. Twenty minutes of dancing had brought each one of us BACK TO LIFE! Like a mutinying crew on a slave ship, we had broken the invisible locks and chains in the hospital and turned it into a sort of holiday camp.

The staff, who were still peering through the lounge window, looked very nervous indeed. Things like this weren't supposed to happen in a psychiatric hospital. After all, weren't THEY, AND NOT US supposed to be IN CONTROL? Besides, when people are deemed 'ill', THEY ARE ILL, and that was all there was to it.

We, the 'inmates', of course knew differently. If only for twenty brief, but glorious minutes these so-called CRAZY PRISONERS HAD ESCAPED!!!!!!!

4

THE DESERT AND THE ENGLISHMAN

AFTER the hospital I returned to my little room slightly more rested than when I had left it, but certainly not in a normal state of health. I was still feeling panicky, so in this respect nothing much had changed, but thankfully the panic wasn't plaguing me on a daily basis as it had done before. Somewhat relieved by this, I tentatively allowed myself to hope that some slight progress in my situation was appearing on my horizon. Nevertheless, despite these encouraging feelings, the time in the hospital had shaken me profoundly and had given me a chance to take stock of what I had actually set in motion.

The truth was that I was in a much more sober mood now than when I had first arrived here in England. My income from the benefits I received was very meagre, and so I quickly settled into a routine based on the fact that I really had no money worth mentioning. ROUTINES COME EASILY UNDER THESE CIRCUMSTANCES!

A large hypermarket was within walking distance of the house, and was almost the only public facility in the area. Since the arrival of my money I had begun to walk to this emporium every day to buy food and get a little exercise, and it was in a cheap, but clean self-service canteen area of this building that I was accosted one morning by one of the regulars there. In fact, given the state of my kitchen annexe back at the shared house, I had also started to become a regular myself.

I will call my friend 'James' and we began talking over hot mugs of tea. The first thing James said on seeing me was that he always recognised someone WITH A BROKEN MIND — according to him that was exactly what I had. I squirmed with a mixture of anger and irritation at this presumptuous and conceited 'psychological assessment' from a total stranger. But James seemed interesting, chiefly because he carried a folder of artwork under his arm. He sat at my table and showed me some of his drawings, and then explained that he was a student at the local art school in town.

He seemed to be surprisingly interested in me, the new face in the canteen – despite, or perhaps BECAUSE of my 'broken mind'. I told him that I had come from Spain where I had been living for many years and that I was hoping to see a psychomagician in Paris later in the year. I was more than well aware that this information made me come across as a rather exotic and unusual type to this young man. However, we got on well as we chatted, and seemed to be able to share ideas about art, psychology and the state of the world. Quite unexpectedly, but in a more than timely way, I had found a desperately needed friend. And so began my wait to see Alejandro Jodorowsky in Paris.

I had phoned Alejandro's number in Paris just before going into the hospital and had been told by a secretary to call back in January 1996. This was now August, and here I was with very little money and many months ahead of me. So, it was only logical that my next question to myself was what on earth was I supposed to do? My immediate rational thought was to go down to the local job centre in town to look for work and earn the money I needed to make the trip to see my 'guru'. But, somehow my logical mind didn't seem to be in control of this journey.

A deeper sense in me, something WAY BEYOND MY INTUITION, was telling me that rational choices were not a part of what was happening to me; instead my focus had to be exclusively on waiting to go to Paris. Work, it seemed, was completely out of the picture. With this decision made, it was thus that my days began to take on a very specific and predictable pattern.

I would wake up, breakfast on the floor of my room, and then tidy up. Later, I would walk to the hypermarket for food, perhaps having a cheap lunch in the cafeteria, and then returning to my room to spend the evening writing or listening to the radio. As I pursued this implacable and seemingly unending routine, I knew most definitely that I was in some kind of emotional and spiritual desert. Why, dear friend was this a desert for me? Well, it was the sheer mind-numbing monotony of each day and each week.

When I awoke in the mornings I faced the same panorama ahead of me. Instead of an endless mass of desert sand as there had been for Santiago in The Alchemist, what permeated my hours were silence and loneliness, and the same tasks which would see me through the next fourteen to sixteen hours of the day.

In a desert, life is stripped down to the most basic elements of existence. The noise and mental distractions of normal living are taken from us, and we are left with nowhere else to go except into the inner world of our hearts and souls. There are many kinds of desert experience in life: illness, bereavement, accidents, failure and other losses, and all of these events plunge us into the little-known world of WHO WE ARE, OR ARE NOT at any given point in our lives. I knew I was journeying to my obsessive goal of seeing Alejandro in Paris, and that my journey was now this monotonous wait in a tiny room with the daily walk to the hypermarket.

However, before I boarded the plane in Malaga at the beginning of June, I hadn't realised that the invisible realm had decided that my quest would take on this precise form in order to force me into:

A PROFOUND ENCOUNTER WITH MYSELF!

***

In this desert terrain, my only relief was James who would appear once or twice a week in my life, either in the canteen of the hypermarket, or at the house where I lived. His presence was in many ways an utterly saving grace, but even though our friendship was vital to me, it proved to be conflict-filled from the very start. This was because we basically operated in totally different ways.

I was an intuitive who gave great importance to the power of that intuition in guiding me through life, whereas James seemed to be my exact opposite. His approach to life was to think his way through it, rather than feel or sense what life was telling him. This conflict was at the heart of every one of our meetings, and seriously undermined and disrupted our ability to communicate with each other. It was as if we had effectively signed up to different political parties and saw the world in totally different ways.

Nevertheless, in spite of all this, for some reason we seemed to keep each other company, and that was most probably because we were both quite obviously misfits or outsiders. The truth was that the world in which we lived was not somewhere either of us could call HOME.

Even though in 1995 I was now thirty-seven years of age, and not a youngster by any means, I most certainly wasn't emotionally equipped to be doing what I was doing in Ambleton. I had never before in my life taken such an apparently 'reckless' leap of faith, and plunged myself into this kind of ALL-OR-NOTHING ADVENTURE. Although it was true that I had been adventurous in the past by leaving my life in England and embarking on a new one in Spain to live with my boyfriend, what I was committed to now was something of a different order all together. I had quite literally thrown myself into this odyssey to find my Holy Grail with no preparation and no resources whatsoever, and here I was, being confronted on a daily basis with the consequences of my actions.

Apart from experiencing great loneliness and anxiety during my long wait in my little room, I made an important new discovery about myself. Slowly it began to dawn on me that I had absolutely no motivation whatsoever for anything material in life. I was exclusively and single-mindedly only interested in the healing ahead of me in Paris. As far as ordinary life was concerned, nothing seemed to interest me at all.

Now, as I look back on those months after many years I realise that I was unconsciously undergoing an initiation into a spiritual awakening. The DESERT I was in was the necessary place of testing and pain for me before any kind of awakening could occur. By leaving Spain, without knowing it, I had left behind the old me, which despite my spiritual yearnings, had still been immersed in the everyday material world. And, now it was only logical that this self-same material world had ceased to hold anything for me.

Yes, here I was, I had stepped away and was now cast adrift from my old self, and yet I was still to give birth to a new me and enter into some kind of spiritual relationship with myself and life.

The desert I was occupying was a no-man's-land BETWIXT AND BETWEEN the old and the new, and in that place all I could do was endure myself, observe myself, and watch, listen and wait.

***

Now, back to Paulo Coelho's The Alchemist, which I haven't mentioned for quite some time.

Like Santiago, the shepherd boy in the fable, I had experienced a powerful dream in Andalusia, but ironically it was not my dream of giving birth to a baby, who was me, which had propelled me on this quest. It had in fact been the book by Alejandro Jodorowsky which had set this whole journey in motion. However, what I hadn't realised at the time was that my dream had been directly provoked by that book. Unbeknownst to me The journey and the dream were actually ONE AND THE SAME THING - two realities were coexisting together.

This meant that although travelling to meet Alejandro for a healing of my soul was my CONSCIOUS MIND'S motivation, the dream of giving birth to myself was in reality my SUBCONSCIOUS MIND'S hidden agenda in order to fulfil that goal.

My birth dream was never in my mind as I went through the days of waiting to phone Alejandro's secretary again in January 1996. However, the universe or God was intimately aware that the dream was actually what this journey was essentially all about, and the invisible realm underlined this with two very concrete signs. The first omen or 'sign' was that there was a couple living in a small attic apartment above my room in Ambleton, and by an apparent 'mere accident of fate' the young woman was pregnant. Not only was she pregnant, but, 'coincidentally' her name, just like mine, was KAREN!

The second 'sign' regarding birth was just as specific because I ended up waiting to see Alejandro for NINE MONTHS, which just so happens to be the physical gestation period for a human pregnancy.

Neither of these signs or 'coincidences' ever registered with me at the time, nevertheless yet again the invisible realm had me firmly in the palm of its hand, and was working out a process I would only begin to decipher many years later. Whilst in this desert did I, just like Santiago in Paulo Coelho's fable, meet and journey with an Englishman, encounter my soul mate at a metaphorical oasis, and then a mysterious person called the alchemist? To the first of these questions I can confidently answer yes - James was most definitely the archetype of the Englishman described in The Alchemist. But to the other two, regretfully I have to answer no.

However, as I made my daily trips to the hypermarket, argued with James, and endured lonely hours of nothingness inside my tiny room when I simply went over and over in my mind my dream to be in Paris, my soul mate was actually not so very far away. Living a mere twenty minutes from my abode, he like me was also walking the streets of this unassuming seaside town. We never met in 1995, but were to come face-to-face with each other just over eight-and-a-half years later when fate conspired that I should return to this very place again!

***

Towards Christmas 1995 my parents decided to send me enough money to be able to pay for the trip to Paris, and also the cost of the psychomagical session with Alejandro. This unexpected blessing from them for my incomprehensible endeavour was, on a cosmic level, far more important than it seemed — things were most definitely looking up! Another 'little miracle' also appeared for me when just before the Christmas holidays I met two Spanish women of my own age in the washrooms of the hypermarket.

I had gone in and heard their voices gabbling away in Spanish, and simply wasn't able to resist the temptation to interrupt them and speak a little Spanish myself. As we chatted away, I learned that Mayka and Susana were from the Canary Islands, and had come to Ambleton for a month to improve their English.

We hit it off immediately because surprisingly it transpired that these two lovely ladies were also misfits, just like me. Neither was married, nor involved in any kind of conventional life path. Instead, both worked hard, saved money and travelled. There and then in the washroom I offered to help them with their English in the time remaining to them in England, and they eagerly agreed, returning to my little room for some tea and more talk. Seated on the grubby carpet of my sanctuary, I spilled out everything about my quest to see a psychomagician in Paris, and they told me of their trips to India and visits to an ashram.

As we shared experiences that day, neither I nor my two new friends had any kind of awareness that only three months later, at the end of February 1996, they would become key players in making my journey to Paris possible.

***

A few weeks after our first meeting in the hypermarket, and just before Mayka and Susana were due to return to the Canaries, I talked to them about my panic attacks. Life in these last seven months had been limited to my room, the walk to the hypermarket, and little else, and yet I still occasionally experienced mild feelings of panic. The idea of going from this reduced and limited existence to making a journey to Paris on my own filled me with terror.

These two angels, who had suddenly and quite magically appeared in my world, weren't in the least bit phased by my confession of angst, and suggested a day out to London to see the Christmas lights and some of the sights. We all agreed that this would be the perfect challenge for me, and an ideal opportunity to restore my lost confidence. If I could get through this successfully, then I would be well prepared for Paris.

The outing to London passed off without a hitch, and although I felt a little panicky towards the end of it, on our return I did sense that I had somehow managed to overcome a large part of the apprehension I had been feeling. I may not have suddenly become totally free of fear, but I was now ready to embrace the challenge of Paris with a healthy measure of courage in my heart. With that loving gift to me, Mayka and Susana returned home to the Canary Islands convinced that I was now well prepared to execute my audacious and crazy-looking plan.

Christmas Day arrived and found me walking along Ambleton beach staring repetitively, and obsessively at the horizon and an invisible French coastline behind it. Boxing Day was spent with

James and his family, and then we were suddenly into January 1996 and the time had come for me to make my phone call to Paris. This extraordinary event took place from a public phone box in the middle of town – as I said earlier, there were no cell phones back then - and within seconds of dialling the number, I found myself once again hearing the voice of Alejandro's secretary.

I spoke very slowly because my French was incredibly rusty and also because, as Odette herself admitted almost immediately, her English was virtually non-existent. She began by asking me in a very steely tone why I needed to see Alejandro. Suddenly I felt I was facing the most important question of my entire life. This young woman at the other end of the line had the power TO MAKE OR BREAK my fragile, life-changing dream, and I knew from her tone that if I gave a stupid or unconvincing answer she most certainly would not book me for a session with Alejandro.

Somehow inspiration came to me, despite the language difficulties, and I explained in the simplest of French that I was English, had a Russian mother, and had lived in Spain for many years, and that my problem was that I DIDN'T REALLY KNOW WHO OR WHAT I WAS.

To my astonishment, and incredible relief Odette accepted this explanation as one of genuine importance, and after a pause confirmed that it would be possible for me to see Alejandro. He had a space on February 27, and I affirmed instantly that that date would be just fine for me. After giving her my address and writing down the time of the appointment, we ended our conversation – my grizzly and nerve-wracking test had resulted in victory!

As I placed the telephone receiver back into its cradle the only words which filled my mind were Oh my God, oh my God! I could not have felt more elated had I won the national lottery!

In the cramped confines of the public telephone box I didn't levitate, scream, or shout for joy, but all of these extraordinarily strong feelings welled up inside me. Something I had set my heart and soul on nearly a year earlier was suddenly becoming a reality! This went way beyond my wildest dreams and fantasies, and I could only conclude that I just had to be the luckiest human being on our planet!

5

THE PYRAMIDS OF PARIS

TO celebrate this wonderful event I walked, or rather 'floated', straight from the phone box to a book shop and bought myself the only thing I could afford - a diary in which to write about the upcoming weeks. On the first page I recorded the details of my conversation with Odette — it was January 12, 1996. About another six and-a-half-weeks lay ahead of me and I continued to wait, finding comfort in writing entries into the diary every evening, no matter how mundane or banal they seemed. And in all honesty, they were exactly that.

Although I had taken the 'rehearsal' trip to London with Mayka and Susana, feelings of panic continued to be a problem for me. With only a month-and-a-half remaining before my longed-for departure, I wasn't in any way able to convince myself that I could accomplish my mission to see Alejandro and return in one piece. Of course, I tried to talk myself out of this gnawing and unrelenting fear, but no amount of self-talk or calming thoughts would take it away. The reality was that time was most definitely not on my side, and so admitting defeat, I decided to abandon any attempts at heroism and look for help.

My first thought was to approach James, explain my predicament, and ask him if he would do me the enormous favour of accompanying me to Paris. I didn't feel very optimistic concerning his reaction, but was completely astonished when, rather than looking down on me, he accepted the challenge with good humour and grace.

Now, anyone would have logically assumed that securing James' participation in my quest should have left me feeling relaxed and relieved, but instead the very opposite began to happen. No sooner had he given me his agreement to travel to Paris than high voltage anxiety assaulted me, appearing as if from nowhere. This time is was the spectre of self-doubt raising its ugly, ignominious head as intense feelings of uncertainty concerning the validity of this whole venture suddenly hit me like a tidal wave.

I hadn't in any way expected this, and the truth was that within the four walls of my tiny womb-like room, with hours alone inside my head, I had begun to seriously - and I mean seriously - question my own sanity. I recorded everything in my diary, trying to express all my fears on paper. Was I totally and utterly mad in wanting to see this psychomagician? Had I created an elaborate fantasy for myself in order to run away, or in other words TO ESCAPE from normal, everyday life? Was this odyssey an act of supreme courage, or just one of self-centred, pathetic cowardice?

Who was the real Karen — a childish, unbalanced neurotic, or a brave, spiritual adventurer? These questions weren't trivial by any means:

THEY HAD TO BE ANSWERED.

Gradually, and almost imperceptibly, my inner wrestling and soul-searching eventually paid off, and after a few weeks the terrifying possibility of my own *madness* began to fade. It was gently replaced by a quiet, calm conviction that this path was truly meant, and I can assure you, dear friend, this really felt like a blessing from on high. Yes, Paris was once more my destiny — **A LIFE-OR-DEATH DESTINY** — to which it seemed that I had somehow been magically summoned by forces far beyond my understanding.

I had managed to survive several unexpected EXISTENTIAL TRIALS, and in so doing had conquered an inner beast, and now I was convinced that this mission would meet with complete and total success.

***

At the beginning of February I set about visiting travel agencies in town looking for a cheap short break deal to the CITY OF LIGHT. Flying there was completely beyond my means, and so the journey would have to be made by coach or train. Fairly quickly, and with not much effort, I was lucky enough to find a package within budget that involved travelling on the new Eurostar train service through the channel tunnel, and staying in an inexpensive hotel for two nights. On Monday, February 19, I finally made the booking for myself and James: Hotel de Nemours: a twin-bedded room to save money, and the Eurostar train leaving London at 10:23 a.m. on February 26, just one short week away.

All through this period of waiting I had kept in contact by phone with Mayka and Susana. Since their return to the Canaries just before Christmas they had been anxious to know of any progress towards my goal of seeing Alejandro. Before booking the deal to Paris I had let them know that I had asked James to come with me because of the unresolved problem of my panic attacks. With great embarrassment I had also mentioned that my calculations told me that if I bought the package for both of us, I would have absolutely no money left for food and metro tickets once we were in the famous city.

Thankfully, Mayka and Susana weren't in the least bit fazed by my confession, and encouraged me to go ahead with the booking. They reassured me that they would send me some money in the post to cover this problem, and so with this unexpected act of generosity I went ahead with paying for the trip.

After February 19 I waited anxiously every morning for a registered letter to arrive from the Canaries, containing the promised money from my friends. Tuesday the 20th came and went, as did Wednesday, and then Thursday the 22nd. On Friday the 23rd I woke up feeling very fearful - there was no post at all that morning — ABSOLUTELY NOTHING! Here I was, only three days away from boarding a bus taking James and me to London on Monday the 26th, and I knew that Saturday was the very last chance for the money from The Canaries to arrive. If it were to come on the Monday morning, when the post arrived at its usual time around 9 a.m., we would miss the bus to London and the Eurostar train by several hours.

Here was a real test for me. I was completely committed to the trip, but the universe seemed to be taking my nervous system to the wire after this nine-month wait. Literally trembling with fear,

I took my steps of faith that Friday morning, even though there had been no post, and paid for two bus tickets to London. Then James appeared in the late afternoon to find out how things were progressing.

Unwilling to reveal what was actually happening, I sent him away with a few white lies, and then in the early evening walked to a local phone box and called Mayka. I was desperate for reassurance that she really had sent the letter with the money more than ten days earlier, and this was exactly what she gave me as I stood panicking and holding the grubby telephone receiver to my ear.

On my way back to my room a brainwave struck me as I suddenly thought of ringing the doorbell belonging to the caretaker of the house in order to ask him if there had been any problem with the post. My agony was brought to a speedy end when he handed me a postal notice and told me that the post had been extremely late that day, but had finally arrived in the late afternoon. In a frenzy of fear I read the notice and discovered that a registered letter was waiting for me at the depot, which unfortunately was now closed. It would be open the following day, just for the morning, on Saturday February 24.

Saturday morning dawned with the rain falling in a monsoon-like torrent. I walked to the post office parcel office in virtually zero visibility, and could hardly believe my eyes when the man at the counter handed me the registered letter with the Spanish stamps on it. I sat on a bench in the office and opened the letter, pulling out one hundred pounds and a note from Mayka and Susana. Floodgates of tension burst in me and I started to cry uncontrollably with relief and gratitude. I couldn't believe that I had come this close to not having enough money for the trip.

Not for the first time in my life I had the distinct feeling that some kind of invisible realm was in control of this whole situation, and had decided exactly how and when it would end.

***

Sunday night was filled with nervous anticipation and adrenalin as sleep eluded me almost completely. After hours of tossing and turning in my bed, I eventually got up at 4:45 a.m., washed and dressed myself, ate a basic breakfast of jam and bread, assembled my bag, checked that money and passport were all where they needed to be, and then walked in the dark for the five minutes it took me to reach the bus pick-up point in town. Needless to say I was far too early, but it was better to be standing in the street waiting rather than lying in my bed, unable to sleep.

Even now I was still unsure whether James would actually honour his word and turn up for this 'crazy' journey. He had been very nervous in the last few days when I had seen him as he had barely travelled anywhere other than around the small county we were living in. I fully expected to wait and wait and eventually board the bus alone. However, finally about twenty minutes before the bus was due to leave, out of the dark and damp foggy air in front of me a lone, lank figure began to appear, walking slowly towards me. James! MY GOD, IT REALLY WAS JAMES! The very last shreds of fear and anxiety fell away from me - the trip was now not a glorious fantasy in my imagination, but about to become a full-blown reality!

Whilst the sky was still pitch black outside, we climbed into a very empty bus and settled into our seats for the journey to London. Everything went smoothly as we arrived in the capital and took the underground to St. Pancras Station for the Eurostar train. James continued to be very nervous, just as he had been on the previous days, but by now I was certain that this was only because of his lack of travelling experience.

We boarded the Eurostar train and along with the rest of the passengers found our reserved seats. Compared to the state of the bus we had travelled on, and even the tube trains we had taken, the Eurostar exuded the glamour of long-distance *voyaging*. It was therefore more than appropriate for what I knew would be THE VOYAGE OF MY LIFE – at long last this was it!

Sandwiches kept fatigue at bay, and the journey passed very quickly. The time we spent in the tunnel at the bottom of the English Channel even seemed relatively short, and in the late afternoon, after hurtling through the north of France at what seemed an impossibly fast speed, we slowly pulled into the Gare du Nord in Paris.

WE HAD ARRIVED IN THE CITY OF LIGHT!

I was exhausted but still in good spirits, even though James had continued to be extremely tense on the train. We stopped at a bench in the huge station forecourt to take some photographs, and then made our way to the Metro to catch a train to the hotel. When we reached our destination, we were pleasantly surprised to find a modest and very appealing-looking building in a quiet side road. On entering Hotel de Nemours, we were greeted by the owner at the reception.

I can't remember now exactly how it happened, but this lady *seemed to recognise me!* Now, as we all know, Paris is an enormous city with millions of inhabitants, so how could I possibly have chosen to stay in a hotel where the owner appeared to know me? After signing myself in, this 'stranger' and I began to try to investigate this sense of DEJA VU she had about me.

I told her that I had lived in Spain, and after a brief exchange of information we discovered that we had both sat together at the same table, chatting and drinking coffee at my local social club in southern Spain a year earlier. She had remembered me from that very brief encounter, and as I recalled the same moment, I instantly recognised her too.

My rational mind took all of this in its stride, but my subconscious mind began to sense something very different. Such a strange 'coincidence' wasn't something it could easily ignore. The invisible realm which I had decided was utterly real back in 1989 seemed to be giving me a very deep message.

IT WAS HERE AGAIN, CONTROLLING AND CREATING THE MOST BIZARRE CIRCUMSTANCES.

This was starting to feel not so much like fate, as me following a prewritten script in which I was being given instructions as to what would happen each day!

***

After finding our room in the hotel, James and I left our bags there and decided to stretch our legs after the long journey. We wanted to take advantage of the remaining daylight to see a little of exactly where we were. We walked for perhaps less than two minutes down some narrow streets, and then suddenly found ourselves in a huge open Parisian square with a grandiose central island filled with an enormous monument and statue.

The street sign announced that this was LA PLACE DE LA REPUBLIQUE. As we both bubbled over with excitement at the sight of something so iconically and quintessentially Parisian, James and I had absolutely no idea that we were in fact within a very short distance of the Louvre Museum and its glass pyramids of light.

I was thrilled that an art student like James could be having his first taste of the artistry and creativity of this amazing city just by standing in this majestic square. We walked the whole way around the square, taking in the space and proportions of the buildings, as well as unfortunately the fumes from the traffic, and then made a circular tour around the monument in the central island. The light was fading fast by then and so we dodged the cars to cross back over to the street we had come down in order to return to the hotel.

Once again, some kind of invisible realm seemed to have pre-programmed events because we were completely unaware that as we walked away from LA PLACE DE LA REPUBLIQUE, we had just turned our backs on a huge statue crowning the central island in the square – a statue that was highly symbolic of this journey. It was the statue of a woman – THE MARIANNE - an allegorical personification the French nation had chosen to embody the values of their new republic in the nineteenth century - the values of: 'liberte, fraternite, igalite'-'liberty, brotherhood, equality'.

The last flickers of daylight had very nearly disappeared as we walked back to the hotel. Suddenly, as we entered a narrow street, James stopped, opened and closed his eyes rapidly several times, and then his body shook gently as he began to speak some kind of incomprehensible gibberish. I instantly panicked, knowing full well that I was witnessing a mild epileptic seizure, but also fearing that a much stronger attack could be on its way.

The trembling and his peculiar speech seemed to go on for an eternity, even though it was more than likely that less than a minute had passed since it had begun.

After about another minute my friend's normal speech returned to him, but I could see that he was still trembling and disorientated. Taking his arm in mine, I very cautiously started to walk towards the hotel, hoping that another seizure wasn't on its way. The irony of what had just happened was not lost on me in the least. James had graciously agreed to be with me in Paris *just in case* I had a severe panic attack, and yet here we were with our roles reversed, and me leading him slowly and nervously back to the hotel.

With my friend still dazed, and me in tears, we eventually arrived at the hotel, negotiated the lift, and safely found our room. I placed James on his bed, and then collapsed onto my own - this had been an extremely long and challenging day!

***

James recovered quickly that night from the seizure, and the next morning both our stress levels were back to within normal limits as we sat eating our traditional French breakfast. This was the big day of seeing Alejandro and yet, bizarrely, it didn't feel so special for me. The appointment was not until 6 p.m., and I wanted to give James something soulful and memorable by way of a thank-you for his real kindness in agreeing to be with me. That meant one thing, and one thing only as far as I was concerned – ART. And so this simply had to be a visit to the Musee D'Orsay to see the impressionist paintings and other great works.

The sun shone and Paris looked magnificent as we crossed the river Seine and headed for the museum. Once inside I gave James my camera and told him to do his own thing. The only concrete stipulation I made was that we should meet up again under the central clock at 4 p.m. Now, free to please ourselves, James went his way and I went mine.

I spent some time wandering aimlessly around the ground floor of the building, now suddenly aware that I was really just killing time before the appointment with Alejandro at 6 pm. I left the building briefly for a coffee and baguette in a nearby café, and then returned determined to at least see the impressionist collection of paintings on the top floor of the museum. What on earth would I say to James if I had seen nothing?

I duly met my friend under the main clock at 4 p.m. as arranged, and we made our way out of the museum and back over the Seine in the direction of the nearest Metro station. We stopped briefly in the Tuilleries Gardens to take photos and enjoy the beauty of a Paris gently awakening to spring, and then it was time to make our way to the suburb where Alejandro lived.

THE TUILLERIES GARDENS, PARIS.

Me in the Tuilleries Gardens just before we headed for the metro station taking us to the suburb where Alejandro Jodorowsky lived.*

*(At that moment, as I sat on the stone wall, I was completely unaware that less than two hundred yards in front of me was the courtyard of the Louvre Museum with its large glass pyramid.

On April 9 2011, flicking through my diary from 1996, I found a photograph from February 27, 1996. Ironically, it was an image of the entrance arch to the Louvre's courtyard, with the glass pyramid behind it.)

THE MAIN GLASS PYRAMID IN THE CENTRAL COURTYARD OF THE LOUVRE MUSEUM.

The journey on the Paris metro was unexpectedly short and we arrived far too early. The street with Alejandro's house was easy to find, and as we began to walk down it, enormous excitement started to well up inside me. It was as if I were inside some powerful fairytale, and now would soon be rewarded with my miraculous HAPPY-EVER-AFTER ENDING!!!

***

When I had received Alejandro's address a few weeks earlier back in Ambleton from Odette, I had been so obsessed with thinking ONLY AND EXCLUSIVELY of getting to Paris that the significance of its name had completely eluded me. Of course, the name of the street sounded magnificently grandiose, as only names can in the

French language, but never for one moment had I noticed that it was talking about FREEDOM.

ALEJANDRO'S STREET WENT BY THE NAME OF '......................*DE LA LIBERATION.*

James and I continued to walk down the street, counting the numbers on the houses to ascertain exactly which one belonged to Alejandro. I knew that we were extremely close when suddenly the peace and tranquillity were shattered by a loud shout. On the other side of the road a tall, thin young man, in a fit of temper, kicked what looked like a piece of dog turd off the pavement, and exploded into very loud French.

"All they do is shit on...............” was what I heard and then I couldn't make out the rest of his words. Suddenly my dream-like thoughts came to an abrupt and violent end. It looked as if this young man was standing right in front of Alejandro's house. Literally, within nanoseconds it dawned on me that yes, this was Alejandro's house, and my intuition told me that the young man was in all probability my exalted 'guru's' son.

Nine months in a cramped, dingy room were now being destroyed in the blink of an eye — and that eye just so happened to be MINE! I fell off my emotional cloud and hit the ground with an almighty crash.

It was around 5:15 p.m. when we stepped forward up the path to the front door. I felt embarrassed that we had arrived so early, but there was a limit as to how slowly we could walk before actually covering the thirty metres or so between the gate and the door. Looking at James to see if he was still morally and emotionally with me in this endeavour, I rang the bell to begin a meeting which had been my one and only reason for living for nearly a year.

Someone appeared fairly quickly. It was a young woman who greeted us, but this was the second shock the universe had prepared for me. She was quite obviously Odette the secretary, but I had never expected to encounter what I saw. All along I had known that this was a spiritual journey for me; one in which I had travelled to see a remarkable man who would heal my soul. And yet, standing in front of me was a young woman with raven black hair, dressed in a very short black miniskirt, black high-heeled thigh boots, a black top, and wearing quite a bit of black eye makeup. Perhaps the only thing missing from her apparel was the whip she may have accidentally dropped in the hallway before she answered the door!!!

To say that I was thrown is probably THE UNDERSTATEMENT OF THE CENTURY! Standing on the doorstep, with my broken dreams still written on my stunned face, my brain desperately scrambled to understand why my paradigm had suddenly shifted in what seemed a totally different direction.

Odette was welcoming, but a little put out that we had arrived so early. She explained that there was a nice café on the other side of the street, less than a hundred metres from the house where we could have a coffee before the appointment at 6 p.m. We all tried to be very friendly and obliging with each other, and then James and I took our leave back down the garden path to find the café Odette had mentioned. Looking right, we saw it immediately and made our way there.

Two coffees later, we sat in the empty café, watching the hands of the clock on the wall. James was graciousness itself and didn't bring up the turd-kicking incident or Odette's extravagant appearance. Time seemed to drag as we sat in the café, unable to buy more coffees because money was running out. I tried to small-talk pathetically with James because I was feeling a little insecure about what was about to happen. Eventually the clock signalled that it was finally approaching 6 p.m. and I guiltily asked my friend to wait for me in the café whilst I had my session with Alejandro.

Back at Alejandro's front door, Odette opened it once again, but was surprised to see that James was no longer with me. I explained that I had asked him to wait for me, however she quickly told me to go and fetch him, assuring me that Alejandro would not mind at all if James was present during the psychomagical session. I ran as fast as I could to the café and told James that he was supposed to come with me. He looked surprised, but followed me out and back to Alejandro's house.

***

It was dark outside when Odette ushered us in. I was understandably nervous about the whole situation, given how much I had staked on this precise moment, and also given the dream-shattering events of the last half hour, but Odette was friendly and my hopes began to rise again. She led us down the hallway and out into a back garden. There were lights at the bottom of the garden, and Odette informed us that this was the studio where Alejandro worked.

As we made our way down the path I could see the dim outline of a single-storey summer house. Once at the side of the building, Odette opened a door and Alejandro was standing in front of us, smiling and greeting us warmly. He looked exactly the same as his photograph in the psychomagical book I had bought back in Andalusia, and as I began to speak Spanish with him I relaxed immediately. I felt that instant Latin informality and ease I had found so often in Spanish-speaking people.

The studio we had entered was very large inside and full of shelves crammed to bursting with books. Alejandro led me to a seat opposite his desk and motioned to Odette and James to sit in two other seats a little way off. Alejandro didn't sit behind the desk, but took a seat in front of me and after a few preliminary salutations to everyone, asked me to begin to explain why I had come. Odette sat a few metres from me on my side of the room, and James sat opposite her on Alejandro's side.

THERE WERE FOUR OF US.

At the time this appeared to be a totally unremarkable, if not utterly irrelevant detail. However, with the gift of hindsight, seven years later the full significance of this number would be revealed to me. I would discover that FOUR is a fundamental structure of the human soul, and that it would also become highly symbolic of my entire quest. That day in February 1996 we were not in fact 'accidentally' or apparently merely 'coincidentally' FOUR individuals facing each other.

I looked briefly in James' direction to check if he was okay, but found myself not wanting to make eye contact with him. This was my crazy adventure and I wasn't sure if he was feeling extremely sceptical or even cynical about the whole affair. My eyes, focus and concentration now returned to Alejandro and his question. I blotted everything and everyone out of my mind and my field of vision - at that moment ONLY MY GURU EXISTED FOR ME.

This was what I had dreamt of for so long, what I had believed in so passionately, and I was going to give my whole being to this encounter. I liked Alejandro. I liked his energy and his personality. I felt totally comfortable with him. After the negative omens during our early arrival, my optimism was beginning to return, and I was sure that this man would not disappoint me.

6

THE BEATING AND THE TREASURE

"As the sun rose, the men began to beat the boy........and he felt that death was near.

THE ALCHEMIST:
PAULO COELHO

AS I sat in front of Alejandro and listened to his first question, I was totally unaware that there was to be one final surprise for me that day. What I thought would be an encounter with this man and his genius had, in fact, been preordained to be:

a quite unexpected type of encounter with
MYSELF!

My 'hero' and 'saviour' began by asking very specific questions related to his psychomagical technique, and then he listened with absolute concentration and dedication as I started to talk. The surprise for me was in what I heard coming from my mouth.

Back in my little room in England I could never have guessed that I would come all the way to Paris to speak about things I had heard myself say or write a million times before. What gushed forth from me was an interminable DRONING ON AND ON ABOUT MY PAST. I went through old hurts, pains, sorrows, frustrations and injustices in a never-ending fashion. Alejandro and I seemed to be locked in a bubble we were creating together whilst Odette and James sat patiently enduring a Spanish they obviously couldn't understand.

At one point I paused to gather my thoughts, and quickly glanced in Odette's direction. I thought I saw a look of extreme irritation on her face; I didn't dare look at James.

Alejandro continued to ask various pointed questions and I continued to unburden myself of these feelings. I squirmed inwardly with embarrassment as I felt myself going over and over a past that was long since obsolete, and to all intent and purposes, actually that – THE PAST. Halfway through the session I began to become incredibly weary of the sound of my own monotonous, complaining voice. I was so familiar with these 'traumas' of mine; the whinging and whining refrain of my one and only song.

Suddenly, at one point, a totally unexpected flash of insight came to me. In an instant, a crystal clear knowing flooded my mind, and I realised that I wanted to LET GO OF THIS PAST and embrace a new beginning. I was truly fed up with my own script. However, this meeting somehow had a life and momentum of its own, and it seemed that I was meant to see just how sick and tired I was of my desire, or perhaps my NEED, to cling to the past.

After about forty minutes Alejandro had asked his last question and I had uttered my last words. There was a long moment of silence as Alejandro left his chair and went to sit behind his desk. He sat quietly looking at the notes he had made during the session, and said absolutely nothing.

***

Staring at the person whom I had charged with the responsibility for the healing of my soul, I immediately realised that his energy had changed. This was not the Alejandro who had greeted me so warmly when Odette had opened the summer house door. I didn't feel any optimism or enthusiasm emanating from him as he continued to just stare at his scribblings.

A flicker of dread went through me. Finally, after a minute or so, Alejandro lifted his head and looked at me. He seemed very tired indeed - depressed even.

"You are the most difficult case I have ever had."

He pronounced this verdict almost as if his words were coming out in slow motion. Another pause ensued; a pause long enough for me to feel an immediate sense of foreboding and doom.

My first thought after hearing his conclusion was, oh no, the next thing he's going to say is that he can't help me. I waited patiently to hear the worst, but at the same time was very unsure of what would happen next. There was more silence and then finally Alejandro spoke again. He repeated that I was a very difficult case and that he really didn't know how he could approach things, but he would do his best to try to come up with something. He returned to staring at the notes he had made and then, after what seemed like an eternity, asked me to give him a blank cassette I had brought from England. He was ready to record a psychomagical act for me.

My relief was enormous. His words had left me floundering in fear of real failure, and now disaster seemed to have been averted by the narrowest of margins. I handed Alejandro the cassette and he placed it into his machine which was standing on the table. Carefully he pressed the record button and then began to speak slowly and deliberately. The psychomagical act he started to prescribe me was this:

I had to come to a house dressed in my old clothes and enter a bathroom containing a large bath. There I would take off my clothes and get into the bath completely naked.

I had to then defecate and urinate in the bath and cover every inch of my body, including my face, with my own faeces and urine. Whilst I did this, Mozart's Death Requiem would be playing in the background. Once completely covered with my own excrement, I had to leave the bath and enter a room where my old clothes would be laid out in the form of a square.

I would be asked to sit in the middle of the square, and there I had to endure the smell of my faeces and urine on every part of my body whilst the music of Ravel's Bolero played. This would go on for the whole length of Ravel's piece. At the end

of the music, if and when I was ready, I would ask to be reborn. When I had made this decision, I could then step out of the square, and two masseurs would take me back to the bath where every bit of excrement needed to be washed off me.

Now clean, I would be massaged by the two masseurs until I gave birth to myself. As this new-born being, the masseurs would then dress me in clothes I had brought with me, which would be specifically sky blue and pale pink in colour. These were the colours traditionally worn by new-born babies: blue for boys and pink for girls. Clothed in these colours, I could then go out into the street and find a machine that printed I.D. and business cards.

Standing in front of the machine, without needing to think, I would intuitively grasp my new identity, and instantly know my new name and new profession. I had to then type this information into the machine so that within minutes I would be holding a card giving the details of my new identity.

Alejandro hesitated many times as he struggled to dictate this psychomagical act into the tape recorder. At one point he paused for so long that I thought he was feeling unable to complete it. When he finally finished speaking, I saw that his positive energy had returned, and a smile of satisfaction broke out over his face - he had cracked it! What had weighed him down before the recording was now a solid achievement. However, I most certainly wasn't feeling the same way.

Never in a million years had I expected anything remotely
LIKE THIS!!

I was totally stunned by what had happened. Alejandro explained that I could take the tape away with me, but that he would dictate a more complete written version to Odette during the week which would be sent on to me at my home address. I thanked

Alejandro as sincerely as I could for his real time and effort, but after more than an hour in his company, divulging my most private thoughts and feelings my guru seemed eager to make our goodbyes quite speedy and formal.

He led James and me to the door of the studio, I paid him the fee for the session, probably said another twenty or so 'thank yous', thanked Odette, and then walked out through the door by which we had entered. Odette escorted James and I up the garden path, through the hallway and back to the front door of the house. Within seconds the door shut behind us, and we were once more in the street in the pitch black night.

As we made our way to the Metro station to make the return trip to the hotel, very little by way of conversation occurred between the two of us. I think I was too dazed and bewildered to make any kind of comment, and perhaps my only feedback to James may have been that I wasn't sure how I felt about what had just happened. We were two very tired souls wending our way back to our hotel after a day filled with shocks, surprises and decidedly new experiences

***

That night we both slept like the dead and awoke the next day with the morning and half the afternoon in front of us before we returned to the Gare du Nord for the Eurostar train back to London. After the stress of the previous day, we both knew that this was a morning for just walking and looking, but not engaging in anything that would need any kind of concentration or attention.

We left our bags at the hotel reception and decided to stroll in a random direction from the hotel to simply experience the city as we went. This was a great way to unwind and relax, and neither of us demanded anything of each other. We must have wandered aimlessly for about two hours, when finally we came to a place which instinctively felt like the end of 'our road.' Three extraordinary things happened on this walk which, like so many 'signs' from the invisible realm, cannot be explained.

Just before we reached the end of the walk, James and I passed a huge billboard on the opposite side of the road. It announced that very shortly there was to be an international conference on epilepsy in Paris. I was dumbstruck when I saw the words on the advertisement, and once again had the very strong feeling that I was following some preordained script written by a cosmic hand. That 'script' said that:

on the morning of Wednesday, February 28, 1996,
James and Karen will walk up this road
and see a billboard about epilepsy.

Within about a minute or so of passing the sign, we came upon a small park with a very tiny pond in the middle of it. It was in a street called Rue du Volga. We approached the pond knowing that we had walked far enough and that this was the end point of our Parisian experience. The incredible thing about this ending was that James had two loves in life: his artwork and frogs. He was simply mad about frogs, and it seemed amazing that we had made our way in a totally random fashion through the streets of Paris for more than two hours to what was, more than likely, a pond with frogs in it.

We didn't see any as we stared down at the water's surface, but I don't think its personal significance for James was lost on either of us.

There was one final miracle awaiting us after this encounter with the pond. In the papers I had received from Odette in the previous month concerning Alejandro's work, there had been information about weekly workshops that he gave for the general public in order to share his psychomagical therapeutic technique. One of the papers said that they were conducted in a suburb of central Paris:

in a street called Rue de Maraichers.

As we turned to leave the park and its pond, I found myself walking slightly off to one side towards a very narrow, dilapidated-looking street. It was the advertisement about epilepsy and then the pond which had awoken my sixth sense and the feeling that there was something more to be discovered before we returned to the hotel. When I arrived at the entrance to the street, the sign on the wall of a house said **'Rue de Maraichers'!** How in heaven's name had this happened I asked myself?

I beckoned to James to come over and tried to explain that we had 'accidentally' walked to the street where Alejandro gave his workshops during the week. James looked completely nonplussed by my words. His expression told me that he most definitely was not going to go down this supernatural road with me – I had tested his credulity and patience beyond any normal parameters, and so enough was enough!

The return journey to London was uneventful and mostly in the dark as we travelled through the night. I recounted the psychomagical act to James on the train, but I don't think he really understood my confusion over it or perhaps why I had needed to see Alejandro in the first place. I arrived back at my little room shortly before midnight, and as I walked in everything was exactly as I had left it just under seventy two hours earlier - my world hadn't changed in the least.

Wearily I dropped my bag on the floor and flopped on to the bed. After nine endless months I had finally had my dreamt-of-encounter with Alejandro, and yet absolutely nothing about it was what I had remotely expected. I had hoped for a dramatic healing of my soul, but as I lay sprawled on my bed, I felt no different to when I had left this tiny room. SOMETHING MUST HAVE HAPPENED, I knew this much – BUT WHAT?

The invisible realm wisely decided that a fraught and emotionally exhausted Karen was not to be given any clues as to what it was that night. However, the next few days did answer this question for me because I WAS CHANGED, but not in any way that I had remotely imagined. Instead of feeling 'healed' within my very depths, I felt confused, let down, despondent, depressed and incredibly tired. I truly did not understand what had taken place in Paris, or why the psychomagical act Alejandro had prescribed had turned out to be so...so... well......... WEIRD!

***

During those first days back in England I decided not to plunge back into the routine of life, but kept to myself, spending most of my time just lying on my bed, exhausted and desperately disappointed. Just about the only thing I did manage to do was to phone Mayka and Susana to tell them that the whole thing had not been quite what I expected.

Alone in my room, I listened to Alejandro's tape several times, but felt no spark of enthusiasm or excitement concerning the psychomagical act. The problem for me was that I didn't feel that I had gone to Paris for what he had given me. So, the burning question was:

why did I go to Paris?
That was something I simply couldn't answer.

In this state of depression and defeat what I didn't realise back then in 1996 was that my spiritual hunger had led me into a world for which I had received absolutely no preparation. I had unwittingly jumped head long into the METAPHYSICAL REALM OF LIFE, and was a complete novice as far as this domain was concerned. It was true that I had kept a record of signs for several years, and had also tried to interpret them, but I was still very much a raw beginner in this field.

Secondly, my emotional involvement with this journey was incredibly intense. I hadn't been so much *immersed* in this quest as *submerged by it*. Here I was - a fledgling in virgin skies - and so emotionally taxed by my mission that I quite literally:

COULDN'T SEE THE WOOD FOR THE TREES!

A few days after arriving back from Paris, Mayka and Susana sent me a telegram to let me know that they were sending me a gift of a book. We had spoken several times on the phone and they wanted me to visit them in the Canaries. However, I was still extremely tired and confused about Paris, and didn't know if I had any energy in me to make such a trip - even if they were to pay for it.

Just over a week after my return, I bumped into my neighbour Karen and her boyfriend on the stairs. He was carrying a very small bundle wrapped in a warm blanket, which was obviously their new-born baby. It was a girl, and the baby seemed to be about a week old, if I remember correctly. I congratulated them both on this wonderful event, and then made my way back to my room. The very blatant coincidence that a baby girl had been born whilst I had been in Paris, or just shortly after I had returned, never registered with me. My nervous system was completely frazzled, to put it mildly, and I found myself totally incapable of reading such an obvious sign as this.

On March 11, a package arrived in the morning from Mayka and Susana. I opened it quickly and found the book they had mentioned. It was in Spanish, and entitled:

THE ALCHEMIST

by a writer called Paulo Coelho.

My friends had written individual dedications to me inside the book in Spanish:

> *'So that the encounter with your dreams continues to become a reality.*
> *I know that you will find your inner treasure, the greatest of all treasures, and you will discover the beautiful being that is in you. Kisses, we love you. Mayka'.*

And, from Susana:

> *'I love you lots. For always.*
> *Our meeting was so intense that we will always be connected'.*

Mayka's reference to treasure intrigued me. It didn't seem to have anything to do with what I had been dreaming of achieving in Paris. I thought my quest had been about the healing of my soul, and certainly not a search for treasure. However, as I held the book in my hands that day in March 1996, what I didn't know was that it had arrived at my door because I had MANIFESTED it.

Now, what exactly do I mean by the word 'manifested'? Am I possessed of supernatural skills? Is the wizardry of Harry Potter really possible?

Put simply, the explanation for this is that whatever we achieve inwardly within the invisible and hidden realm of our spirit will then appear for us in the outside world as a concrete material manifestation. This manifestation may already exist in the outside world, but comes specifically into our lives outwardly AS A RESULT OF WHAT HAS HAPPENED INSIDE US.

Right there and then in 1996, I had absolutely no idea that I had taken the shepherd boy Santiago's journey by going to Paris, and that I had experienced a 'beating' and also found my treasure. I would only be given the understanding of this process several years later, and 'coincidentally' also in the month of March.

***

I began reading The Alchemist that afternoon. I read quickly even though my Spanish was not as good as it could have been. I was hungry for some kind of answer to my journey, and Mayka seemed to have hinted at the possibility of one in her dedication.

That evening, I noted down a coincidence I had found in the book: 'TARIFA-TANGIERS.' How strange, I thought to myself. The hero in the book had been to these two places, and I had done EXACTLY THE SAME THING! I also noted that my journey had started in Andalusia, just as it had for this enigmatic shepherd boy Santiago. I cast my mind back a year to when I had been reading Alejandro's book and remembered my dream about giving birth to a baby, and that I was both the mother and the baby in the dream. I wrote the words: 'being born again' in my diary.

Then, over the next two days I continued to read the book, skimming through it because I wanted to get to the end as quickly as possible and find out if there was any explanation for my odyssey to Paris. When I finally finished it, one thought stood out for me - Alejandro had given me back my original dream of rebirth, and it appeared that The Alchemist told exactly the same tale.

In Paulo Coelho's story, Santiago the shepherd had been given back his dream of buried treasure by the leader of the refugees who had led his beating - albeit in a different location. All along, his treasure had been under the ruin in Andalusia where he had had his recurrent dream. But, the fable had necessitated that he make this long journey to the Pyramids of Egypt in order to be told where his treasure really was.

I looked at my own journey and realised that Alejandro's psychomagical act had been all about THE BIRTH OF A NEW ME. Coincidentally, or not so 'coincidentally', in my original dream from February 1995, which I had never mentioned to him, it too had been about the birth, or rather THE REBIRTH OF A NEW ME. In the dream I had given birth to myself and the gory, putrid blood of the placenta had been on my cheek, whereas in the psychomagical act things were THE OTHER WAY AROUND. Gore and dead matter symbolised by my body being covered in my own excrement and urine were there BEFORE I gave birth to myself.

Either way, quite serendipitously, both my dream and Alejandro's solution were about REBIRTH and what seemed to be the negative, downside which went with it. But, what was that downside? At that precise moment in time I didn't really know, nor could I even hazard a guess as to what it might be. So, turning away from this puzzling and enigmatic element, I decided to refer myself back to the pattern of Paulo Coelho's The Alchemist.

It seemed that, just like Santiago, I had left Andalusia, travelled to Tarifa and Tangiers, and then journeyed to a far-off land to experience a rebirth. Through that rebirth I was able to discover that my treasure was exactly where I had left it just over a year earlier. In other words:

BACK IN ANDALUSIA.

***

The true significance of the story of The Alchemist did not really touch me that March. I had read the book so quickly to find out if it contained any answers for me, and I had also read it in a foreign language, that much of its message was lost on me. As I have already said, the only real clarity I had was that the book had shown me that Alejandro had given me back my original dream, albeit in a back-to-front form. Also, I had journeyed and waited for so long because I had needed to learn that my treasure was where I had been in the first place.

Four days after receiving the book, the universe seemed once again to intervene in my journey because I experienced a powerful dream. In it an old man - a lecturer of some sort - was telling me that I had to learn how to die, or in other words, accept my own mortality. He was pointing out to me that time wasn't exactly on my side. I was nearly thirty-eight, and it was vital that I confronted the inevitability of my own death.

When I awoke from the dream, I knew with absolute certainty that it was connected to my journey to Paris. As I reflected on its message I began to suspect that covering myself in my own faeces and urine was probably symbolic of the acceptance of death as the inevitable 'other side of life.' Then I remembered that Alejandro had said that Mozart's Death Requiem would be playing as I sat in the bath tub and covered myself with my own excrement. A glimmer of understanding was beginning to emerge for me.

I thought of my dream with the baby and mother a year earlier, and realised that the blood of the placenta on the baby's cheek was also a symbol of death, just like the faeces Alejandro had prescribed for me. This was because after the birth the blood was no longer living tissue inside the womb, but decaying matter in the outside world.

Amazingly, the invisible realm had given me a prophetic sign about what was to come in the psychomagical session when James and I had witnessed the turd-kicking incident in the street, just outside Alejandro's house only moments before we arrived. Slowly, and almost imperceptibly I began to see more clearly. My rebirth, both in Alejandro's psychomagical act and in my dream, required:

an acceptance of the reality of death.

This insight finally made it totally obvious as to what the 'downside' of rebirth was. Yes, it was DEATH - the other side of life's coin - its inevitable companion.

Aha, now I understood!

That was absolutely as far as I got in my understanding of the events of the last ten months, and my thoughts now turned to whether I should return to Spain or go to Paris and perform the psychomagical act at some point in the future.

Somehow, remaining in England, and saving the money I needed to go back to Paris didn't inspire me in any way. The truth was that this prospect didn't fill my exhausted heart with excitement and unbounded passion. I let the days pass and as the emotional and mental fatigue from the trip left me, gradually the feeling of returning to Spain became stronger. After all, I had reasoned that The Alchemist had told me exactly where my treasure had always been – ANDALUSIA - and that meant that my mission had truly been accomplished!

James did not understand my desire to return to Spain when I gave him the news. I think he felt a little hurt and rejected. He implied with his attitude that I was acting as if England wasn't good enough for me, and this, of course, wasn't true at all. However, thankfully wisdom prevailed, and I knew better than to argue with him at this sensitive time in our friendship. And so, a few days later I phoned 'home' to my parents to tell them that I had been to Paris and that I would be coming back within the next few weeks. To my relief, their reaction was positive, and this allowed me to set about getting a flight booked and tying up loose ends with a sense of calm and happy completion.

During the long and difficult wait in Ambleton my life in my little room had been frugal and austere to say the least: no television, no furniture, no books, and no possessions of any kind really. This meant that the process of leaving was quite a simple affair, only requiring getting rid of a couple of items and then saying goodbye to a few people. I knew exactly what I would give James as a parting gift:

Paulo Coelho's book The Alchemist, plus a ceramic
frog I had seen in a shop window.

I bought both a few days before I was due to leave, and wrote a
sincere and heart-felt dedication inside the book. For me it summed
up completely what I had learned about my odyssey to find healing
in Paris. After writing the dedication to James on the front page of
the book, I made a record of it for posterity in my beloved diary:

Tuesday, March 26, 1996.

*And so we dream, and follow the passion to its
irrevocable end. But all ends are but rebirths, new
beginnings.*
*I go to my new beginning James, to where my
treasure lies, and hope that this book, and my dream
that you shared with me, will guide you to your own
destiny.*
*Be brave and bold, be foolish in your passion for
wresting your destiny from the life around you.*
*'Spew forth my treasure' may be your battle cry,
and be sure that life will answer back— your heart will
hear this answer. Follow her. She is your destiny.*

With love, James,
Karen.

For some peculiar reason, in the last two days before I left, I
couldn't find James when I called at his apartment, and so I had
to leave the book and frog with a friend. After all we had been
through together, poignantly there was to be no proper goodbye
between the two of us.

On Saturday, March 30, after an overnight stay with my brother,
I boarded a plane bound for southern Spain. I felt calm and at
peace with this return; it was exactly what I was meant to be doing.
The journey back passed very quickly and in good company, as I sat
next to a friendly woman called Marika and her young daughter

Harriet. She looked about eight years old and was reading a children's book called Misery Guts.

This instantly made me think about my English roots and how much our identities depend on the language we speak. For a very brief moment I found myself wondering whether I was doing the right thing in leaving England, but this doubt was fleeting for me, and soon we were touching down on Spanish soil. The sun was shining and everything felt so familiar - it was as if I had never been away. It seemed as though for ten months I had entered a time capsule which had cut me off from the world, and now someone had opened the door and let me out.

I waited with everyone else at the luggage carousel to pick up my bags, said my goodbyes to Marika and Harriet, and then walked slowly towards the automatic doors leading to the arrivals hall. I knew my parents had agreed to meet me and would be waiting on the other side of the doors. Momentary fear and apprehension suddenly overcame me as I wondered how they would receive me, but I knew this feeling was a fairly normal one for such a transcendental moment. My arrival was so heavy with significance and emotion that I reacted in the only way available to me. I coped by putting myself on automatic pilot and walked through the automatic doors, which were doing the very same thing.

This took me into the arrivals hall where the usual sea of faces stood anxiously behind the airport barriers, waiting to greet their 'long-lost' loved ones. I spotted my mother and father close by, and saw my mother's face light up immediately when she caught sight of me. Then she shouted out four small words I shall never forget:

"MY BABY IS BACK!!!"

For the most imperceptible of nanoseconds my brain registered utter consternation as I took in what I had just heard. Then, still stunned, but outwardly looking totally relaxed and normal, I put one foot in front of the other and walked forward into what I hoped and prayed would be my brand new beginning — YES: A NEW KAREN WITH A NEWLY REBORN SOUL.

7

WHY THE ALCHEMIST?

THE subconscious mind is truly an extraordinary thing! It is our most direct connection with our souls and the Jungian* concept of the collective unconscious, or **Soul of the World** as Paulo Coelho named it in The Alchemist. Here was my mother acting as some kind of 'cosmic messenger' for me, and blurting out a clear and completely unambiguous fact.

> But how did my mother know that I was returning to Spain
> as a new-born being?

The words have stuck with me for all these years because this was the first time in my life I had ever heard my mother call me her 'baby'

As a small child I spoke Russian with her, and have no recollection of her ever using the word 'baby' in English during my entire life. I knew that my mother's cry came straight from her subconscious mind, but I suspected it also emanated from the much deeper **Soul of the World.** However, the one and only incongruity in all of this was that I DID NOT IN ANY WAY FEEL LIKE A NEWBORN BEING.

On a conscious level I knew perfectly well that I was *supposed* to have been reborn in Paris, but this was more of a theoretical understanding of what had happened to me than a living reality. As I look back more than eighteen years to the events of 1995 and 1996, I realise that the signs about this odyssey were incredibly abundant and obvious - but unfortunately not to me.

(The famous twentieth century Swiss psychiatrist C.G. Jung's concept.)

The reason for this, as I have already said, was because I was engaged in an emotional and spiritual challenge far beyond my experience. I had quite literally been on *an unknown and unmapped path*. And yes, hindsight is truly a wonderful thing!

Another question you may be asking yourself is how what transpired in Paris when I saw Alejandro has anything to do with what happened to Santiago in Paulo Coelho's The Alchemist? In the title to Chapter 6, and also the quotation from The Alchemist, I allude to the fact that Paris had been all about experiencing a 'beating' and then receiving my treasure, just as it had been for Paulo's shepherd boy right at the end of Paulo Coelho's iconic fable. However, I will acknowledge that perhaps this is less than obvious – so let me explain.

In The Alchemist, Santiago's beating at the hands of refugees from the clan wars is symbolic, as is so much of what happens to the shepherd on his journey. Paulo never explains this symbol, but gives us a clear hint as to its meaning. When Santiago feels himself close to death from the beating, he recalls something the mysterious alchemist told him earlier on his journey. This man's words were a reminder to Santiago that money was of no use in saving a person from death. And it was in that fleeting moment of recall that the shepherd boy experienced his epiphany.

He 'saw the light'

With it, he had the immediate realisation, even if only subconsciously, of what and where his treasure truly was. It most definitely wasn't a vast sum of money buried in a hole in the ground of an Egyptian desert dune. Instead, he saw with complete certainty that it was within his very own essence or being.

His treasure Santiago realised was life, and more specifically

HIS OWN PRECIOUS LIFE.

With that sudden awareness, he abandoned his digging in the sands of the Egyptian desert and was rewarded by being given his true treasure by the leader of the refugees. This was Santiago's moment of spiritual rebirth, and curious as it may seem, what happened to me in Alejandro's study at the bottom of his garden in Paris was symbolically almost identical to what happened to Santiago.

***

In The Alchemist the shepherd's beating is both metaphorical and literal: he is BEATEN by his own digging inside the hole, but also physically beaten by the refugees when his digging produces no results. For me, even though there was only one type of 'beating' - the metaphorical – a BEATING is what I got.

When I began to talk about myself and my past, locked in that bubble with Alejandro, the two of us were metaphorically DIGGING a hole which, like Santiago's, was also giving us absolutely nothing. Well, when I say nothing, I have to qualify this and show you that this was not quite true. Mirroring the shepherd's experience, as I dug my hole with Alejandro's help, I experienced the futility and emptiness of what I was doing. The 'beating' I received was the pain of listening to my own monologue, and the feeling of being sick and tired of my interminable complaints and dramas.

In many ways Alejandro, like the refugees in Paulo's book who found gold on Santiago and had forced him to carry on digging in the desert sand, performed exactly the same role as these men. With his periodic, highly specific questions, his task was to push me on to keep EXCAVATING INSIDE MY PERSONAL HOLE. In a sense, Alejandro was like the conductor of an orchestra holding the baton, and I the soloist 'playing away' in response to the movements of that baton.

Did I, as a result, see my own death close at hand as Santiago had in Paulo's fable? Well, not exactly, in the purely literal sense. My monologue didn't lead me into a sudden encounter with mortality, but I did experience a sort of feeling of BEING DEAD as I listened to words I had repeated so many times in the past. Everything I brought to Alejandro, and which he unveiled for me with his questioning, was DEAD MATTER; a past that could no longer bring me any kind of vitality, joy and life.

As I have said, it was in one brief moment, sitting inside Alejandro's study, when consciously the thought flickered through my mind that I wanted to let go of all this 'stuff' and move forward into the new – A NEW ME! This realisation was my own epiphany, and the moment when my soul was reborn.

THE MAGIC OF ALCHEMY

The central metaphor of The Alchemist is alchemy.

Paulo Coelho studied alchemy intensively, even somewhat obsessively, in his twenties when he discovered that he had no answer to the fear of his own mortality. His initial fascination with alchemy had come about because he discovered that the ancient alchemists had tried to find the fabled ELIXIR OF LIFE - a substance that would grant a person eternal youth. However, by the time Paulo came to write The Alchemist, he had long ago abandoned this very material concept of alchemy and uncovered its metaphorical and symbolic meaning.

Although the original medieval alchemists had tried to change base metals into gold, the essence of alchemy had always been spiritual. Since its very inception it had always been a search for the transformative spiritual power locked inside nature, and Paulo Coelho's story of Santiago is a tale of a young man's search for that transformative power.

This is not a conscious intent on the part of the shepherd boy; consciously, he is only aware of wanting to find a treasure that appeared to him in a dream. However, the process he unconsciously submits himself to is that of his own personal transformation. On his long journey to find that 'treasure', Santiago learns about himself and the whisperings of his heart. He discovers how the **Soul of the World** speaks to each of us through signs or omens, if we are only willing to be still and listen and watch.

He is transformed by the process of journeying he undergoes and is finally rewarded with THE GREATEST OF ALL POSSIBLE TRANSFORMATIONS:

THE ALCHEMICAL 'UNLOCKING' OF HIS PERSONAL TREASURE

In the language of fables, he finds gold and jewels where he originally had his dream, but of course these are only symbols of the inner gold and jewels he actually finds within himself. By crazily following the passion of his heart, he works alchemy on himself and transforms his ordinary 'base metal' self into the gold of his new REBORN SPIRITUAL SELF. Equally, and seemingly 'coincidentally', it was this very same process of personal transformation which happened to me.

I began my journey with a dream about my own rebirth in Andalusia, and the journey ended with this rebirth taking place. However, the process I engaged with was so extraordinarily subtle - in fact so much so - that I never actually came *to feel as if I had been reborn*. Nevertheless, the moment in which I despaired of listening to the mini Hell that was my interminable churning over of my past in front of Alejandro Jodorowsky, and suddenly in a flash consciously wished to let go of it all:

> this was the fleeting and conscious
> rebirth of my spirit and soul.

However, besides this 'cosmic miracle', the journey to Paris, which took nine months from the time I arrived in England, was also more than just a deep search for my soul. Without me knowing it, my meeting with Alejandro had been two events rolled into one.

It was actually a rite of passage and also a rite of initiation.

Rites of passage are common place events in all our lives marking the end of a certain phase of our lives, and the beginning of a new one. The invisible realm has a very intimate relationship with all of us, even though we may be completely unaware of this, and will invariably bring into our lives specific circumstances or situations to let us know that we are making an important transition. Divorces, marriages, deaths, accidents, loss of jobs, house moves, births of babies, promotions, holidays, are the many ways we 'DIE' to our old self and embrace and enter into a relationship with our new self.

Paris was a rite of passage for me from youth into middle age, but, on a deeper, invisible level, it turned out to be something much, much bigger than that. It was a rite of initiation into a spiritual journey which would take me another eighteen years to complete.

***

The Alchemist is a truly magical book because, having been written in the form of a fable, its simplicity speaks directly to our subconscious minds and hearts.

The head or conscious mind is not directly engaged; instead it is our spirit which resonates with the story. But the fable is far more profound and transcendental than it seems. In the following years after Paris, as my own journey progressed, I began to learn that Paulo Coelho's book is, in fact, an archetypal myth of the human spiritual quest for God. Wow – now that is a huge and amazingly audacious statement!

What is an archetype and what exactly do I mean?

The Swiss psychiatrist Carl Gustav Jung, who revolutionised psychology and psychiatry in the twentieth century, was the pioneer in discovering the primal nature of archetypes as part of the organisation and pattern of the human soul. These patterns, for Jung, were the universals which underlay all human experience, but which are expressed as different rituals, symbols and metaphors in all our various cultures.

He initially called these subconscious patterns of the human soul 'primordial images', but later adopted the term 'archetype'. Examples of some archetypes are birth, marriage, death, parenting, courtship, initiation and transcendence, and it is this very last archetype which is the deepest of them all. By transcendence I refer to the universal quest of the human spirit to overcome THE DUALITY OF HUMAN EXISTENCE and find the transcendent, unifying source of everything - in other words GOD!

In our physical lives we live in a world of opposites or what we call duality: night-day, male-female, hot-cold, life-death, growth-decay, happiness-sadness, and so on.

Duality is what underpins our material existence on this planet, and is the fundamental organisation of our manifest world.

However, within the soul the archetype we call TRANSCENDENCE seeks the reality of what exists beyond this yo-yo, to-and-fro experience of life. The soul knows that there is a reality which is able to unite these opposites, and in so doing, TRANSCEND THEM. This domain is THE INVISIBLE REALM OF OUR SPIRITS.

Jung proposed that archetypes were not just to be found within the human psyche or soul, but also existed in the world around us. For Jung our physical world was, if you like, a mirror showing us on the outside what was also inside us, and so this was why the physical book The Alchemist appeared to 'manifest' for me on my return from Paris.

As I said earlier, what I had achieved
INSIDE MYSELF
through the journey came into being
OUTSIDE ME
In the form of the book.

Even though I had studied psychology at University back in the 1970s, I didn't know any of this when I took the first steps on my spiritual quest to find and live from my soul. However, over the years my experiences would show me that Jung was an extraordinarily intuitive genius, and completely right in his thinking. And, apart from being a pioneering psychiatrist, he was also a dedicated alchemist. He had studied alchemy with enormous passion because he knew that it was the science and art of the human soul. It was Jung, more than anyone else, who was responsible for bringing alchemy into the twentieth century, and revealing its spiritual dimension.

One particular Renaissance alchemist Jung revered and whose work he studied meticulously was the man Paracelsus. Paracelsus, like Jung, had been born in Switzerland - only several centuries earlier in 1493.

He had been a physician, alchemist, astrologer and botanist. From Paracelsus Jung learned that we humans have two sources of knowledge of the divine. One is called LUMEN DEI, and is the apprehension of light coming directly from God. This is what we experience when our spirits are illuminated directly through revelation. The other source is called LUMEN NATURAE, which is the divine light *hidden* in physical matter and nature itself.

Unlike Lumen Dei, this counterpart light can only be experienced by releasing it from nature through alchemy. In other words Lumen Naturae is seen as caught or IMPRISONED in our physical world, and needs to be 'liberated' by an alchemical process of transformation.

'There's gold in them there hills', so the miners' saying goes, and for the alchemists, there was metaphorical 'gold' hidden in nature, if only the transformative formula could be found.

It was this 'gold' - the light of his spirit — for which
the shepherd Santiago went in search.

***

As I have already stated, our human species being one that is physically incarnated, inevitably exists within the dual nature of the physical world. Our material bodies faithfully reflect this physical duality as in our two eyes, two lungs, two arms and so on. But, what we perhaps have never seriously considered before in our modern, materially-based culture is the possibility that OUR SOULS ARE ALSO OF THIS DUAL NATURE.

Yes, for me the soul is not one unified whole, but
made up of two distinct halves.

My hypothesis is that these two halves can be distinguished from one another by the two different ways in which each knows our world, and also connects with the divine light we call God. My suggestion is that these 'ways' are Paracelsus' two sources of divine knowledge - Lumen Dei and Lumen Naturae.

My other suggestion is that Santiago's alchemical journey to the Pyramids of Egypt was his journey in search of overcoming and transcending that dual nature of his own soul. However, before he could achieve this goal, he would need to access the Lumen Naturae 'IMPRISONED' WITHIN THE OPPOSITE HALF OF HIMSELF. And, the only way in which the shepherd boy could do this would be by making a physical journey into the material world outside himself.

That is the central paradox of The Alchemist.
It would only be through an OUTWARD encounter with the other
half of his own soul that he would then experience a simultaneous
INNER encounter with that other half's spirit inside himself.

This was not theoretical alchemy he chose to perform, nor alchemy in a laboratory, but the alchemy of life experience - transformation through living and learning.

All of this may seem rather heavy and esoteric, and in many ways it is. This was complicated knowledge I didn't have in any shape or form when I began my nineteen year quest to discover my soul. And yet, with complete dedication to this search, through my intuition and a little basic understanding of Jungian psychology, I was able to live and discover these seemingly rather rarefied truths for myself - and also know them in a much simpler form.

At the bottom of Alejandro Jodorowky's garden, metaphorically WITHING SIGHT of a large glass pyramid of light in Paris, I initiated a journey encapsulated by Paulo Coelho's modern version of an ancient allegory; an allegory relating man's quest for:

SELF-DISCOVERY AND TRANSCENDENCE.

So, dear reader, through this account of my personal search for soul rebirth, and alchemical transformation, you will see that Paulo's The Alchemist is far deeper than it appears. In the years that followed I learned that Santiago's beating at the very end of the fable was actually THE MOST IMPORTANT PART OF THE STORY. In fact, although Paulo Coelho dedicates very few words to its description, it is:

THE ALCHEMICAL HEART OF HIS TALE.

Without it, there is no alchemy, and no discovery by Santiago of his Lumen Naturae within the other half of his soul.

This ending is not, as many seem to think when you read study guides for The Alchemist on the internet, an elegant paradoxical twist to the end of a supernatural story of self-discovery, In reality, it is a description of the ACTUAL ALCHEMICAL PROCESS by which Santiago experiences the rebirth of his soul. Without it, absolutely no transformation within himself was possible – no matter how much he had learned before this moment of beating at the very end of the fable.

The reason for this is because that apparently 'enigmatic beating' right at the end of the shepherd boy's odyssey was his cosmic encounter with HIS OWN SHADOW – the 'impurities' within himself which needed to be ALCHEMICALLY BURNED OFF inside the metaphorical furnace of his soul before any transformation could take place.

Following in the shepherd boy's footsteps, I too would journey to receive a 'beating' from my own shadow, and in so doing, bring about the rebirth of my soul. However, unlike Santiago, for me there would be more than just one 'beating'. My journey would last for so many years because I would find myself 'pounded into a pulp' by more 'beatings' than I could ever count, as impurity after impurity would be brought up into the light of conscious awareness.

Through my long years of questing, and these innumerable, and painful alchemical transformations, I was also destined to uncover A SECOND GREAT TRUTH regarding the meaning of The Alchemist – something I have never heard anyone mention before in all the commentaries I have read about Paulo Coelho's fable. It is that the story also hides another reality, apart from that of a confrontation with one's shadow.

Santiago's original dream in which he was told that he would find 'treasure' at the Pyramids of Egypt, WAS ACTUALLY TRUE.

THERE REALLY WAS TREASURE BURIED
IN THE SANDS OF EGYPT!!!

If only Santiago's heart had been in a *different space*, and he had carried on digging for just a little longer, in a slightly different spot, he would have found it.

This treasure belonged to the men who beat him at the end of Paulo's fable, and specifically their leader, who finally revealed the true location of Santiago's treasure to him. All of that I was to uncover for myself ten very long years later in 2006.

However, for more than a decade and a half after my return from Paris, my spirit would push me to continue this quest, journeying to countless metaphorical Egypts in order to endure a 'beating' at each one, and experience MANY REBIRTHS OF MY SOUL. Here was a giant metaphysical pyramid my spirit was obsessively set on climbing - an invisible Mount Everest stretched out over time - and if anyone had told me that all this lay ahead of me, I would never, but never have allowed myself to venture onto this path.

Through innumerable acts of grace, God, or the supreme intelligence which governs our lives, hides so many things from all of us. We are not told about accidents, divorces, deaths and all manner of other trials we will encounter when we agree to sign up for life. He/She or It knows that we spirits clothed in human bodies could never face any of it if we were given prior knowledge of what lay ahead. Our spirit is the one and only part of us that has this knowledge, and from deep within our subconscious minds it calls to us to follow our God-given paths.

In the end, the destination we all long to reach, whether it be over metaphorical seas, up symbolic mountains, or across imaginary deserts, is paradoxically THE SAME FOR EACH AND EVERY ONE OF US. It is what I have called Divine Love or our BIG DREAM; that transcendent light of our spirit within the two unified halves of our soul.

The Love that is the very essence of who we are.

**The mighty pyramids of stone
That wedge-like cleave the desert airs,
when nearer seen, and better known,
are but gigantic flights of stairs.**

THE LADDER OF SAINT AUGUSTINE, LONGFELLOW

BOOK TWO:
THE QUEST

If you want to eliminate the suffering in the world, then eliminate all that is dark and negative in yourself. Truly, the greatest gift you have to give is that of your own self-transformation.

LAO-TZU.

PROLOGUE

ANWAR hated Cairo and Cairo hated Anwar; at least that was how he felt on the rare occasions whenever he was forced to visit the city. Anwar was a man of the desert, not of crowded, noisy, dusty streets and the endless streams of nameless strangers who were too busy to notice anything around them.

However, unfortunately today was completely different. Much as he loathed to admit it to himself, he needed help, and Amira the fortune teller was the only person who could provide that for him. She had guided him once before, more than ten years earlier, when she had told him that he needed to go out into the desert to find himself.

Now, he was lost for a second time. No one knew this but Anwar, and he could see that without Amira's special gift he would no longer be able to lead his men. The truth was that even if his friends and cohorts couldn't detect it, Anwar felt utterly incapable of disguising his inner fear from himself.

When he arrived at the bottom of an alleyway he saw that the old woman's house was unchanged. The decorative terracotta tiles around the door were still chipped and grimy. Anwar knocked on the door and instantly remembered his younger, troubled self.

Amira barely glanced at him when she opened the door, and directed him to sit on the old Persian carpet in the middle of the room – exactly the same one he had sat on ten years ago. She was undeniably much older now, and Anwar only prayed that she would still be capable of discerning his destiny.

Amira sat down beside him, and gently brushed the palm of his left hand with aromatic oil. Then, rubbing her thumb over the centre of his palm she spoke. "Your life is about to change, my son. You have travelled a long and hard road, and you have been strong, but your heart is tired."

Anwar closed his eyes with relief. Amira had seen his dilemma – thankfully her powers were still intact. She continued to speak. "You will meet a stranger near the pyramids, and he will give you your treasure. Without this treasure, you cannot go on.

"When?" Anwar demanded suddenly, grasping hold of the old woman's wrists with both hands in an unexpected act of desperation.

"WHEN YOU ARE READY," Amira replied, fixing Anwar with a steely glare. He instantly withdrew his hands and lowered his gaze in shame, for he knew that his violent reaction had offended her.

"Am I ready?" he asked apologetically, and with his eyes firmly fixed to the ground.

"Perhaps," said Amira, "but then again, perhaps not. Your heart is ready, of that I have no doubt, but as for you – well I can't do your work for you."

Anwar bravely hid his disappointment; he had hoped for just a little more from this old woman with the gift.

"Amira, will my heart speak to me?" he asked almost pleadingly now.

"As I have just told you my son, when you are ready - when you are ready. Now, I have given you all that you need to know, so you must go. The future is waiting for you."

Amira slowly rose to her feet as she gripped the side of a large wooden chest in order to maintain her balance. Then, once again she dipped her thumb into the bowl of aromatic oil. Leaning over Anwar, she pressed her thumb hard between his jet black brows:

"As Allah knows - IT IS WRITTEN, MY SON, IT IS WRITTEN."

PART I: SHADOWLANDS (REDEMPTION ROAD)

Love is the only game
that is not called on account of darkness.

AUTHOR UNKNOWN

8

ME AND MY SHADOW

**Escaping the true nature of life is not an option
when you have set your heart on knowing it.**

ANON

BACK in Spain my parents made no mention whatsoever of my
odyssey to Paris, apart from one short sentence from my mother
when she declared: "You certainly needed guts to do what you did."
Then, by mutual consent the subject was closed.

In May, when Mayka and Susana came from the Canaries to
see me for my birthday, little was said between us about it either.
All in all, it was almost as if the ten months in England had never
happened – an aberration no one wanted to examine. As I stated
before, although on my return from Paris I had eventually grasped
that my rebirth involved a confrontation with and acceptance of
death, the ten month journey was still something I hadn't really
understood. I had barely taken in the meaning of The Alchemist in
England, and just before my return to Spain I had given the book
away to a young Spanish man I had met in the hypermarket, hoping
that it might help him in his own journey through life.

Now, finding myself on Andalusian soil once again, and with
no one to talk to about what I had been through, I felt cut off
emotionally and spiritually from the experience. But, looking
back, perhaps fate had organised things to be this way so that I
would temporarily FORGET about my Parisian 'ADVENTURE' and
concentrate on what was in front of me in the here and now. And so,
that is exactly what I decided to do.

However, even if I was feeling more or less unchanged by my quest, whether I realised it or not, a change had taken place and the universe didn't waste any time in letting me know it. I moved back into an apartment my parents owned, and in which I had lived on-and-off for several years, and the next stage of my spiritual search moved in with me as *the worst of all possible flatmates!* She made her appearance at the beginning of July, and introduced herself one night as my long-lost 'friend' **DEATH!!!**

Again, as with most things on this spiritual journey, there was never any warning of what was about to happen. One night I simply went to bed as usual and fell asleep, only to find myself waking up in a total state of panic at around two in the morning. Sweat was pouring off the back of my head and my pillow was completely saturated.

DEATH HAD COME TO SAY 'HELLO'!!!

***

At that moment I simply sat bolt upright in my bed and felt the most horrible terror inside me concerning my own mortality. Naturally, I hoped that this was just a one-off event and that normal sleep would soon return – but how very wrong I was. The waking at two in the morning, with my pillow soaked, and feeling each fibre of my being consumed with the fear of my own death, went on every night for about four weeks. This was incredibly draining.

Each night as I awoke with a start and sat up in my bed rigid with fear I remembered the dream I had experienced on my return from Paris about coming to terms with my own mortality. Its message had been clear and unequivocal - time was not exactly on my side. I also thought about the excrement in the psychomagical act, and realised that this terror I felt night after night certainly wasn't something new. I had been terrified of death as a child, and this fear had been lying buried inside me for decades. Now, it had caught up with me, and was asking to be faced if I wanted to progress spiritually.

Although the four weeks of terror suddenly ended one night as abruptly and mysteriously as they had started, I found myself deeply traumatised by this unexpected turn of events. I was also exhausted from a lack of sleep and the nervous exhaustion that comes with experiencing such extreme fear on a daily basis.

Normal sleep did return, but during the day I quite unexpectedly developed other problems which I could never have anticipated. It seemed that I had suddenly lost contact with my body, and couldn't feel when I was hungry or thirsty, or if I needed to urinate or defecate. It really didn't require much thought on my part to realise with alarm that this was a completely new scenario in my life, and a very serious one at that.

Knowing that I was in desperate need of help, on my shopping trips into town my spirit frantically scanned innumerable advertisements in shop windows in an attempt to find a therapist. I needed someone – ANYONE - with whom I could talk; I was an utter and total mess. Luckily, I found that person fairly quickly and felt I had hit upon an authentic genius. The therapist told me that I was encountering a syndrome very common to drug addicts - I had lost touch with my body and was totally stuck inside my head. He prescribed me a simple diet of fruits and brown bread in order to 'break' this condition and help me reconnect with my body.

I followed the diet for two weeks, and to my great surprise it worked. Thus started a period of several weeks during which I visited my 'guru' regularly and talked incoherently and frantically about all my most deep-seated fears. During these 'therapy' sessions I was obliged by the therapist to read THE TIBETAN BOOK OF THE DEAD to help me deal with my overwhelming terror of death, but rather than helping me, the book seemed to make my fear even worse.

One day I realised that I was getting absolutely nowhere with this approach; there appeared to be an inherent air of cold, compassionless detachment coming from the therapist which unnerved me. The 'shine' was fading fast from my spiritual guide and 'friend', and so I decided to abandon my visits to him and his esoteric methodology.

Now, to walk away from a so-called 'expert' because you somehow trust yourself more is one of the hardest things to do in life. One usually does this at a point in time when there is no Plan B on the horizon, and that inevitably makes the decision taken even more risky or courageous, depending on your personal levels of fear or faith. However, despite this almost disastrous return to Spain, the one thing that was totally clear to me was that I was still on a spiritual path in search of my soul — or what I now understood would be SOUL REBIRTH.

I felt this to be my on-going reality because I couldn't in any way sense HOW my odyssey to Paris had brought me any closer to an encounter with this core part of me. In 1996 I didn't exactly know where my soul was located inside me, or when I would find it, but I knew for certain that my intuition was the royal road to a close contact with this centre of truth within me.

Apart from the few weeks in early August when I had temporarily found myself completely disconnected from my own body, since my original soul dream of 1993 I had religiously practised the discipline of being as closely connected to that intuition as I possibly could. Central to this effort was trying to keep my ego at bay in the passenger seat of myself. Using the metaphor of a car, every morning on waking I would concentrate on putting my intuition in the driving seat, and each day became a process of willing myself to keep it there. Of course, nothing is ever plain sailing, and my ego was a much tougher adversary than I had ever imagined.

It would regularly overwhelm me, and jump straight into the front seat of my 'vehicle', taking over the driving for several hours. However, overall, I was able to say that most of each sixteen-hour day was 'dominated' by my intuition.

***

After my return from England, and with it the sudden unexpected appearance of my life-long fear of death, the next three-and-a-half years turned into a time of deep pain and learning. Even though this was not what I had anticipated by any stretch of the imagination when I had gleefully returned to Andalusia, in a sense whatever came up for me couldn't be avoided because I had already committed myself to a very specific path back in 1993.

My obsessive hunger for my soul was so strong that I simply had no option but to accept what was happening around and within me, even if I had no way of understanding it. And so I faced those forty two months by continuing with my spiritual discipline, and I also used what little energy I had left for meticulous self-observation.

For some peculiar reason I never bought myself another copy of The Alchemist in order to re-read it, but I did discover other books written by Paulo Coelho, and proceeded to devour them voraciously. One in particular spoke incredibly directly to me. It was called:

Manual of the Warrior of the Light.

In its pages I discovered that my constant effort to subordinate my ego and keep my intuition in control of my behaviour was exactly the same discipline described in this book. The text was a revelation to me and cut through my feelings of isolation and loneliness. Through its meditative reflections on the nature of the spiritual path, Mr Coelho became my most prized and intimate mentor on my continuing spiritual quest.

During this three-and-a-half year period, I found myself journeying along a varied, unpredictable and diversely constructed learning curve full of ups, downs, bumps and surprises. The naive Karen who had jumped on a plane back in June 1995 to journey to England, and who really believed that life could be one great, big fairy-tale, would never have foreseen any of this.

In my first year back in Andalusia I avoided a nervous breakdown, and then returned to England for a few months. The following year saw me in Andalusia once again, and joining an English-speaking Christian Evangelical church. In the spring of the third year I left the aforementioned church and met a Spanish gentleman who lived in Madrid. We set up home together for six months, each of us 'high' on a dream of finding true love, but our crazy leap into the unknown revealed that this was not to be. I ended the relationship at the beginning of August of that year and returned to the only place I could truly call 'home' - my parent's house amongst the olive groves, next to *my magical ruin*.

Although painful, and more than confusing, all of these experiences only served to confirm for me that my intuition was, as I had always suspected, my most direct connection to my inner spirit. It seemed that this spirit inhabited my soul, which, in turn, lived somewhere in or possibly around my heart – at least that is what it felt like. I wasn't sure if my heart was inside my soul, or my soul inside my heart, but I refused to read esoteric literature on the subject; I was determined to make real experiential discoveries, and access spiritual truth directly on my own.

***

Such dedication and passion on my part bore fruit and I learnt an enormous amount about myself and the human condition in general. During this bumpy, 42 month learning period I discovered that my constant 'enemy' was still my ego, and my heroic efforts to keep her under control revealed so much about this 'other' aspect of my nature.

By observing myself almost forensically, I could see that my ego was essentially the antithesis of my spirit. It was highly intelligent, but selfish, insensitive, heartless, controlling, and extremely fearful and domineering. My spirit however was gentle, patient, wise, loving and trusting. I also saw that my ego was incredibly addictive; it was obsessive in the extreme and clung tenaciously to its passions.

As well as all of this, I learnt that the ego had a travelling companion; the strongest force we human beings possess. And, for something so powerful, you will be surprised to know that we only need three letters in order to spell it out – **S.E.X.** Did I just say sex? Yes, I most certainly did. During this time of accelerated learning, I experienced my sexual feelings flaring up inside me at what seemed like 'the drop of a hat'. When they did so, they were never connected to my spiritual values. On the contrary, it was shocking and deeply mortifying to see what kinds of situations and types of men provoked such feelings in me.

By saying this directly to you, dear friend, I am making a very public and uncomfortable confession of a very personal weakness, but I do this for A VERY IMPORTANT REASON. At a point in history where we feel we have shaken off the shackles of sexual repression, we have blindly not bargained for the fact that we have never fully understood the utterly primal nature of this force. That was what I now found myself encountering inside my own mortal flesh. Like any addict facing their personal demon, many of the ways in which I was 'tempted' were utterly degrading to say the least.

Through sheer will power I never acted on the sexual arousal I experienced, but simply watched it wage a war inside my body, fighting to annihilate every one of my most cherished spiritual ideals and values. These sexual feelings wanted one thing, and one thing only - their own pleasure-seeking satisfaction and consummation.

To make matters worse in my daily battles with my ego, I found that the material world used sex and erotic feelings as its prime language of communication. But this 'language', which sold food, cars, houses, drugs, clothes, animals, furniture, happiness and a cornucopia of dreams, was ultimately totally disconnected from any moral parameters. It was — and please forgive the pun - a naked instrument of power.

From the havoc it had caused inside my own body and mind, I could understand the terrible danger of sexual feelings when they were disconnected from genuine feelings of love coming from our souls. I also saw how they could control and humiliate a person who was caught in their grip. The fact that there now seems to be an 'epidemic' of internet pornography, incidences of paedophilia and also sexual violence around the world only bears testament to the truth of what I am saying.

Let us not complacently and smugly distance ourselves from this reality, dear friend, which appears to be rising exponentially as I write these words. The human shadow should never be underestimated, for it is a deceptively treacherous beast. Truly it can be said of all of us that BUT FOR THE GRACE OF GOD, THERE GO WE!!!

It is something we will all have to face and examine, sooner rather than later, as a globally interconnected society. Anyway, let me end this short digression, and return to my personal battle.

***

These two tyrants - the ego and sex - became the companions I observed, studied and controlled day in and day out for forty two long months. Each morning when I awoke, there would be four of us facing the new day - me, my spirit, and my two very material UGLY

SISTERS. Their only mission was to gain control of me and derail me from living in search of my soul. Nevertheless, my spiritual passion went far deeper than either of them, and I managed to win my often excruciating battles almost all of the time. I was determined to stay connected to my spirit, come hell or high water – and that is not merely a neat turn of phrase dear friend. Oh, no. I found myself in a real spiritual war, and intuition was my only compass and North star.

It was during this time that I started to refer to my ego and sex as my shadow. I was vaguely aware of a Jungian concept of the shadow, and knew that the universal shadow of Mankind was death. This allowed me to begin to slowly half-understand why I had been assaulted by the terrible fear of my own death on my return to Spain back in 1996.

It seemed to me that the human condition which raged inside me, and which I obviously shared with every other individual on the planet, was about each person's encounter and battle with the human shadow - those aspects of their character that demeaned, degraded or destroyed them and others in some way.

If death was the parent of this aspect of
ourselves then the ego and sex were most definitely
her offspring.

I was aware that Jung had defined the shadow as an archetype which we relegated to the realms of unconsciousness, or simply chose to deny – never admitting to ourselves the existence of this murky, dark and treacherous aspect of our being. He described how the 'bad' side of our psyche would be cast out of consciousness like a hideous and unwelcome guest in order to inhabit the unconscious part of us. And yet, paradoxically it could not be banished forever. Inexorably, it would find its way back into our lives through projections, psychosomatic disorders or sudden breakdowns in our conscious personalities.

I knew Jung was a genius, but found anything that I read about his work extremely complicated and somewhat inaccessible. Nevertheless, even though I was not of the same intellectual calibre as this man, or a so-called 'expert' in this field, I was also beginning to see that my spiritual journeying wasn't of the more commonly experienced type of spiritual 'awakenings' which the average person might touch in themselves.

Much like Jung, and others who had come before and after him, my questing was taking me into very, very deep levels of my own human condition, and I felt confident that I could comprehend what I was learning about life, and also theorise about these insights, on my own terms - even if I were borrowing half-understood ideas from this giant of the twentieth century.

***

As well as encountering my shadow during this three-and-a-half year period, several very significant events happened to me. The first came about after I joined a Christian evangelical church in 1997. That spring I found an English-speaking church in Salveira and felt a deep desire to break free of my lone walk in order to share my faith with others. So it was that I brought my tired heart into this apparently welcoming fold, hoping to find like-minds and like-souls. However, the experience very soon proved to be a mixed one.

On the positive side I learnt an enormous amount about the history of Christianity. Some preachers seemed to know the Old Testament inside out, and it was fascinating to listen to their sermons. But, on the negative side I didn't find the fellowship and sharing I so desperately needed. Instead, I encountered a lot of religious zeal, bigotry and passion for evangelising- AT WHATEVER COST. When I tried to point out that the Christian gospel was about love – A LOVE OF EVERYONE - I saw eyes glaze over and minds shut down. The expression on people's faces was generally one of, 'she's not getting it, is she?'

It was whilst I attended the church that one night I had a very vivid and unforgettable dream. I dreamt that I was in Guatemala in Central America, and that I had gone there to teach English to the native children. In the dream I was in a large town, possibly the capital city, and the streets were paved with huge, heavy flagstones which looked as though they had been laid by the Spanish conquistadors.

I stood outside a cathedral made of the same stone. In one part of the dream I entered the building, and decided to climb one of the towers which happened to be a clock tower. I climbed up a winding, spiral staircase, until I reached the top of the tower, and then suddenly the dream ended. This dream was so strong and memorable that a few days later I sought out one of the elderly Christians I knew at the fellowship to share it with him.

His verdict was simple and straight forward. He felt it probably meant that at some time in the future I would travel to Guatemala to teach English there – and climb the cathedrals clock tower. Great, I thought, SO MUCH FOR THE WISDOM OF AGE!

At that moment I was not to know that this was in fact a prophetic dream about my future, and that seven years later I would indeed be standing outside this great cathedral staring up at the clock tower I had climbed in my dream. But, this was not to be in Guatemala.

Instead, the place would be the famous pilgrimage
town of SANTIAGO DE COMPOSTELA
in northern Spain.

Something else that was of great importance during these three-and-a-half years of painful spiritual growth was the awakening I experienced during my short relationship with my Spanish boyfriend, which began after I had decided to abandon the evangelical fellowship. Alberto was sixteen years older than me, and had a wealth of life experience under his belt.

It was during my stay with him in Madrid that I began to see and feel on a much deeper level than ever before. Where my physical eyes had dominated my vision and feelings, suddenly I started to 'see' and feel the invisible realm. It was my heart that began to have 'eyes' and used a totally different 'light' from that of the physical spectrum in order to see another reality beneath the surface appearance of life. And, even though the relationship between Alberto and I finally ended painfully after only six months, this change in me was due to him alone.

Through all the pain we shared, I could clearly see the greatness and depth of his very noble heart. Our time together represented a true quantum leap in my spirit, because if I had arrived in Madrid still clinging to my girlhood, I left the city as a woman - and a more spiritual one at that.

***

The final extremely significant event which took place between April 1996 and October 1999 occurred right at the end of that period. In the first week of October I found myself inside a deep and unremitting state of depression. Was it being triggered by the stress of my break from Alberto, or the strain of living in search of my soul, or the sheer agonising loneliness of it all? Probably everything combined to making me feel desolate and emotionally wrung dry.

One afternoon I left my parents' house and walked up the fennel-covered hill and its terraces to sit at the foot of *'my ruin'*. As I looked out at the glittering Mediterranean Sea I wondered where I was going with my journey. It was something I couldn't talk to anyone about, and yet it was at the centre of my very reason for being. In that moment, I found myself experiencing a deep and terrible loneliness inside the very core of my being. I suddenly felt incredibly weak, but paradoxically and strangely very strong at the same time. Could I leave this crazy path I was on was the question in my head? Life would become a lot easier if I did. But as I sat with my back pressed against its warm, rugged stones, I knew that *'my ruin'* was tangible physical proof that I couldn't.

After about twenty minutes of these conflicting emotions, I climbed down the hill as slowly as my legs would allow, not wanting to leave the magic of that place of broken walls and crumbling stones. Going back to the house seemed like a return to my depression and despair, and so I slowed down even more in order to delay my departure. Just before the hill finally ended and met the main road, I saw a patch of bare earth hidden from view of the adjacent villas and the road itself. I made my way to the spot and sat down.

The October sun was still hot, and its rays warmed my body and the earth. Suddenly, my intuition told me to take off my T-shirt and lie down on the ground with my naked torso touching the warm soil. I did just that and felt the sweet freedom of leaving civilisation behind.

I lay there for a few minutes and then again my intuition spoke to me, telling me to start making circular movements with my arms to create semi-circles on either side of my body in the earth. I obeyed.

As my arms circled the surface of the ground, the smells of the adjacent wild herbs filled my nose. I persevered with my arm movements for several minutes and then rested for a while. The sensations I felt were delicious. The sun, still high in the sky, continued to warm my skin and the ground I lay on. Nothing disturbed the silence all around except the occasional sound of a car passing on the road. I didn't bother to analyse what I was doing, but just let myself connect with this huge, natural world surrounding me.

After a few minutes of bliss, I once again started the circular movements with my arms, stopping occasionally to grasp a stalk of fennel, and smelling the luxurious odour of this wild herb. I stayed on that patch of ground for over an hour making these incomprehensible movements, and feeling myself to be almost in a trance-like state. Finally, the sun dipped below a nearby hill and my body lying sprawled on the earth fell into shade. I knew instantly that this was a sign telling me that it was time to stop what I was doing. As I succumbed to fatigue, quite suddenly and unexpectedly this experience revealed an astonishing mystery to me.

At the beginning of the ritual I had been so close to the ground and the roots of the surrounding wild herbs and grasses that the gentle breeze had continuously wafted their scents into my nostrils. But, the longer I lay there, continuing to make the semi-circles in the soil, a change took place. Instead of the scent of the herbs, I began to smell all the rotting carcasses of animals that had died and decayed on this spot over countless number of years.

This smell was very familiar to me because years earlier my red setter had often found the corpse of a dead animal in bushes when I had taken her for a walk in the hills here in Andalusia. With her highly attuned instincts, she would roll in the corpse to cover herself with the scent. My boyfriend had explained to me that this was part of the dog's hunting behaviour when she was out looking for prey.

Now, I was experiencing this smell coming from
every inch of the ground I lay on.

My logical mind briefly tried to take hold of what I was experiencing, wanting to know how this could be happening, but my trance-like state was still strong and I just surrendered to what was going on. When I finally raised my torso from the earth, I saw that my arms were thickly covered with the dust from the ground where I had been creating the circles.

My back was also covered in fine earth and dust. But most noticeable of all was the fact that my whole upper body, including my hair, was completely impregnated with the smell of these dead animal corpses. I smelled exactly like my beloved dog all those years ago.

I did my best to brush most of the earth off my arms and the rest of my body, and then slowly put my T-shirt back on. Wearily I got up and tried to return myself to a normal state of consciousness in order to be in a fit state to walk back down safely to the house. I hoped I wouldn't meet any neighbours on the way because the smell of corpses on my body was so strong that no one could fail to notice it. Luckily nobody was around, and once in the house I rushed into the shower to wash the smell off.

What was this all about I asked myself? What had I done? I understood nothing when I stepped out of the shower, but something very mysterious, and other-worldly had happened. I thought briefly about ancient shamans and their rituals with nature. Had I unconsciously performed a shamanic ritual at the base of the hill? It seemed to me that this was more than a possibility. But, as to why it had happened and what it meant, I had absolutely no idea.

***

Now, after all these years, the meaning of this experience is crystal clear to me. I can see that this three-and-a-half year period began with DEATH, and also ended with DEATH.

In my parents' apartment on my return from England in 1996, DEATH had come to introduce herself to me, and shake my hand. Then, on that spot of ground at the bottom of the hill three-and-a-half years later, she had re-emerged, but this time it seemed she had wanted a much more intimate relationship with me – CO-HABITATION UNDER THE SAME ROOF!

Yet again, a rite of passage had entered my life as I pushed forward on my journey, but at the time I was completely unaware of this fact. On the warm ground at the base of the hill a part of this odyssey had come to an end, and it seemed as if I had quite unconsciously passed some kind of cosmic test and was now being initiated into a new phase. The universal shadow of Mankind was no longer VISITING ME as I slept, and then awakening me suddenly from that sleep to leave me in a state of abject terror. Oh, no, things had most definitely changed.

She was now letting me know that she was an intrinsic part of me – something from which it would be completely impossible for me to escape. DEATH had finally caught up with me, and had well and truly come to stay.

9

LET THERE BE LIGHT

At any moment, you have a choice that leads you closer to your spirit or further away from it.

THICH NHAT HANH.

IF 1996 to 1999 had been a steep learning curve during which I was given an in-depth insight into my own darkness, then the year 2000 brought the arrival of light:

THE LIGHT OF AWARENESS.

I was to be blessed with making real progress in my understanding of this spiritual path. However, once again it began with my shadow, and this time it came in the form of a massive panic attack at the end of November 1999. I only became fully aware of the reason as to why my shadow would somehow 'appear' at the beginning of a new phase in my life three years later on - in 2002. But now, as I found myself facing a new millennium, and a new decade, I didn't have the slightest idea whatsoever as to why certain things happened to me as they did.

This particular panic attack was so bad in fact that my parents had to call out the local doctor to give me an intravenous injection of some kind of sedative which rendered me unconscious within seconds. The severity of the attack was partly due to my actual state of mind at the time, but also due to the lingering effects on my brain of the cocaine-based dental anaesthetic I had been administered back in 1993.

For some reason, a DOOR inside my brain had been forced open by that anaesthetic, and had never properly shut again. This meant that it seemed to be able to swing wide open given the right combination of stressors.

Well, those 'stressors' were more than self-evident as I came to the close of 1999 and the end of so many life-changing events. In that period an important relationship had collapsed around me, an intense learning process had emerged, and a stage of my life when I had turned forty the previous year had come and gone. It was therefore not surprising that perhaps the recent past had exhausted me emotionally, and the future I now looked out on seemed like a great, unfathomable abyss.

My mother, ever a loving soul, felt I needed help and so set about finding me a psychiatrist in the capital city of the province in which we lived. During the early weeks of January 2000 one of Malaga's practitioners, Don Pablo, welcomed me into his consulting room in the heart of the city. A brand new year lay in front of me and perhaps, my battered heart whispered to me: THE CHANCE OF A NEW BEGINNING!

***

From the word go Don Pablo and I seemed to get on famously. It was impossible to tell his age - somewhere in his middle fifties or early sixties. He had a gentle, compassionate manner and a little twinkle in his eye that hinted at his mischievous sense of humour. He ticked all my boxes for what a good psychiatrist should be.

In the quiet sanctuary of his consulting room I found a listening ear for my pent-up feelings concerning my spiritual journey. Don Pablo prescribed a few pills to help me with anxiety and mitigate any possible future panic attacks, and then assured me that I was basically an emotionally sound person who might just need a little 'tweaking' here and there. I began to see 'my friend and confidante' once a week, and unexpectedly found myself experiencing great relief at being able to unburden myself. At last, here was someone with whom I could talk about the things I had lived through in the last few years.

Towards the end of February, after one of my weekly visits to Don Pablo, I decided to delay returning home because I wanted to go to one of the book shops in the centre of the city. It was as if my intuition were telling me that I was now ready to once again embrace the mighty current of my spiritual search. On my arrival at the shop, as usual I wandered over to the esoteric section and scanned the shelves to see if there was anything of any interest. After an incredibly long time during which I pulled out book after book from the shelves in the shop, I finally hit on a volume with a very alluring cover.

It was a reproduction of part of the painting PRIMAVERA - The Spring - by the Renaissance artist Botticelli. It showed the goddess of spring, Flora, and the title was intriguing, too:

El Juego de La Vida: The Game of Life.

I opened to the introduction of the book and found that it was a novel based on the twenty-two Major Arcanas of the Tarot. The author, Ram, made an esoteric connection between the twenty-two letters of the Hebrew alphabet, and these Major Arcanas.

It was an allegorical tale of a young woman's encounter with all twenty-two of these major Tarot Arcanas in her daily life. She experienced them in their numerical order from zero to twenty-one. The idea behind the story was that in a very short space of time the heroine would gain a deep understanding of herself through taking this rapid crash course in the archetypical spiritual journey of THE FOOL. The author explained in simple terms how the Tarot's FOOL is an archetype of the questing human spirit — in other words each person's search for their true spiritual identity.

The twenty-two 'stages' symbolised in the Arcanas were the trials, tests and encounters THE FOOL would need to experience before being able to penetrate and realise his/her spiritual self. Wow, the invisible realm had metaphorically 'come up trumps' for me! Just as an injection of energy was returning to me, renewing my desire to continue on my path, EXACTLY THE BOOK I NEEDED HAD MADE ITS WAY INTO MY HANDS!

Since reading a little about the Swiss psychiatrist C.G. Jung back in the early nineties I had realised that he had been aware that long before our modern, technological age, mysticism, symbolism and revelations concerning the nature of the supernatural realm were studied as intensely as were the sciences of our present era. There and then I knew *I just had to buy the book,* and so, that very night I returned to my parent's villa and started the journey mapped out by the novel.

"But, wait a minute", I here you cry,
"WHAT ABOUT THE ALCHEMIST?"

"You've been telling us that your odyssey was psychically predicted by Paulo Coelho's fable, and now we seem to heading off in a completely unrelated direction. And not only that, but we are at Chapter Nine of this book! Where exactly is this story going?"

Well, fear not, dear reader. With just a little more patience on your part, you will discover that my account truly does lead us to Paulo Coelho's The Alchemist — and far sooner than you may imagine.

***

It was after a week when I had just finished reading the chapter about the protagonist's encounter with the thirteenth Arcana, and had started to read the fourteenth known as Temperance, that a most incredible thing happened. On my way to see Don Pablo for our weekly session, once again fate appeared to take control of events.

I always followed the same route to my appointment because I had long ago made the commitment to heed my intuition at all times That inner knowing had instructed me not to take a more direct route to Don Pablo's consulting room, but instead it had guided me to a much longer, but far more interesting path. Each week it instructed me to cross the busy road outside the train station and walk past a church next to the main river in the city. I obeyed my intuition unquestioningly, because it had so far shown me that this spiritual path was 'hidden' in apparently small, and seemingly inconsequential little details - everything was vitally important.

This regular and unvarying trajectory would always take me to the back of the church to cross a bridge spanning the river. As I did so, I would pass a beautiful ceramic tile freeze on the back wall of the church. Spain is a living outdoor museum of religious art, and I adored these freezes which appeared on the outside walls of most of the churches here in Andalusia. The vast majority were always of Christ with the Virgin Mary, and were also invariably accompanied by words at the bottom, describing their meaning. As usual, this particular freeze at the back of the church was that of Christ and the Virgin, and the words accompanying the images were:

Cristo de la Buena Muerte: Christ of the Good Death
and
Maria de Los Dolores: Mary of the Pains.*

*(Because I have lost my diary entry for that year, I am only 90% sure that the Virgin was Maria de Los Dolores. It is possible that she could also have been Maria de La Soledad, which means solitude or loneliness in English. Either way, the insight I explain below remains the same.)

That afternoon, before crossing the bridge, I stopped for just a little longer than normal to enjoy the spiritual artistry of the freeze. Suddenly, a flash of insight came to me. My God, I thought to myself, this freeze looks just like the Temperance Arcana I have been reading about!

I made a mental note of the images and words in my mind, and when Don Pablo and I had come to the end of our session, I rushed home to finish the chapter on Arcana number fourteen. My flash of understanding hadn't been in vain, because after going through the chapter I felt I had hit on something extraordinarily deep.

The Temperance image in the book was the figure of an androgynous angel (see the author's version of the Temperance card) standing with one foot in a pool of water, and its other foot on dry ground. It held two flasks - one in each hand. The liquid from one of the flasks was being poured into the other. Well, this was not exactly what it was doing, because the liquid wasn't falling vertically. Instead, it seemed to be flowing diagonally as though it were moving from both flasks and then somehow joining together in the middle and blending.

I thought of the freeze I had seen that afternoon and immediately 'saw' the connection. The freeze was telling precisely the same story as this Major Arcana of the Tarot. Or rather, to be precise, it was telling two stories— ONE OVERT AND THE OTHER COVERT. The overt message was of a Christ who had died on the cross for humanity whilst his mother Mary had looked on in horrified anguish. However, the covert message of the freeze appeared to be something which had come directly from the artist's subconscious mind.

In this subtext imagery
I could see that
Christ was like one
of the flasks in the Temperance Arcana
and the Virgin was the other flask.

Even though I had never had this kind of esoteric understanding before in my entire life, they suddenly took on another totally new meaning for me. It seemed that the two flasks were also representations of *the two halves of the human soul in symbolic form*. In the book, the author appeared to be suggesting that the Temperance card meant that the heroine had reached a stage on her journey when she would be able to unite THE TWO HALVES OF HER SOUL. This could only happen if she was willing to move away from being a person of two halves, and allow these two halves to mix and merge together.

Yes, the religious symbolism in the Freeze was unintentionally telling the exact same story as the Tarot Card.

Here were the two separate halves of the human soul – CHRIST AND MARY - and the words at the bottom of the freeze told us that something completely new was occurring.

The Christ half was willing to 'die' to his position of separateness— hence the title: CHRIST OF THE GOOD DEATH — and move towards and meld with his 'other' half. Equally, the Virgin Mary half of the soul was also willing to 'die' to her state of separateness, and blend with her 'opposite' half, symbolised by Christ. This was why in the pain of this mini 'death' she was called MARY OF THE PAINS.

***

Well, well, well, I had truly astonished myself with these insights! I had intuitively seen that the religious freeze and the Temperance card were exactly the same archetype. They were both showing how each of us needs TO OVERCOME THE SEPARATION, OR DUALITY OF THE TWO HALVES OF OUR SOUL. The excitement of my discovery went way beyond words. But, that wasn't all.

Just as I thought that my epiphanies had come to an end, I suddenly went onto a further realisation. These poetic religious images from the Catholic Church, which I so loved and admired for their spiritual beauty, were actually images flowing from the collective unconscious of Mankind, or what Paulo Coelho had named the **Soul of the World.** Unconsciously, they were the outer depictions of the archetypes of the human soul Jung had worked so hard to communicate to the world.

By this, I didn't mean, and wasn't in any way saying that Christ and the Virgin were myths. For me, with my faith, these were real people who had lived real lives. However, what I was beginning to understand was that man's artistic imagery flowed unconsciously from the deep knowledge we all held of the essential nature of our souls.

What we could not know consciously in words,
we most certainly knew subconsciously in
PICTURES.

With this apparent 'quantum leap' in my personal understanding of human spirituality, I felt absolutely ecstatic. If I — my soul - were really two halves, then knowing this would surely make it so much easier to find the path by which they merged together to make me whole. My Holy Grail was potentially closer than ever before!

The extraordinary continued after this. As I made my way through the Tarot book over the next two weeks, I began to notice that signs would appear around me in the outside world which corresponded exactly to the particular Arcana I was reading about at that very moment. And I can assure you, dear friend that this most definitely WAS NOT my imagination. Of course I knew it was true that I was always obsessively on the lookout for signs. But this was only because I needed them to confirm that the intuitive impulses I followed so religiously were leading me in the right direction. However, in this instance, no, I most certainly was not being dishonest with myself; the signs truly were appearing in a synchronistic fashion as I read my way through the book.

The other extraordinary event which happened at around that time of seeing Don Pablo was yet one more amazing dream. Because of the depth of this dream, I made a record in my diary of when it had occurred. It was the night of April 6 that year. In the evening I had been talking to my ex-boyfriend Alberto on the phone. In my heart I was still hoping for reconciliation between us, and as we said our goodbyes, I ended our conversation by wishing him protection from lots and lots of angels. That night I dreamt the following:

I was in my ninth month of a pregnancy and was lying on a flat table being watched over by an old family friend. Labour pains started and I gave birth quickly to a baby.

The baby was a girl and she came out of me feet first instead of head first. What was strange was that although she was just a new-born, she seemed to have already learned how to speak. As the baby emerged from inside of me, she appeared to be talking non-stop.

When she was completely free of my body, I saw that she had some large capital letters written across her chest. The letters spelt out the name AURORA.

The instant I saw these letters, I knew that I shouldn't let anyone know for a few months that this baby had been born. And there the dream ended.

Now, at this juncture in my story this is the fifth time I have mentioned having had an important dream, and it may seem to you, dear reader, that I am some sort of dream-making machine. However, that is not remotely how I experienced life.

Five years had elapsed since the dream about giving birth to myself in 1995, and three more since the dream about the stone cathedral in Guatemala. The truth was that this road which I had embarked on was a very lonely one for me. Months and years would pass in which I simply pushed myself onward, often feeling intense pain and isolation – dreams or no amazing dreams!

On waking the following day in April 2000, I knew without any doubt that the dream had been about my spiritual rebirth. I remembered my birthing dream of 1995 and felt that here was a concrete sign telling me that I had made very substantial progress. It seemed highly significant to me that this baby girl, Aurora, had been born FEET FIRST. Given what I had learned about the probable source of the meaning of the Temperance card only weeks earlier, my mind immediately suspected that this unusual detail in the dream was the symbolism of Jung's collective unconscious.

Physical births I knew were head first in the human species, so could it be that spiritual births were symbolically the other way around? The name of the baby was also quite amazing on a symbolic level. Aurora was a girl's name in Spanish, but it was also the Spanish word used to describe in a very poetic way the light of the dawn.

It was that moment of the birth and coming of light in the sky at the break of each new day. Wow! You couldn't get a stronger message concerning the arrival of spiritual light in your life than this name! Aurora also happened to be a Roman Goddess, and when I looked her up in an encyclopaedia that day, I discovered that she was the roman Goddess of the Dawn.

My experience with my dreams told me that I hadn't necessarily been spiritually reborn that night in April. The dream was in all likelihood prescient and foretelling a time in the future when this rebirth would take place for me. Nevertheless, my excitement when I woke up was huge. It was an incredibly strong affirmation for me that I was on a real journey, and not some kind of bizarre invention of my tortured, and neurotic mind.

***

To fill me with even greater energy and enthusiasm for my quest, another miraculous event happened towards the end of April that year. One afternoon, I took my camera and decided to walk along a path that overlooked my beloved ruin. I had climbed up to it so many times, but had never thought of photographing it.*

(The roll of film I used that day in April remained in my wardrobe for a year, and then one morning, in a fit of frustration at how long my journey was becoming, I threw it into a rubbish bin. For this reason you only have my sketch of the ruin.)

I stood on the path and took several pictures of the ruin from varying angles. To my eyes, its shape was incredibly photogenic.

After the last picture, I stopped to gaze lovingly at this romantic pile of stones, when suddenly I was caught in a psychic flash of knowing. MY GOD I heard my inner voice cry out silently, THAT'S SANTIAGO'S RUIN IN THE ALCHEMIST!!! And, then less than two seconds later, another flash of awareness came to me:

that means
YOU ARE SANTIAGO, KAREN!

It was as if the obvious had been staring me hard and fast in the face for years, and I had never been able to see it. At that precise moment my inner world quite literally shifted on its axis; the supernatural invisible realm, which I had BELIEVED to be a reality, had suddenly decided to reveal itself to me. Now, I was being shown that I no longer needed to believe it existed, I KNEW IT EXISTED, and that knowing was in every corner of my heart and soul. Nothing could ever be the same for me after this revelation of truth.

Before I continue with this story, I need to address you dear reader directly concerning what I have just said. I am making the seemingly preposterous claim that I am the real-life Santiago of Paulo Coelho's story The Alchemist. For many, I know this may appear utterly ridiculous – even though I have clearly stated that I know for certain that Paulo unconsciously channelled his fable from the invisible realm where all of the past, present and future coexist together.

When we humans are gripped by powerful intuitive flashes of insight, as I was that day, unfortunately it is almost impossible to 'prove' or 'give evidence' that what we have discovered is actually true. Paulo Coelho understood this dilemma implicitly, and in creating his hero Santiago in The Alchemist, he had followed the archetypal pattern of the anti-hero - the archetype of THE FOOL – set out in the original Persian tale. Fate conspired that I too chose to take this very same path.

The shepherd Santiago's 'heroism' lies not in fantastic deeds of valour and courage, but in the fact that he dares to be incomprehensible to himself and to the world around him. He cannot, and **doesn't even try to explain himself to the rational world**. And, this is because his quest is not about rationality - it is all about his soul. At one point in The Alchemist Paulo Coelho says of his protagonist:

"The boy was beginning to understand that intuition is really a sudden immersion of the soul into the universal current of life,.........and we are able to know everything, because it's all written there."

I quoted this passage in the preface to my book, and I do so again to show how it was that a SUDDEN IMMERSION of my own intuition *'into the universal current of life'* produced my unexpected realisation. Without that 'immersion' I could never have known who I really was, and what was happening to me as I stood looking at *'my ruin'* that April day in the year 2000.

The famous twentieth century genius Albert Einstein once said:

"I believe in intuitions and inspirations.....I sometimes FEEL that I am right. I don't KNOW that I am."

Einstein knew only too well that rational KNOWING has very precise and concrete limitations when we resort to it in order to explain our world of real-life experiences. But, let us return to my story.

***

Naturally, I wanted to share some of this spiritual 'treasure' with my great 'confidante and friend' Don Pablo. I had enough wisdom to realise that I wouldn't be able to share my dream about Aurora with him, or the psychic flash I had experienced whilst looking at *'my ruin'*. But I knew I just had to tell him about the signs that had appeared synchronistically with each Arcana that I had read about in the Tarot novel.

I thus enthusiastically and zealously returned to the book shop in Malaga and bought a second copy of **THE GAME OF LIFE** and presented it to Don Pablo one day during one of my therapeutic sessions. Then, from the beginning of May till the middle of August I bombarded my ally with incessant talk about the archetypal pattern of THE FOOL'S journey in these Tarot Arcanas, and all the signs and amazing coincidences I was experiencing.

With passion and a conviction of steel I made it clear to Don Pablo that all of these pointed to one thing, and one thing only — the fact that I was engaged in this very same journey myself!

My 'mentor', though apparently somewhat taken aback by what he was witnessing in his client, seemed genuinely interested in what I had to say. It was obvious to both of us that I was not the average type of patient he was used to seeing. On a few occasions Don Pablo made notes on what I felt I had discovered about my own shadow and also the nature of humanity's shadow in general. All in all, I felt I had his complete support for my spiritual 'investigations', but how blind and naive I was. None of this illusion of mine was to last.

At the beginning of August I made a fatal error. I became so immersed in interpreting the signs which were appearing for me that I went *just a little too far* with my zeal. August was the month of a very large, end-of-summer lottery. I bought myself a lottery ticket and became convinced that because the numbers on the ticket added up to twenty-one, they were part of my odyssey through the Tarot Arcanas. This 'cosmic coincidence' would therefore inevitably guarantee me a huge win that month, and even the actual jackpot.

The invisible realm was most definitely working its magic in my life, and so I announced this prediction to Don Pablo one afternoon with an air of triumph. Here would be my 'coup de grace' and an incontrovertible manifestation that I had truly deciphered the workings of the spiritual realm I had so passionately been talking to him about.

Don Pablo adjourned for his summer holiday after this session, and when we next saw each other at the beginning of September, inevitably I had to report that I had been too LITERAL in my interpretation of the lottery ticket. No, oh dear, no, I hadn't won anything at all. That afternoon, in Don Pablo's consulting room he gently led me away from my usual seat in front of his desk, and asked me to sit in an armchair next to one of his impressive book cases. Then suddenly, without any warning, my genial friend CHANGED.

It seemed that he had detected a serious problem in me which he hadn't noticed before. I wasn't sure what exactly he was getting at as he talked to me in a much more severe and troubled tone. However, reality hit me over the head incredibly abruptly when I heard Don Pablo say that he felt it would be necessary to prescribe me a stronger type of medication. In that instant, a small current of shock suddenly passed through my head and my heart. Uh oh, I thought, he had unpredictably moved the goal posts! My friend was now calling a very different tune, and it sounded only too familiar to me - it was called POWER.

In emergencies, it is amazing how quickly adrenalin allows us to regroup internally and respond from wisdom and experiences buried deep inside our subconscious minds, even when our conscious minds have barely grasped what has happened. This is exactly what I found myself doing. Keeping as calm as I possibly could, my subconscious gave me the words to tell Don Pablo emphatically, but without aggression, that I had no intention whatsoever of taking any stronger kind of medication.

I admitted that it was true that I had been stupid and foolish about the lottery ticket, but this was the sort of mistake all of us made once in a while. I think Don Pablo was utterly shocked to meet with this kind of resistance from me, albeit summoned out of my depths from a courage I barely felt. I saw his normal composure begin to unravel right in front of me. After all, patients didn't usually stare one down and contradict a professional diagnosis with such certainty and apparent self-belief.

The two of us then quite suddenly found ourselves briefly wrestling in a short verbal spat of extremely thinly disguised anger, and then just as suddenly as it had started, the whole thing was over. Don Pablo called an end to our session and left me with his incensed ultimatum - the medication or I could leave.

Our wonderful relationship of mutual bonhomie, which had lasted more than eight months, was now over in the space of a few brief minutes. I raised myself from my seat, feigning a self-assurance I most definitely didn't feel, and once again made my choice clear to Don

Pablo. His silent, wordless glare was my cue to leave the room. As I walked away into yet another new unknown, I sensed that I had turned my back on a test which I had only just passed by the very skin of my teeth!

***

Needless to say my parents were not in the least bit pleased when I revealed to them what had gone on between Don Pablo and me. When I finally plucked up enough courage to confess the decision I had made, I knew that I was not just making myself incomprehensible to them, but probably to the rest of the world around me.

Here they had tried to help me, and yet again I had somehow failed to stick it out and make some tangible progress that this world recognised as 'becoming adjusted'. Of course, they had no way of knowing that I was actually deeply shaken by the incident and felt more alone than ever before. Nevertheless, I knew that I had somehow succeeded in rescuing myself from a subtle, power-driven lie, and that was why I had to do what I had done.

Briefly the thought passed through my head that what had transpired in Don Pablo's consulting room was possibly a repetition of the 'beating' at the end of The Alchemist. This time, it wasn't me metaphorically 'beating' myself up with the collusion and assistance of another person, as it had been in Paris. Instead, it seemed that this had been a more direct pummelling; an intentional, but nevertheless probably unconscious 'attack' from Don Pablo - based on the assumption that I was flawed.

The thought stayed with me for an ominously long period of time, and I felt my emotions contract with fear. I really didn't want to believe that this might be true for I knew only too well that:

life could prove to be very difficult and extremely painful
for me if it were.

10

THE INVISIBLE REALM SPEAKS

The spirit never sleeps – instead it dreams.

ANON

THE end of the year 2000 marked almost six years since I had stood in the basement of my local book shop holding Alejandro Jodorowsky's magical book in my hands. I had worked long and hard in following an invisible path in search of my soul, and although I was gaining in understanding, I had absolutely no idea how far I was along this path, or how much further I had to go.

Despite this, my reward had been to have learned several new things. I now understood that my soul was made up of two halves. Apparently, these two halves needed to JOIN OR MERGE for a spiritual 'rebirth' to take place, and somehow this process of merging involved 'mini-deaths' for each half as they abandoned their separate identities.* Added to this, the spiritual path seemed to consist of twenty-two stages, if one included The Fool Arcana of the Major Arcanas of the Tarot.

Finally, I had discovered that *my mystical ruin* at the top of the hill next to my parents' villa was the ruin which Paulo Coelho had described in The Alchemist – the ruin where Santiago had dreamt once more of finding treasure near the Pyramids of Egypt. This meant, therefore, that the universe had decided to let me know that:

I WAS SANTIAGO – PAULO'S SHEPHERD IN THE FABLE!

(This insight was premature for what I had undertaken, but would eventually reveal what happens to the soul AFTER the journey of The Alchemist has ended.)

***

At the beginning of 2001 I finally bought a copy of The Alchemist in order to go over the story again. This would be my first reencounter with the book since reading it in England back in March 1996. This time I went through it much more slowly, knowing that it was a story I had lived out in my own flesh. But, much to my disappointment, no great insights came to me, nor any sudden flashes of understanding. It was the journey I had experienced five years earlier to see Alejandro Jodorowsky, and which had in a way marked the beginning of my quest for my soul - and that was just about it.

In April 2001, feeling I needed a greater degree of independence, I decided to move out of my parents' house and into a small one bedroom apartment slightly higher up the mountain from where they lived. The views of the coast and mountains were spectacular from the apartment's spacious outdoor terrace, and when I leant over the wall to look directly at the sea, I could see the top of **'my ruin'** a mere two hundred metres in front of me.

Much to my surprise, things began badly in my new home. Barely a week into my move I started to experience severe headaches when I woke up in the mornings, or came round from an afternoon's siesta. It felt as though my head were being tightly squeezed inside a vice, and this was very frightening to say the least. Naturally, my imagination ran riot as I panicked with thoughts that I was possibly developing a brain tumour or some other life-threatening condition. One night, the pain was so bad that as I lay in bed I cried out to God in complete desperation, "Please, please, help me Lord. Tell me what this is."

For the first, and almost only time in my life, the Almighty did just that. I fell asleep and had the most astonishing dream. I dreamt that a healer lived on the other side of the mountain from where my apartment was situated, and that if I went to see him, he would heal me from these head pains. The dream was truly unforgettable. It was as if I had received a direct reply to my plea from the invisible realm. There were no symbols, no metaphors or cryptic clues this time - just a straight forward answer to my prayer.

A few days later I was on a local bus returning from having seen my girl-friend living in the next village when I heard a conversation that completely defied belief. A young man stood at the front of the bus, talking to the driver, and was telling him about a healer he knew who lived near one of the local mountain villages!

I could see that the young man had got up because he was about to leave the bus, and I knew that I had to act very quickly and speak to him before the bus stopped and he disappeared for good. In that instant, I quite literally catapulted myself out of my seat at the back of the bus and rushed to the front where he was standing. Breathlessly, I tried to sound normal as I asked him if he had just been talking about a healer. He casually confirmed that this was so. I then quickly asked him where exactly this healer was, well aware that as I spoke the driver was slowing down on his approach to the bus stop.

"Oh, he lives just outside Gancho, near Monte C," he replied as he picked up his bag and prepared to leave the vehicle. I thanked him and watched his back disappear down the steps, and into the open air. DONE - he had given me the location! Had I hesitated for just a split second longer about whether or not to leave my seat, I would never have had enough time to ask him this vital question. Although his answer was basic and completely lacking in detail, it was all I needed. In a rural setting this was enough information for me to be able to find the healer.

***

It goes without saying that I found the dream, and then the incident on the bus only a few days later, quite mind boggling. However, life is not about sitting around feeling mesmerised or confused by strange events. It is about daring to act on what may seem miraculous or even downright bizarre. So, a few days later, I packed myself some sandwiches and headed out to catch the local bus to the village of Gancho on the other side of the mountain.

The bus climbed up the mountain road, and then made its way along the sierra, following each fold and contour of the mountain, finally arriving at Gancho after about forty minutes. I made a short stop at the village to eat and rest, and then asked a passing stranger for directions to the road which led to Monte C. The villager pointed to one of the few tracks leaving the village, telling me that this was the one I needed to take. But he also warned me that Monte C was probably a good six-kilometre walk from where we stood. I thanked this person for his help and headed for the road he had indicated.

It was spring and a cloudy day so I imagined that I was more than up to walking the distance. However, around three quarters of an hour into that walk I felt utterly exhausted. Physically I wasn't in the best of shape, and walking along the side of a dusty, winding road, tripping over stones and bumps along the way, was not as easy as I had thought. Ahead of me I spotted a roadside restaurant and cafeteria, and decided to stop for a while for a drink and some fresh information on the whereabouts of Monte C.

I sat in the cafeteria with a hot tea and reassessed my plans. I was adrenalin-charged with the desire to find this healer, but it was already the middle of the afternoon and I knew that even if I managed to walk to Monte C, I had the problem of getting back. Perhaps my only option was just to keep going.

I made my way to the bar to pay for the tea and whilst I stood there waiting for my change I decided to ask the waitress if I was close to Monte C. She asked me if I had a car, and when I said no, it was then that she seemed to look at me in a rather strange way and shook her head pessimistically, "You've got another four kilometres at least," she said. "It's a long walk."

The mostly male customers drinking at the bar were obviously listening to our conversation, and heads nodded around me with the same expression of doubt as was worn by the waitress. I stood by the bar unsure of what to do next and intensely aware of being a blonde foreigner who, true to type, did rather peculiar things like walking four kilometres along a country road instead of staying at home to look after her clearly neglected husband and children.

Then, quite out of the blue a very sunburnt, deeply-lined face turned to me and spoke.

"I know where Monte C is. I'm going that way. I can give you a lift."

It was the man standing next to me at the bar who was just finishing his extremely black coffee. He looked somewhere in his mid-fifties, and had the wrinkled brown skin of someone who had spent his whole life working outside. I had only a fraction of a second to weigh up the whole situation and decide if this person was safe, before any hesitation on my part became too long, and I risked offending an upstanding and much loved local man. Luckily, it was my subconscious mind that gave me the answer.

"Oh, that would be great," I replied, trying to show genuine gratitude, but not out-and-out enthusiasm.

There were nods of approval coming from the men at the bar and the waitress. Obviously, a problem had been solved in a manner that left everyone satisfied. My 'rescuer' introduced himself as Salvador, which in English means saviour, and we shook hands. I then followed him out to the car park where we got into his very rusty old van. Almost immediately I felt completely at ease with this man. His manner was unpretentious and down to earth, and it became clear that I was in absolutely no danger; Salvador was a countryman through and through.

He headed down the road for about two kilometres until we came to a roundabout. There, Salvador turned right and then left onto a dirt road which ran through a large olive grove. The van bumped along the track whilst Salvador and I small-talked about the weather, the time of year and other neutral topics. The path seemed to go on and on forever, and I commented to my new friend that I would never have been able to find the healer on my own. He nodded sagely in agreement.

Eventually, after taking another bumpy track, we passed a large hill standing alone amongst the olive trees. Salvador pointed out that this was Monte C, and that we were almost at our destination. Within a few minutes the track ended in front of a large modern villa with spectacular views over the valley. My friend brought the van to a halt in what seemed to be the visitors' car park, and the two of us got out.

***

The property was deadly quiet except for two or three guard dogs in a pen who greeted our arrival with frenetic barking. The shutters on some of the windows were lowered and no one appeared in response to the barking. We walked up to the front door and rang the bell - complete silence. I noticed that there was an image of THE SACRED HEART OF JESUS next to the door, and felt somewhat comforted because this was my favourite of all the images I had come across in the Catholic Church.

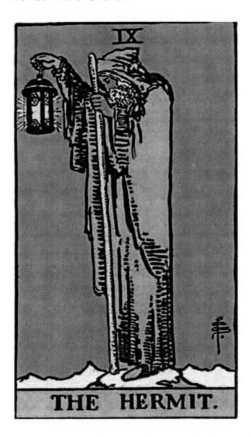

I rang the bell again, but nobody emerged from inside the building. My disappointment was intense. I felt fatigue take hold of my mind and body where adrenalin had been. We stepped away from the villa and walked towards the van. Turning back, Salvador and I took in the view. Acres of olive groves covered the north face of the sierra, giving way to orange and lemon groves further down the valley. The villa had extensive grounds, and my estimation was that it must have been quite costly to build. Whoever the healer who ran this centre was, he/she evidently had plenty of financial support.

The dogs carried on barking at us, and I felt Salvador's disappointment too. He had been so generous in bringing me here over dusty, potholed terrain that I didn't know what to say. I muttered something about us being really unlucky, and Salvador assented with a philosophical shrug.

"Do you know anything about this healer, Salvador?" I ventured.

"Yes", he replied, to my surprise. "My son-in-law came here once because he had a problem with his back, and the man healed him."

This was comforting to hear, given that the place didn't just look shut for the season, but positively abandoned.

My mind rewound to my dream, the man on the bus a few days later, and then Salvador's offer to bring me here when I was standing at the bar. It was all too supernatural to end this way. Suddenly, I surprised myself as a question came from me that even I didn't expect.

"Salvador, do you believe in miracles?

There was silence. Afraid that he might not have heard me, I repeated the question. "Do you believe in miracles, Salvador?" My companion looked pensive, but not in the least bit fazed by what I had just asked him. In fact he seemed to have taken this peculiar question of mine very seriously.

Yes, I do," he answered, "because we had a miracle in the village where I come from not so long ago." And it was then that he started to recount this story.

"We have a shepherd who looks after a herd of goats, and every day he used to take them to the sierra and always have his siesta in the same place, next to a big boulder that his black goat stood on top of whilst he was sleeping.

"One day, he had a dream next to that boulder, and the dream told him that there was treasure buried somewhere on the quay in Malaga. Well, you can imagine, he made sure he found a way of getting to Malaga.

"He spent the whole day walking up and down that quay, but, for the life of him, he couldn't see any place

where treasure was buried. One of the harbour men saw him doing this for hours, and eventually came up to him and asked him what he was doing.

"This shepherd told him that he had had a dream that there was treasure buried somewhere along the quay, but he couldn't find anything. The harbour man just laughed at him. He didn't expect to hear that. And then he said the most amazing thing.

"He told the shepherd that he had dreams too, and one night he had dreamt that there was treasure buried under a big boulder where a black goat always stood, but, of course, he knew it was just a stupid dream. Well, you can imagine what happened next.

"That shepherd couldn't get back to his boulder quickly enough, and, just like the harbour man said, when he started digging at the base, he found a whole lot of money. He's a rich man now in our village. So, yes, miracles do happen, because that was a real miracle."

***

Time seemed to stand still as Salvador came to the end of his story, and I found myself caught in a never-ending space between my own heartbeats. I knew for certain that I had heard what he had said, but this moment was utterly, but utterly surreal. Good grief, my inner voice whispered to me:

He's just told me another version of
The Alchemist,
and in all probability he knows nothing
about the existence of this book.
What's more, he believes the story he has told me is true.
But, then again,
MAYBE IT IS!

If I had desperately wanted a miracle, I was certainly right in the middle of one now. I tried not to look at Salvador, but attempted to seem as if I were mulling over the details of the story. Finally, I replied with an 'incredible' in Spanish. Yes, this whole day was turning out to be incredible and totally unbelievable!!!

Salvador indicated to me that it was time to leave, and that he would be quite happy to drop me off at a neighbouring village which we could see in front of us etched into the slopes of the sierra. The kindness of this man knew no limits. We clambered back into the van, manoeuvred onto another dirt track, and slowly made our way out of the olive groves in the direction of the main road. An hour and a half later I was back in my apartment, reliving the events of the day.

This journey had accustomed me to many extraordinary coincidences, but what had happened with Salvador went far beyond anything I had previously encountered. I knew the invisible realm was a reality that we could access for ourselves if we were willing to be intuitive and open-hearted, but here was something beyond even the intuitive mind. It was as if I had been spoken to in a private dialogue between me and, did I dare believe, the Almighty Himself?

What was crystal clear for me was that He, She or It was telling me that:

THE ALCHEMIST WAS MY STORY

Not only that, but He was also showing me that the cosmic events which had transpired in Paris five years earlier still weren't truly over. My quest to find my soul was this magical story written by Paulo Coelho back in 1987, and my task was to unravel its meaning, which would then guide me to finding my inner treasure.

I slept deeply that night, and strangely the next week saw me completely free of headaches. I certainly hadn't experienced any healing on my trip out to the healing centre, so why did they disappear as mysteriously as they had arrived? What I didn't know was that subconscious forces were at work in me, speaking the language of the spirit, and this language was taking me step by step closer to my goal.

Under these circumstances what I most needed was blind faith in this path, and an unquestioning trust which would allow me to obey the apparently irrational, inexplicable signs and promptings that were coming my way. If Don Pablo had doubted my coherence and mental stability back in September, 2000, I shuddered to think what his opinion of me would be now!

***

The next two months in my new apartment after this 'cosmic' encounter with Salvador were total misery. I was stuck three quarters of the way up a mountain road, with no neighbours and only the local village bus to take me down to town or up to the village above me. I was so desperately lonely in my new abode that I even temporarily re-joined my old evangelical Christian fellowship.

My mother, who is gifted with a beautiful loving heart, could see that I was isolated and stuck, and always a person *to act* rather than wait around and watch a disaster unfold, she sat me down one day for a heart-to-heart.

Her idea was that if I moved down into the town I would be close to amenities and other people, and she had a most wonderful proposition. She had spoken to my father and they had both agreed that life was too short for frittering away precious moments. The plan was that if I were prepared to hunt for a suitable apartment, then they would buy it for me with my inheritance, rather than waiting to give me the money after their respective demises.

If this is not love in action, then I don't know what is. Genuinely humbled by the generosity of my parents, I set about the job of finding a property, and by August we had signed the papers on a small, but well-maintained apartment in a working-class area of town. I moved into it at the end of August and began a new phase of life as the owner of my very own 'Spanish Castle'.

Other events moved swiftly too, and by October of 2001, I had found a job working as a translator, and was also sharing my brand new nest with a close friend and her three-year-old son. Cecilia had found herself homeless at the beginning of October and I just so happened to have the spare bedrooms.

In January 2002 she left, and briefly I had the company of a Colombian friend before ties with my old flame Alberto were reignited. He had phoned several times over the Christmas holidays in 2001, and it seemed that I had been on his mind and perhaps his heart as well.

I visited Alberto in Madrid in the early part of 2002 to help him move into a new apartment, and then what I had dreamed of for so long happened - he felt we could give our relationship another try. In March I moved back up to Madrid and began in earnest trying to make what hadn't worked in the past, a renewed venture in love. But, very quickly it became obvious that this dream was only a fantasy for both of us. Alberto was the same person I had lived with back in 1999, and so was I; the truth was that in two-and-a-half years of our separation neither of us had changed.

During those six months in Madrid, Alberto's stepfather had died, and so I spent most of my time inside this departed gentleman's old apartment, selling off furniture and pictures and arranging for auctioneers to take the rest of the contents to auction. I was alone for much of this period and had space and time to think.

My thoughts always revolved around this spiritual path I was on. I was still disciplining myself to live from my intuition, which meant keeping my ego and my sexual feelings well and truly in the back seat of my personal car. I knew implicitly that I couldn't explain any of this to anybody. To me it seemed that my life was like that of a nun - although, not a celibate one - who had decided that, rather than live her spiritual practices inside the confines of convent walls, she would use the outside world as her spiritual domain.

I wore no habit, or cross, or anything else which could identify me to others as being committed to a spiritual discipline, but that was exactly what my whole purpose in life was. I also thought a lot about The Alchemist, knowing that I still couldn't fully understand the true meaning of the story.

My hero Paulo Coelho was constantly on my mind, and in my heart, and I re-read his book THE FIFITH MOUNTATIN, and also used MANUAL OF THE WARRIOR OF THE LIGHT as my spiritual compass and Bible. More and more I began to feel that this man and I needed to meet. Deep within my soul I sensed that Paulo simply had to know that THERE REALLY WAS A RUIN IN ANDALUSIA, and that I, just like Santiago, had experienced a powerful dream and had taken THE SHEPHERD BOY'S JOURNEY TO THE PYRAMIDS.

***

It was during these long hours in between attending to buyers coming to the apartment that I also thought about everything I had learned so far about my soul. I remembered that back in 1989, in a remote mountain village in Spain, a friend had introduced me to Jung's work, and also that of some of his collaborators. In particular, I recalled that one of these individuals had dedicated much effort to analysing the archetypes hidden in our much-loved children's fairy-tales.

Quite spontaneously an intuitive flash of insight came to me that the story of Beauty and the Beast was possibly another version of my soul journey! In 2000 I had learned that the Temperance card and the subconscious symbolism of the religious freeze on the church wall in Malaga had been telling me that my soul was made up of two halves. And I also knew that a spiritual quest was about these two halves journeying to meet each other. So, the more I thought about the Beauty and the Beast fairy-tale, the more it seemed that it was another version of this duality of the soul.

I therefore jumped to a very logical conclusion: Beauty and the Beast were not two different people, but the two halves of my soul I had identified so far. But why had I fixated specifically on this fairy-tale rather than another? So many stories were about true love and two halves joining together to make a whole, but I somehow knew instinctively that it was the Beast that had clinched it for me. My intuition appeared to understand that my soul was not just some ethereal, spiritual entity within me, but was also intimately connected with my physical being.

It was as I thought about the character of the Beast that I experienced the sudden realisation that his 'beastliness' or 'ugliness' was my shadow. I had named my ego and my sexual passions my shadow, but now I could see that the fairy-tale had PERSONIFIED these physical aspects of the soul in the form of the Beast's physical ugliness. My soul, although spiritual in essence, was confined to my physical body during my lifetime and so it would only make sense that part of it - perhaps half of it - would be very much bound to the physical aspect of my being.

YES, THAT WAS IT, THE BEAST WAS SPIRIT 'CLOTHED' IN A MATERIAL GUISE!

The ego, sexual passions and DEATH were the inevitable and inescapable realities of our physical selves, and part of the soul would have to live with this reality, even though the soul's true identity was always spiritual - hence the prince 'hidden' within the outer physical appearance of a Beast.

In the fairy-tale it was Beauty's spiritual eyes that were able to see BEYOND the material form of her other half and into its essence – spirit. This act of love enabled the Beast to transcend his physical level of manifestation, and merge with Beauty to form a new spiritual whole. My God, I was incredibly excited about this discovery. Pieces of a confusing and muddled puzzle were slowly coming together for me.

The daily battles I endured with my dual nature, which had gone on for so many years – in other words my spiritual self versus my **material** self, with the latter comprising my ego and sex - now made complete and total sense. Beauty and the Beast was telling me that, although the Beast in me felt ugly and abhorrent to my spirit, the spiritual light hidden inside this half of me could connect with the spiritual light of the Beauty half of my soul, and bring about my soul rebirth.

With these unexpected insights, from that moment on I felt confident that I could now give the two halves of my soul names. Beauty I named the MYSTICAL part of my soul, and Beast the MATERIAL aspect. PROGRESS INDEED! However, how all of this was related to the archetypal journey of The Alchemist still baffled me. I thus began to turn over in my mind what I knew about the essence of Paulo's fable.

Santiago, the shepherd, and I had both encountered the face of death at the end of our quests; Santiago literally, and I symbolically. This encounter had awoken each of us to our inner treasure - the inner light of our spirits, and death, of course, was the UNIVERSAL PHYSICAL SHADOW of Mankind. Was Beauty and the Beast connected in any way to The Alchemist? Both seemed to be tales of soul rebirth and transcendence, but try as I might, the link between the two completely eluded me.

Meanwhile, after six months in Madrid, my fraught relationship with Alberto eventually ground to a halt. We had revisited the painful place we had discovered on our first attempt to live together in loving harmony in 1999, and in late August WE READ THE WRITING ON THE WALL and accepted defeat. I packed my bags once again, and boarded the train to return to my little castle in Andalusia.

With yet another 'battering' of sorts 'acquired', it seemed that I was some kind of expert at throwing myself into challenges and then walking away from them with the wounds and scars to prove that I had embraced everything with my whole being. Thankfully my Andalusian home welcomed me back without judgement. Perhaps the apartment had patiently been waiting all along for me to come back.

But what had I learned in those six months in Madrid? What had the challenge really been? The thought popped into my head again: THAT WAS ANOTHER BEATING KAREN. YES, MY DEAR, ANOTHER BEATING. I didn't like what I was hearing, but all my life I had known that nothing worthwhile is ever learnt easily, and that suffering is invariably the price to be paid for personal growth.

At that moment, at the end of the summer of 2002, I was bruised, exhausted and confused, but I was also far too close to the break up with Alberto to understand how this experience had made me grow. Nevertheless, growing I most certainly was; the light was really there, beginning to DAWN on my horizon - even if metaphorically it was still very much DARK OUTSIDE.

11

IF THESE WALLS COULD TALK

**Life doesn't allow us to hide from it. Sooner or
later it 'reveals' itself.**

ANON

TO recover from a second failure in romance with Alberto, I took
refuge inside the walls of my private FORTRESS. Home is where the
heart is, and my heart needed quiet, rest and the soothing comfort
of my own domain.

I did what most of us do when we are tired and worn out - I
pottered. I got up late, breakfasted late, ambled from room to room
picking up books, flicking through magazines, and then flopping onto
my bed at regular intervals. And, as the hours turned into days, I
began to notice that this apartment I had bought just over a year
earlier did not really reflect who I was as a person.

The reason for this was because the previous owners had sold
it to me fully-furnished - and this was quite a common practice in
southern Spain. Most sellers didn't want the aggravation of having
to move furniture out of their sold property and into a new one
because invariably the next home often came with furniture left by
those owners too. So, for me a fully-equipped apartment right at the
beginning of this new phase was a total Godsend - I had no further
expenses to face beyond the purchase price.

But now, as I walked from room to room healing my wounded
heart, I realised that I was living with someone else's taste in decor,
and their values and choices were not necessarily my own. The living
room was where this fact shouted out at me the loudest.

The room was long and narrow and the longest wall was taken up by a huge fake mahogany wall cabinet. Like most pieces of furniture of its type, it was narrow in width, but as far as length was concerned, it was easily the size of a small automobile. I had bought the apartment from a Spanish family consisting of two adults and three teenagers, and obviously the cabinet had served a very useful purpose for a family of this size. However, for little old me, alone in the apartment, with my very limited needs, it stood against the wall like some kind of decorative war memorial; I couldn't have filled it even if I'd tried!

One day, staring at the cabinet, I knew that it would have to go if I were to be able to reclaim the living room for myself. On a trip to a local supermarket a few days later, I spied a large warehouse run by a Christian charity which bought and sold second-hand furniture. When I spoke to a man who looked as if he was in charge, he assured me that, provided the cabinet was in good condition, they would be more than happy to take it away for sale. There and then I arranged a time and day for his team to come and release my living room of its major occupant.

Life is full of surprises, revealing its secrets to us in extraordinary ways, and so it was with the cabinet and its removal. This relatively minor event wasn't what it seemed. In fact, it was actually about me being able to move forward and create a living space which would be A MANIFESTATION OF MY ESSENCE.

The men arrived on the agreed day to take away this part of the past, and worked valiantly as they unscrewed each shelf and panel of the monster. I felt extremely guilty as I watched the work progress. I could see that there was more than an hour's labour involved, and as we all know, there are some things in life that are simply not worth the time or the effort. The team groaned and rolled their eyes throughout the whole proceedings but at no time signalled to me that they weren't prepared to carry on.

Eventually, the cabinet lay dead on the living room floor - a mass of planks, panels and drawers ready to be taken away. I thanked the men from the bottom of my deeply contrite heart, and helped them take the pieces down the two flights of stairs to the removal van parked in the street. After the customary 'thank-yous' and exchange of good wishes, I returned to my apartment to sit in what was now wholly and totally my domain. And then, that was when it happened.

Suddenly, out of the blue the revelation came. As I stared at the empty space I had been gifted, I saw a huge shadow on the wall where the cabinet had been. I sat in my chair in awestruck amazement, instantly knowing exactly what I was looking at. This was:

MY SHADOW

The interior walls of my apartment were all painted white in the traditional style here in Andalusia. The removal of the cabinet had shown me that the previous owners had placed this monstrosity against the long wall of the living room, and then painted the whole room with a fresh coat of white paint.

Removing the cabinet had revealed the shadow of the unpainted section of wall behind it. But for me, this shadow I sat staring at was much more than a long rectangle of unpainted wall space. It allowed me to suddenly grasp a great truth about the nature of spiritual growth, and also the nature of my own spiritual journey in particular.

***

I had decided to get rid of the cabinet because I needed to move forward towards my own inner light – in other words MY SPIRIT NEEDED A HOME. The action of moving towards that light within me had necessitated *an outer change*, and the removal of the cabinet had been THAT CHANGE. But, what it had revealed was the shadow on the wall which had been hidden by the presence of this piece of furniture. Now, my mind suddenly comprehended the 'cosmic' message I was being given.

In reality, this shadow wasn't what it seemed, but something far more transcendental. It was a PHYSICAL MANIFESTATION of what had happened *inside me* within the invisible realm of my soul during this whole process. It was the part of my own inner shadow that had been hidden from me, but which was now exposed and open to the light because I had decided to move forward.

What had happened on the
OUTSIDE
in my living room
faithfully reflected what had happened
INSIDE ME.

This was an enormous discovery for me, and suddenly allowed me to make sense of so many things that had occurred on my spiritual quest, all of which, up until this very moment, I had never truly understood.

Now I could see so clearly why my journey to Paris back in 1995 had begun with a stay in a psychiatric hospital. I could also understand why, at the beginning of my return to Spain in 1996, I had been surprised by the appearance of my life-long fear of death, and then why the new phase of the journey I began at the end of 1999 had started with a massive panic attack. These were all moments of MOVING FORWARD on my journey and, in doing so, the hidden aspect of my shadow had MANIFESTED or come out into the open – it had literally:

COME TO LIGHT.

This 'light' was, of course, a metaphor for my shadow coming out of the realm of the unseen area of my subconscious and into the awareness of my conscious mind.

Then, looking back on those events of 1995, 1996 and 1999, my intuition seemed to suddenly give me an even greater insight - it also appeared as if *an aspect* of my shadow, but not all of it, was possibly some form of mental illness, hence the panic attacks I had experienced in the past.

As I sat contemplating the space where the cabinet had been, and the perfectly rectangular shadow, another transcendental insight emerged - once again as if from nowhere. In a flash I realised that, if this last 'hypothesis' were true, then this part of my shadow also belonged to a large spectrum of conditions shared by the entire human race.

My intuition seemed to be telling me that my individual malaises lay within a universal spectrum of mental health issues which formed the SHADOW OF OUR HUMAN SPECIES. These would include, amongst many others, conditions such as manic depression, schizophrenia, obsessive compulsive disorder, anorexia, bulimia, epilepsy, phobias and others. Then, quite unexpectedly a memory popped into my head.

I remembered that back in 1999, when I had made my first attempt at a relationship with Alberto, he had taken me to see a nutritionist and iridologist because we were both overweight and needed advice on dietary changes. The iridologist had examined my eyes and announced to my shock and consternation that he could see an epilepsy mark on my brain. Within less than a second of being told this I had made the connection with my past, and knew that the mark had been produced by the cocaine-based dental anaesthetic which had entered my bloodstream in 1993.

That day in Madrid was a watershed for me, allowing an impenetrable enigma to be solved after six long years. I had finally found an explanation as to why I had felt that I was going to have convulsions in those few hours after returning home from the dentist. But now, more importantly, something else was happening with this memory. It was also giving me a fresh insight and a new connection to what had just occurred with the removal of the cabinet.

The shadow on the apartment wall was quite clearly a manifestation of humanity's UNIVERSAL SHADOW. But, at the same time it was also a 'cosmic' confirmation that I obviously had a genetic potential within my personal shadow for manifesting epilepsy.

These discoveries, gleaned from the apparently innocuous removal of an unwanted piece of furniture then went even deeper. It seemed as if my intuition and mind were on some kind of a 'metaphysical roll' because yet another insight suddenly revealed itself to me as I continued to sit in front of the empty wall. Now I knew why when I had embarked on my odyssey to see Alejandro Jodorowsky, I had met and befriended as if by pure chance a person who suffered from epilepsy – my dear friend James. The insight was showing me with total clarity that chance had had ABSOLUTELY NOTHING TO DO WITH IT AT ALL.

In reality, I had 'jumped' into a relationship with the unseen, metaphysical side of life, and in moving forward into my adventure back in 1995, a part of my shadow had emerged into the light - exactly as it had done here in the apartment. That inner 'aspect' of my shadow had then MANIFESTED itself outwardly in the outside world in the form of meeting my epileptic friend James. MY GOD, I muttered to myself under my breath, barely able to take on board what I had just learnt in the space of five very short minutes. It was truly astonishing how much this patch of unpainted wall was revealing to me!

***

In the next few days after these incredible revelations, and buoyed up by my discoveries, I began tentatively to venture forward mentally hoping that I would be able to find some kind of integrated understanding of my quest. I needed an intelligible picture of where I was and where I might be going, and so with this in mind I started to mull over what I had come to understand about the duality of my soul.

I knew from working with my intuition that my soul was largely buried deep within my unconscious mind, but I began to suspect that a part of it was also connected to my conscious mind. The reason I came to this conclusion was in some ways due to what had been revealed to me with the shadow on the wall. But, another factor was that I couldn't overlook the fact that the human brain 'coincidentally' comprises two halves - the left and right cerebral hemispheres.

Logic told me that if my soul were two halves, then it would inevitably be connected in some way to these left and right conscious hemispheres of my brain. Perhaps the **mystical** half of my soul was partially connected to my right hemisphere, and the **material** half of my soul to my left hemisphere. I visualised the soul as being similar to an iceberg, with most of its mass below water — in other words on a subconscious level. However, using this same analogy, a small area of my soul would also be above water, or part of my conscious mind. If this were true, then my shadow - *the **material** aspect of my soul* - was part subconscious and part conscious.

So far I had only been dealing with the conscious part of my shadow, which was my ego and sexual passions. However, with this reasoning I realised that a myriad of fears, anxieties and terrors, as well as disease states belonging to my shadow, also inhabited my subconscious mind. Like the shadow on my living room wall, a move forward towards my inner light caused the metaphorical waters around the iceberg to recede, and part of my 'submerged' shadow EMERGED to be felt and experienced consciously.

All of this reinforced a conviction I had held for several years which was that spiritual growth was more about getting to know one's own shadow than anything else. The shadow was the aspect of our souls which, unless examined through the light of consciousness, had the power to sabotage or destroy any movement towards the light of our spirits. Wow, amazing, so much insight into the nature of the human spiritual path in so short a space of time was incredibly heady stuff!

In the week or so after the removal of the cabinet these quantum leaps in my understanding started to coalesce for me, and I became convinced that the morning of seeing the shadow of unpainted wall had truly been my rebirth - THE REBIRTH OF MY SOUL! It just had to have been the definitive sign marking the birth of AURORA!!! Surely, I told myself, the baby Aurora of my dream from April 2000 was the 'illumination' I had experienced only seconds after that fateful moment when I had seen what was on the empty wall of my apartment.

Wasn't it the invisible realm speaking to me yet again in its seemingly 'invisible' language of manifestations and signs?

MISSION ACCOMPLISHED!

With this thought i I relaxed and breathed an enormous sigh of relief. I had finally achieved what I had blindly set out to do seven years earlier, and to be honest, I couldn't quite believe I had DONE IT!

***

Now, I decided to turn my energies away from my completed odyssey, and set about the task of creating a new home and a new life for my newly reborn soul. To achieve this end the first thing I did was to move my existing sofa into the space where the cabinet had been. I then spent the little money I had in the bank on a bamboo chest of drawers for the opposite wall, and emptied the smallest of the three bedrooms in order to convert it into an office.

With a new life beckoning to me I realised that I would need to move away from the old and look for a total change of direction, and so with this I quickly, and almost unthinkingly decided that I wouldn't return to English teaching. Instead, I felt a possible profession for me could be that of a freelance translator - hence the need for an office.

Whilst I was in the throes of rearranging my home, a close friend invited me to see a film which was apparently turning into a huge box-office hit all around the world. It was called **MY BIG FAT GREEK WEDDING,** and Sophie and I took ourselves off to the local cinema to see it dubbed into Spanish. I saw this same film a year later in its original English version, and I can honestly say that it wasn't the same experience. Watching the film in Spanish was truly astonishing.

Because a large part of Spain borders the Mediterranean Sea, its culture and customs closely resemble those of other Mediterranean countries like Italy or Greece. This meant that the experience of listening to the characters speaking Spanish was almost as if they were speaking to each other in Greek. The effect created was that the film appeared to exist INSIDE the Greek mind-set and culture, with the American characters having to speak Greek too in order to be able to communicate. The film was brilliantly funny, but as I watched it, because of the dubbing, I became aware that I was watching two films in one.

The second film was a subtext, and an extraordinary revelation of the true goal of the spiritual path I was on. The depth of this revelation was mind-bogglingly amazing, to say the least. Again, just as had happened with the religious freeze I had seen on my way to Don Pablo's office in the spring of 2000, the wisdom and knowing of the human collective unconscious, or **Soul of the World**, was being communicated through the film in the form of this subtext.

I will explain the spiritual message of the film at the end of this book, because it pertains to the ultimate direction of our spiritual strivings as a human race.

Suffice to say that in the autumn of 2002 the invisible realm had mysteriously 'popped up' once again, and simply whispered to me that I was on a path which was revealing itself to me through what others might dismiss as mere coincidences, or the flights of fancy of someone with an over-active imagination.

***

By the beginning of December I had moved considerably further forward in creating my new life. I had completed a course to orientate women in setting up their own businesses, finished a crash course on surfing the Internet and emailing, installed a fax machine and computer in my office, and found Paulo Coelho's website and address on the Internet. Ecstatic that I had finally been able to access a point of contact with my hero, I wrote Paulo a long letter in which I told him all about *'my ruin'* and my journey to Paris.

Almost seven years had elapsed since I had lived out my odyssey in 1996, and knowing that Paulo would finally read my testimony filled me with a glorious hope. It was a hope which seemed to be bursting out of my heart as I had never felt it before on this long and arduous quest.

The invisible realm seemed to be most definitely on my side, and now, with my little office all organized and 'ready-to- go', and a 'door' open to Paulo in Rio de Janeiro, I was ready to step into my new beginning. But, then again…I….. I….I……well…. I wasn't. The next few days revealed to me that my heart and soul weren't in the least bit committed to this new life and game plan.

Setting myself up as a translator was a logically sound idea, and even an inspired initiative, but my spirit seemed to be somewhere else altogether. During all these preparations in my apartment, the longing to live a different kind of life had somehow CREPT IN and taken root in me.

The truth was that I had become tired of the dusty streets outside my windows, the noise of traffic, and the endless bustle of people around me. My heart never responded to logic, but yearned to look up at vast stretches of empty blue sky, hear birds singing in the morning, and see fields of grasses and wild flowers swaying gently in a summer breeze. I was of course dreaming of HEAVEN HERE ON EARTH, and my spirit suddenly came up with a 'brainwave'. I needed to move out of town and buy a small piece of land somewhere out in the hills to be able to put a very inexpensive wooden house on it.

My heart imagined that this could be the seed of a retreat centre for anyone suffering from burn out; a place for them to come to find themselves again through simple contact with nature. Now that I had discovered the Internet, I saw that there was a worldwide community of potentially like-minded souls out there in cyberspace. Even if my money would only stretch to buying a very small piece of land, I could always communicate my vision for a retreat on the Web, and I was sure to attract people willing to work with me to bring about this dream!

And, so it was that a new passion and dream were born for me and my logical plans ground to a total halt. At this point I suddenly realised that I had been premature in thinking that AURORA had been born with the removal of the cabinet back in September. Slowly it was dawning on me that in actual fact this had been just one more STAGE in my odyssey, and there now seemed to be much more mileage ahead of me on this quest. My intuition pointed me firmly in the direction of the wooden house on its idyllic piece of land.

**

Alberto visited me for the Christmas holidays and I told him enthusiastically about this new vision of mine. His reaction was muted, and it became clear that we were speaking different languages and our spirits were set in different directions. My heart took in the sad reality that, though never outwardly mentioned in words, our relationship was well and truly over.

With the New Year approaching, all my plans for the freelance translation business came to a complete standstill as my whole focus became the dream of finding my piece of HEAVEN ON EARTH here in Andalusia. My thoughts also returned to The Alchemist. I knew that this allegory was in effect the template or pattern of my spiritual journey, but I still didn't have a clear understanding of its true meaning. Life had shown me that a superficial interpretation of something, be it a person, a situation, a picture, a film, or a book, always missed the deeper underlying truth and significance of what we were experiencing.

So in January 2003 I decided to dedicate myself even more intensively to my path — not the slightest, small detail could be overlooked. That would mean cutting out all distractions from my life, and so I wouldn't read any books other than The Alchemist, and Coelho's Warrior of the Light, and I also needed to keep my TV watching down to a bare minimum.

My spirit knew that it was time to move much closer to my goal of that encounter with the LIGHT OF MY SOUL for which I had been searching so very long and hard. I knew that deciphering The Alchemist and my dream of the land with the wooden house would both get me there. My journey was turning into a marathon of far too many years, and AURORA was calling me, if not screaming at me that I ABSOLUTELY HAD TO FIND HER.

I was now almost frantic in my desire to get this quest over and done with, and I felt the end point to be so very, very close. Everything I was discovering and doing, although largely 'invisible' to the outside world, was of vital importance to our human race, and I figured that for better or worse, and no matter the consequences, THE REST OF LIFE COULD WAIT!

12

THE PYRAMID OF LOVE

**True discovery is a very lonely business. You're
out on a limb which only you suspect is there,
reaching for a prize that only you suspect exists.**

ELISE BAXTER

I have just spoken about my spirit being in search of the light of my soul, and this may seem contradictory and illogical. If the light of my soul is also my spirit, then how can something be in search of itself? Of course, the explanation for all of this is THE DUAL NATURE OF THE SOUL. As Jung knew, there is the Lumen Dei of the soul, and the Lumen Naturae. Each of these halves carries divine light or spirit, and the one goes in search of the other — ITS TWIN IF YOU WILL.

I had understood this much when I discovered the symbolic meaning of the Beauty and the Beast fairy-tale, and had named the two halves of my soul the **mystical** and the **material**. However, the connection with The Alchemist was still proving to be an elusive and mysterious enigma. I was now entering the ninth year of my search and the only two things on my mind were deciphering the meaning of The Alchemist and finding my precious piece of land. The invisible realm knew all of this much better than I did, and decided to move into action far more quickly than I could have anticipated.

Two weeks into January I walked past a local shop window, and caught sight of an advertisement for the sale of a plot of land. The appearance of such a manifestation so soon after setting my intention was completely thrilling. Without any kind of hesitation or doubt on my part I immediately contacted the owner to arrange a viewing. A few days later, the gentleman concerned drove me out into the hills to see this little piece of Heaven most people only dream about. However, when I saw the plot, I suddenly understood precisely why it was well within my calculated budget.

It was the north-facing side of a low terraced hill which hardly ever saw any sunlight. In the shade of a January afternoon sun the land was cold, steep and extremely uninviting. As I stared at the antithesis of everything I had hoped for, it took only seconds for me to realise the discrepancy between my dream and the realities available to me with my limited funds. And so it was that after a brief tour with my expectant guide, I politely told him that I would need to think it over.

Back in my little castle, and licking my 'wounds', I decided that my dream was a long-term project - possibly a year or more - and that I would be better off dedicating my energies to undoing the riddle of The Alchemist. Far too much time had gone by without me being able to read this cryptic map of my soul quest.

***

I turned to Paulo's fable once again, and began to go through it for a third time, making notes of any signs or coincidences I might find in the book. Towards the end of February, as I was reading the final pages of the book, a friend asked me if I had a spare room for a friend of hers from Argentina. Being very short of money I agreed to rent out the remaining bedroom in my apartment to this person. Marta arrived with the intention of staying for a month or two before returning to Buenos Aires.

Looking back on these events I can see that the life I was leading at the time must have seemed rather strange to my guest. Each morning would involve me waking up, breakfasting, and then keeping myself silent for at least forty-five minutes. This was my religious discipline of trying to tune in to my intuition and my deepest, subconscious feelings. Most of the day would then proceed in the same way for me as I took my contemplative nature to a new level of intensity.

Nevertheless, despite this unusual behaviour on my part, Marta and I managed to get on. We were both spiritual seekers, trying to live out a spiritual path based on love, tolerance, peace, and personal honesty.

Life was not completely and solely a dedication to the contemplative way because just before Marta's arrival I had decided to give my artistic and creative temperament an outlet. This took the form of me attending Flamenco dance classes given by a teacher living nearby. I had begun the classes in January whilst reading The Alchemist, and before the start of each class I used to chat to my teacher's father who ran a gift shop where the classes were held.

During one of our conversations, he mentioned that he had been healed of a very serious illness by going to a healing mass held once a month at a catholic chapel in one of the towns along the coast. Anything related to healing immediately had my full attention and interest. This man's testimony was extremely impressive, and so at the beginning of February I accompanied him, along with many others, on a hired bus to attend the mass for that particular month. My scepticism regarding the trip was high and so, just as I had expected, I returned from the healing mass totally unchanged and more significantly UNHEALED. However, the experience set me thinking about what I had been reading in The Alchemist.

Trying hard to understand the allegory I stripped my knowledge down to the bare minimum. All I knew was that Santiago, the shepherd, had journeyed to a place where his treasure WAS NOT and there, in this very place, had discovered the true location of his treasure.

After the mass in the chapel, each of us attending had been given a small gift before leaving. I can't remember now what this gift was on my first visit, but the fact that I had been given something at the end of the service impacted me strongly. As I thought about The Alchemist and my visit to the healing mass I suddenly felt there was a connection. Perhaps in some way my journey to the little chapel and participation in the mass was exactly the same as:

Santiago's journey to the pyramids of Egypt.

To me it seemed that we had both gone to places where our treasure WAS NOT, and yet paradoxically before leaving, we were shown or given the location of our true treasure. I concluded that the gift I had received, along with everyone else at the end of the mass, was a PHYSICAL MANIFESTATION of my inner treasure which I had somehow found by making the journey and participating in the service. Then quite unexpectedly, my intuitions began to deepen as I continued to pursue this line of thought.

Mysteriously, I came to realise that TWO THING WERE HAPPENING AT THE SAME TIME whenever we made a journey. Santiago's journey to the pyramids, like my own to the chapel, was actually two journeys occurring simultaneously. As Santiago moved forward physically towards his destination in the OUTER material world, inwardly and unseen, an equal but opposite movement to an INNER destination within his own psyche was taking place.

He was effectively travelling in two directions at once:
OUTWARDLY AND INWARDLY.

Finding 'the cupboard bare', so to speak, at the pyramids, or as I had found it at the healing mass because I experienced no kind of healing there, awoke him — and also me - to the inner treasure located deep within our souls. This awakening always subsequently led to a manifestation on the material plane of this inner treasure.

In The Alchemist that manifestation had come from the leader of the refugees who told Santiago of his own dream concerning finding treasure buried under the roots of a sycamore tree growing inside the ruin of a church in Andalusia. For me, the manifestation was that of being given a material gift at the end of the mass.

Naturally, this was a totally oversimplified analysis of my journey to the healing mass. I had conveniently overlooked the fact that even though no healing had occurred for me, there were people, like my dance teacher's father, who *did receive their treasure* at the service.

However, my reality was that I was trying to decipher a riddle and enigma, and if simplifying helped me to advance even a little in my understanding, then this was what I needed to do.

***

In March I had finished reading The Alchemist, and was now fired up with this latest insight. I persuaded Marta to accompany me to another of the masses because I was determined to test out my theory with this second visit, and she would be my witness.

Sure enough and to my great delight, the experience turned out to be the same as what had transpired on my visit in February. I found no healing there - no treasure - but my effort was rewarded with yet another small gift at the end of the service. This time I do remember what it was - a minute reproduction of the image of the VIRGIN MARY. This excited me greatly.

For quite some time now I had come to the conclusion that, even though the Virgin was a real historical figure, in the language of the collective unconscious she was most likely a symbol of the human soul. Jung had always postulated that the soul was a feminine entity, and my knowledge of world mythologies, although scant, told me that the soul was invariably portrayed as a feminine figure. Had I been given this gift of an image of the Virgin as an outward manifestation of my inner treasure?

Was this my feminine soul found within me, and
reborn through taking this outer journey?

Marta left towards the end of March, and I returned to a rereading of The Alchemist — I simply HAD TO understand this story! It was clear to me that I was now embroiled in a new phase of this search, and not one bit of me was considering living a conventional life.

In order to continue with my inexplicable quest I knew I desperately needed money, as stopping to look for work was nowhere on my horizon. I turned to the most obvious place from which I could raise some funds — my bank. Thankfully I managed to obtain a loan using my apartment as security. Clearly this was not a wise thing to do, but my journey was so transcendentally important to me, that making so-called sensible decisions was logically not an option.

My passionate faith that I was intimately part of an invisible path and destiny was rewarded fairly immediately when near the end of

April a letter arrived through the post. It was an electoral registration form which I needed to submit to an office in Malaga in order to appear on the voting register for the province. At first I didn't pay any attention to the form, until I accidentally spotted the name of the street where the office was located. It was called *Calle Puerta del Mar*, which in English translates as Door of the Sea Street.

MY GOD, THE SEA!
Was I finally beginning to understand
THE MESSAGE OF THE ALCHEMIST?

After eight long years on this quest, I had become familiar with poetic metaphors for the spiritual journey, and one often used by writers of all cultures was the metaphor of rivers journeying to the sea. We humans were akin to rivers that traversed mountains, deserts, plains and valleys, always with only one goal in mind - a return to our source, the sea. The sea in these metaphors was our spiritual home, and where a river could be reborn to a new existence.

I also knew from my psychological studies at university that the sea was a symbol of the unconscious in man - the realm of the soul and our spirits. Instantly I felt that I had received a sign from the invisible realm, and it was telling me that my personal river had finally reached her sea! With this intuitive realisation, I knew my insight could mean only one thing – THE DOOR TO SPIRITUAL REBIRTH WAS AT HAND!

Ever eager to put into practice everything I was learning, I applied the theory I had arrived at for what had happened to me at the healing mass to this new situation. Like the name of the mass, because the name of the street where the registration office was located promised rebirth, then I could confidently predict that I wouldn't find any treasure there. The obvious reason for this was that in making the journey to Malaga I would in effect be once more metaphorically JOURNEYING TO THE PYRAMIDS OF THE ALCHEMIST. And true to the pattern of this archetypal path, I would find 'the cupboard bare'

That moment of EMPTINESS would then be the pivotal epiphany and, as with the mass, lead to the discovery of my inner treasure and where it really lay. This discovery would then automatically produce a MATERIAL MANIFESTATION in the outer world of what I had found inside me.

Bingo, I had struck spiritual gold!

With this realisation, in a flash a huge horizon of new understanding seemed to open up before me. Suddenly I felt myself to be standing at the threshold of an extremely exciting point on my journey. This was rather like the moment when a scientist makes his or her breakthrough discovery of a universal natural law. However, the realm I was unlocking was far deeper than the physical world all around us.

By engaging with 'signs' and my intuitions, I was penetrating the workings of the metaphysical side of life – in other words, our INVISIBLE SPIRITUAL REALM.

***

On Saturday May 3, 2003 I filled out my electoral registration form and on Sunday the fourth I made my way to the office in Malaga, not to test out my theory as I had done before at the healing mass, but to actually *put it into practice*. This was no longer observation and hypothesising on my part, but a conscious quantum leap into:

co-creating with the universe.

My attention was incredibly heightened that afternoon when I entered Malaga, as each of my footsteps felt as though they were engaged in the making of history. I walked very slowly in the direction of *Calle Puerta del Mar*, knowing that this would lead to the amazing rebirth of my soul. The adrenalin coursing through my body was galvanizing all of my senses because I knew full well that I was on the cusp of finding the Holy Grail which had fuelled every waking moment of my days for more than eight long and arduous years.

True to the theory I had elaborated before coming up to Malaga, there was ABSOLUTELY NO TREASURE at the door to the office when I arrived. Being a Sunday, everything was shut, and so I lifted the flap of the letter box located in the main door, and silently praying for strength dropped my form through onto the floor of the entrance hall visible through the glass door.

YES, I HAD FINALLY ACHIEVED MY GOAL!

I had made the two journeys –
the outer one here to the office in Malaga,
and
simultaneously the inner one,
to a place deep inside my psyche.

The cupboard was, as I had hypothesised, predictably BARE and I knew that even if I couldn't feel it, I had indirectly found the true location of my treasure:

MY SPIRIT AND MY SOUL HAD BOTH FINALLY BEEN REBORN!!!

I stood stock still for several seconds to feel the enormity of this instant in my whole being. Yet again, as on past occasions, the feelings of being someone new weren't present within me, but according to my theorizing I most definitely was supposed to be a new creation. Elated by this apparent certainty, I now understood what the next step which awaited me needed to be. It was time to receive the material manifestation of this rebirth in the outside world, and my intuition instantly told me that I needed to head in the direction of a church.

I didn't analyse this impulse, but simply obeyed. I left *Calle Puerta del Mar* and began to walk in the direction of the river because I knew there were two churches on its west bank. The universe seemed to want *to* 'hold my hand', so to speak, as I crossed the bridge over the river by giving me an enormous sign. Was it watching me from its

INVISIBLE HOME to let me know that I was one of its star pupils? The bridge was called:

Puente de la Esperanza
THE BRIDGE OF HOPE.

As far as signs went, this was something that left me incredulous. It seemed that the invisible realm could speak more eloquently and directly than any person on our planet! I continued to walk in the direction of the two churches, and decided on the one that was on the opposite side of the road. The church on my side was familiar to me as it was the church I had passed each time I had been to see Don Pablo.

It had the ceramic freeze on its back wall which had shown me so much about my spiritual path. However, the other church was one I had passed but never stopped to look at, so it was the obvious contender for this end-of-journey moment.

As I walked up to a set of traffic lights next to a zebra crossing in order to be able to cross the busy main road, I noticed a large piece of paper stuck to one of the traffic light poles. I stopped to read what was on it, and was astonished to see that it was a flyer advertising a Chi Kung weekend at the end of May. It was to be held in the town of Granada, only around an hour's bus journey from Malaga. Now, there is nothing particularly or necessarily astonishing about the discipline of Chi Kung, but the appearance of this flyer had a very special meaning for me.

Whilst living with Alberto in Madrid the previous year, I had found some books about Chi Kung on his eclectic book shelves. Somehow this Chinese martial art had captured my imagination and enthusiasm. Here, in the middle of Malaga, I couldn't quite believe that I was standing in front of a traffic light pole looking at what I concluded just had to be A MANIFESTATION OF MY TREASURE!

I dug inside my bag for a piece of paper and a pen, and quickly scribbled down the contact telephone number for the weekend. I stayed for a while staring at the flyer, still feeling dumbfounded by what was happening to me. But then suddenly some people approached the lights and it was time to resume a normal demeanour and at least look as if I too wanted to cross the road.

The little green luminous man attached to the traffic light appeared, and a small group of us made our way across the multiple lanes of highway to the other side of the road. Still reeling from the Chi Kung flyer, I approached the outside of this church I had been guided to. What happened next may seem utterly stupid to you dear reader, given what you have read about my quest. I was about to be shown probably one of the biggest and clearest signs of my journey, and yet I would be completely unable to interpret its meaning.

As I walked up to the church, I could see the vague outline of the typical ceramic tile freeze of the churches in Andalusia on the long sidewall of the western side of the building. I approached it slowly as I always did when I met with religious images or artwork. Spirituality, of whatever faith, demands a degree of reverence and respect on our part, and this was my way of expressing these attitudes. Suddenly, what I saw before me was way beyond astonishing.

The freeze was once again the typical pairing of CHRIST AND THE VIRGIN, but the truly mind-boggling feature was not any part of this image. It was in fact an innocuous and inconspicuous municipal plaque screwed to the wall of the church by the side of the freeze. Quite simply, it gave the name of the road where I was standing:

Avenida de la Aurora.
AURORA, for God's sake!!!

Although I had travelled down this road in a car many, many times, I had never been aware of its name. What was my reaction? Shock is the best way to describe my feelings as I stared up at the plaque. I had just found my treasure glued to a traffic light pole on the other side of the road, and now this!

***

My brain simply couldn't process what I was seeing. Yet again, here was a situation where, had I been given access to hindsight;

I would have understood what was happening with no difficulty whatsoever. But standing alone by the side of the church on a quiet Sunday afternoon, when most people were at home having lunch, I simply wasn't able to comprehend a totally unexpected event of this magnitude.

Then, quite unexpectedly I felt my brain begin to turn to putty as the adrenalin of the last few hours began to leave my bloodstream. This whole 'experiment' was proving to be much more than I could take. Hunger pangs gripped my stomach and I looked around me for somewhere to sit and eat. Luckily, there was a restaurant behind the church which was visible from where I stood. I walked quickly to the tables and chairs on the terrace; my blood sugar suddenly feeling dangerously low. Whenever this happened to me, alarm bells began to ring inside my head telling me that a panic attack was a distinct possibility.

I sat alone, and ate a hearty lunch in what can only be described as a totally dazed state. My brain appeared to have shut down completely, and the hour I spent on the restaurant terrace was one of utter mindlessness. Once replenished, I paid my bill, and wended my way back home in the same state - bemused, astonished and exhausted. The universe had more than endorsed my theory. It had positively SCREAMED AT ME that I was out there, like so many mavericks before me, discovering new horizons and new worlds.

However, unknown to me on that amazing Sunday in Malaga, my interpretation that *The Door of the Sea Street* was a sign signifying that the river of my soul had finally reached the sea and its point of spiritual rebirth was erroneous. What it had really meant was that my soul journey was about to enter a new and completely virgin phase: THE SEA REALM OF MY UNCONSCIOUS. The iceberg that I had imagined my soul to be, with most of it below the surface of the water and therefore within my unconscious mind, was what I was about to climb.

Icebergs are often drawn in the shape of giant pyramids, and this is how I have represented my soul journey in the diagram you see on the next page. At this stage of my journey, I had no idea that going up to Malaga and *Calle Puerta del Mar* had been a *rite of initiation* in which the invisible realm had begun to prepare me for the journey into this UNCONSCIOUS DOMAIN OF MY SOUL. The universe, knowing that I was an able but novice apprentice on this quest, hadn't been signalling to me that my journey had ended, but that the most important part was just about to begin.

Self-realisation awaited me at the top in the form of SOUL REBIRTH, but until that time level upon level of upward ascent stood before me - MY VERY OWN PERSONAL EVEREST - and no one, but absolutely no one, could tell me the height of this particular peak.

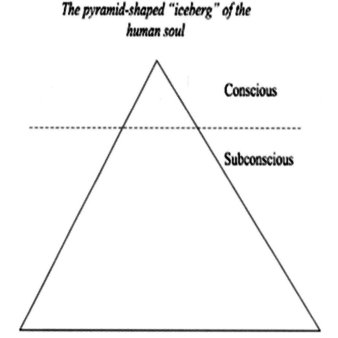

The pyramid-shaped "iceberg" of the
human soul

Conscious

Subconscious

MY PERSONAL EVEREST

13

THE MYSTERY UNCOVERED

**The most beautiful thing we can experience
is the mysterious.
It is the source of all true art and science.**

ALBERT EINSTEIN

ALTHOUGH Everest loomed on my horizon, and with it the start of an encounter with my unconscious, as I have just said I was completely unaware that this new stage awaited me. For the moment all I knew and felt was that my journey appeared to have ended. Soul rebirth had taken place in Malaga and a new life in the spirit was opening up before me. I couldn't have been happier!

It seemed more than synchronistic of the universe to allow this to happen just before my forty-fifth birthday in the middle of May. Where my fortieth birthday had been a time of depression, this birthday felt like the start of a brand new phase and my optimism about the future was high. My intuition appeared to be guiding me to celebrate this new beginning in some way, and so I put into action a desire I had harboured for quite a while.

On a visit to a travel agency in town I chose a hotel stay for a few days in a remote mountain village a few hours from my home. Nature was what I longed for: mountains, sky, streams and fields; a balm of tranquillity and peace to set me up for the next part of my life.

With my soul enraptured by this prospect in the second week of May I boarded a bus into the mountains. However, just before leaving I had sat down and engaged in a heart-to-heart talk with the universe. In the past I had learned that doors only open when we let go of the old, and so with this in mind, and knowing that I needed to be open to the new, I made the decision not to take any books with me. In fact, I decided not to take any reading material at all. I would go to the hotel as a totally clean slate, and thus allow the universe to write whatever it had prepared for me.

***

I arrived in this remote area of sierra to find that the summer tourist season hadn't as yet started and that I was the only person in the hotel. I had been allocated a sumptuous, airy room at the top of the building, and the magical, Andalusian countryside I longed to connect with was right on my doorstep. On my first morning I walked down to the river which ran alongside the entrance to the village. There I discovered a trail which led to a huge, natural pool further upstream. This was obviously used by the villagers for summer bathing.

I breathed in the delicious country air and watched turtles swimming gracefully just below the surface of the water. Later in the day, I returned from the river and explored the silent streets and alleyways of the village.

Then, hours later and alone in the hotel that evening, my solitariness was a little more difficult to deal with. After a good meal, I had the choice of either returning to my room or sitting in the empty hotel lounge where I could flick through magazines. All the magazines on the lounge table were in Spanish so this was a welcome opportunity to practice my reading. However, with absolutely no warning signs, I was in for a very big surprise:

the invisible realm had me well and truly in its sights.

After ploughing through several light-weight magazines I hit on one which was the weekend supplement to a national newspaper. There were at least six back copies of this magazine, and I knew from the quality of the publication that there would be some interesting articles well worth looking at. I picked up another one of the supplements and turned to the back pages, and it was then that I was utterly astonished by what I saw.

There, right before my eyes was an essay by Paulo Coelho!!! Instantly realising that this was probably a regular weekly column in the magazine I opened up another copy of the group of supplements lying on the table to check if this was the case.

Sure enough that copy also had an essay by Paulo Coelho. In fact, when I checked all the copies, each one contained an essay. This was truly extraordinary! The only two books I had been reading all year were The Alchemist and Warrior of the Light, both by Paulo, and I had deliberately left them behind in my apartment to allow the universe to bring me SOMETHING NEW. Yet, here in a remote mountain village, inside this empty hotel lounge, Paulo Coelho had somehow 'followed me' on my journey.

These essays were most definitely signs from the invisible realm, but what kind of signs were they? I retired to my room to think, and within less than a minute my intuition provided me with the answer I needed well before my reasoning head. The odyssey hadn't ended at The Door of the Sea Street, in Malaga, as I had thought – oh, no, I was being shown that THERE WAS MORE TO COME!

Journeying to this remote area was clearly my intuition extracting me from the world and allowing me to assimilate the fact that more of this invisible path to soul rebirth lay ahead of me. So it was that instead of engaging in relaxed tourism as I had expected, I began to use the four days in the mountains to walk and sense where I was on my quest.

I climbed hills covered in almond trees, and walked down empty country roads, taking in the fields and mountain ridges, but always trying to tune into my intuition. I felt that I was on the edge of something – SOMETHING VERY BIG - but the future was shrouded in silence and mystery. Much as I so desperately wanted answers, I couldn't see anything of the path ahead.

On my last night in the hotel, and anxious for some kind of understanding before I left, I sat down in the lounge and systematically went through all the essays by Paulo Coelho in the copies of the weekend supplement lying on the coffee table. However, after seeing absolutely nothing which could be interpreted as a sign, I despondently admitted defeat and decided to abandon my search.

Just as I was about to leave the room, I turned my gaze back towards the coffee table almost despairingly, and then quite accidentally spied one final copy I had missed. It had been buried under a pile of gossip magazines, and I returned to the table at almost lightning speed to pull it out. As I did this, several layers of other magazines scattered onto the wooden floor, but ignoring the chaos I was creating, and with excitement mounting inside me, I turned once more to the back pages in a frenzied anticipation of what I might be about to find.

Sure enough this last essay was once again by Paulo, and had a very interesting title:

ITHACA – THE LONG ROAD OF RETURN

In it the Brazilian writer described how he had used a poem written by a contemporary Greek poet as a source of inspiration whilst he had had been travelling along The Camino de Santiago in 1986. The poem was about the mythological journey of the ancient Greek hero Ulysses. It used Ulysses' adventures and trials as he made his way back to the island of Ithaca, where his great love Penelope awaited him, as a metaphor for the nature of the journey of life. However, it was the title of the essay that really held my attention: THE LONG ROAD OF RETURN

Immediately my mind understood that this was yet again one of the central metaphors used to describe the human spiritual quest; a journey *outward into tests and trials* that eventually brought us back to where we had started, but now INWARDLY REBORN IN OUR SPIRITS. Wow, I couldn't quite believe what was happening to me! Here was most definitely a sign from the invisible realm concerning my own journey, but sitting there in the silence of the hotel lounge, I couldn't quite fathom what it meant.

In a split second I did something which I normally never allowed myself to do. I tore out the page from the magazine on which the essay was printed and pocketed it. It was going home with me; I couldn't possibly leave such an important sign behind, and back in my apartment I would have the time to go over it again in order to decipher its significance for the journey ahead of me.

***

Two days after my return home I suddenly grasped the meaning of Paulo Coelho's Ithaca essay. The mythological Greek tale of Ulysses was in fact a story of two halves. Ulysses and Penelope were another example of how deep inside the **Soul of the World** of Mankind humanity understood that our souls were made up of two distinct and separate halves. Ulysses, with his trials in the outer world, was the **material** half of the soul, and Penelope, who remained quietly constant, weaving a death shroud on the island of Ithaca awaiting his return, was the **mystical** half of this soul.

Paulo had compared Ulysses' journey in the poem to his own struggle to complete the Camino de Santiago without ever realising that the myth was actually about the unification of the two separate halves of the soul! With this unexpected inspirational insight, it appeared that I had now identified two distinct tales describing the journey to soul rebirth: they were Beauty and the Beast and the myth of Ulysses and Penelope. Surely, my excited heart seemed to be saying, these signs meant that I was finally approaching my own end point and the longed-for REBIRTH OF MY SOUL!

I looked ahead to the end of the month when I knew that I would be participating in the Chi Kung weekend which had been advertised on the traffic light pole in Malaga. Before my stay at the hotel in the mountains I had assumed that a journey to this weekend would represent a magnificent encounter with my treasure, but now with my latest discovery, everything had been turned well and truly upside down.

Would going to Granada in fact be yet another journey like the one I had made to the healing mass - and would it be my last? Was it to be somewhere I would be heading where my treasure WAS NOT, and in the process I would discover where my treasure REALLY WAS?

I realised that these questions had absolutely no possibility of being answered inside my head. As ever, there was only one way of finding those answers, and that was if I stopped wondering and speculating and actually went. Armed with renewed valour, I waited for my birthday to come and go, and then on May 30 journeyed to Malaga to catch a bus to Granada for the 'enigmatic' Chi Kung weekend.

On my arrival, I checked in to a cheap hotel and then made my way to a large hall the following day to begin the first session. As soon as I entered the building I was somewhat disconcerted to see that the venue was full of aspiring Chi Kungists who all looked rather like me. Reluctantly I had to admit to myself that it was just a little obvious that we were what you would call society's outsiders. We were the ones — THOSE 'TROUBLED' SOULS - who couldn't seem to find a place for ourselves within the conventional parameters of so-called 'normal life', and it appeared that Chi Kung was just one of many ways in which we were looking for meaning in a world that had little room or time for the spiritual.

Everything started well enough that morning. Even though the Chi Kung Master didn't speak any Spanish, one of the participants acted as a translator as we warmed up with a few exercises and then began the serious stuff. However, within less than an hour I knew I was *in the wrong place* doing *the wrong thing*. Try as I might, I simply couldn't connect with the spirit of what was going on at all.

This left me feeling decidedly uncomfortable, and somewhat anxious. Why was I always this 'weirdo' constantly looking in on life, instead of being an integral part of it — even when I found myself amongst other so-called 'weirdoes'? Everyone else in the hall looked as if they were completely wrapped up in the explanations the Master was giving, and doing their utmost to perform the movements to the best of their ability — all that is, except for me.

I carried on in this state of discomfort for another hour until suddenly an extraordinary flash of insight came to me: I couldn't relate to what was happening because there was no feminine energy present in the room.

> The feminine energy of the soul, or what we call
> intuition, was more than conspicuous for
> its total absence.

Now, I beg of you, dear reader, not to misunderstand or misinterpret what I am saying here. I am by no means stating that soul energy is absent from Chi Kung in general. I have neither the knowledge nor the understanding of this discipline to make such a bold and unequivocal statement. However, what I can say is that at this particular weekend seminar I was attending intuition was the one thing most notably *not present*.

Immediately I understood that I was only able to sense this because of my years of practise in developing a connection with the intuitive side of myself. As I looked around the room I was sure that the vast majority of the people there were not aware of this missing element. I guessed that some might perhaps have a feeling of dissatisfaction at the end of the weekend, but I was pretty convinced that they wouldn't be able to identify the reason as to why they felt this way.

In the instant when this insight came to me, I realised that I had metaphorically COME TO THE PYRAMIDS YET AGAIN! Yes, just as at the healing mass, and also when I had gone to Malaga at the beginning of May, my treasure wasn't here. However, the great discovery with this trip was how clearly I had sensed WHAT AND WHERE MY TRUE TREASURE WAS:

It was the intuitive feminine energy inside my soul.

When we broke for lunch I decided that, having found my treasure, there was no point in returning for the afternoon session, or the two sessions scheduled for the following day. Instead, it was time to go in search of a church my intuition told me, and an OUTWARD MANIFESTATION of my treasure. I knew that if I did this, what had happened for me in Malaga when I had completed my mission at *Calle Puerta del Mar* would also happen once again here in Granada.

***

I left the hall, and using my internal radar, turned down a street which looked promising. After walking about a hundred metres it came to an end, joining with a broad, modern boulevard. I looked to my right and saw the distinctive outline of a church about another hundred metres in front of me.

How on earth did I manage to do these things, I asked myself excitedly? I had never been to this part of Granada in my life, and yet within a minute or so I had found a church! I walked the remaining distance to where the edifice stood and took in this wonderful sight in all its glory. It was a modern building, and I could see that the whole boulevard in which it stood was a recent development of high-quality apartments for the well-off in this part of town. I read the name of the church:

Santo Tomas de Villa Nueva
St. Thomas of New Town.

Amazing, I thought to myself, I didn't even have to go hunting for the 'manifestation' of my treasure because my intuition had led me right to it, just as it had in Malaga. 'Coincidentally, or perhaps *not so coincidentally*, my father's name was also Thomas – he being one of the great treasures of my life. Suddenly, something deep inside me began to smile.

The invisible realm really did speak a specific language to us human beings, and I was beginning to be able to READ IT! If that wasn't truly COSMIC, then I didn't know what was!

As I stared at the church, I found myself standing on a segment of pavement outside a cafeteria and decided that this would be as good a place as any in which to have lunch. I sat down at one of the tables on the terrace, and looked up at the name of the establishment. It was called CAFETERIA SIGLO 21, which in English means '*Cafeteria 21ˢᵗ Century*'. My God, ANOTHER MANIFESTATION I thought! Yes, we – humanity - were at the beginning of a new century, and my journey was all about bringing forth new light and a brand new consciousness within my soul. By any standards, what was now transpiring was really quite extraordinary!

Then, as I was still processing the astonishing nature of the signs which the invisible realm had led me to, whilst simultaneously eating an assortment of tapas, I began to go over what I had discovered since my arrival in Granada.

The Chi Kung weekend had revealed its meaning and purpose to me, and this was that it was not a manifestation of my treasure as I had presumed back at the beginning of May. My suspicions after my return from my stay in the mountains had been confirmed, and as I had just realised earlier, it was now quite obviously another journey to the metaphorical pyramids of Egypt. Then, casting my mind back over the last few months, I could see that all of this had started in February with my first journey to the healing mass. That too had been a journey to Egypt, and likewise the trip to Malaga had been exactly that.

Suddenly I felt I was beginning to detect a pattern in all of this. Once more I stared back at the church as I sat eating my tapas, and once more smiled to myself. I read its name again - Santo Tomas—and then, quite unexpectedly, the realisation came in an instant:

I knew the true meaning of The Alchemist!!!

Yes, I'll say it again:
I knew
the true meaning of The Alchemist!!!

Miraculously, as if I were someone who had been digging for what had started to feel like an eternity, my pale had abruptly and quite spontaneously hit a solid seam of gold. Yes, that was it! The Alchemist, just like Beauty and the Beast, and also the myth of Ulysses and Penelope was the story of:

THE TWO HALVES OF THE HUMAN SOUL!

***

Santiago's journey to the pyramids had been his journey towards an encounter *with the other half of his soul,* and since February I had been doing the very same thing. I had metaphorically been making journeys to symbolic Egypts in order to encounter this other half of my inner self. The half both Santiago and I had journeyed to meet was what I had earlier named the **material** aspect of the soul, and so this logically meant that each of us was personifying the **mystical** half of the human soul.

And now, in an instant I understood with total clarity why neither of us had been able to find treasure in the places we had been to. The **material** half of the soul was the shadow I had identified back in chapter 8 – in other words the controlling, fearful ego and its rational, logical and reasoning approach to life. And this ego didn't believe in treasure because treasure was of the spirit. Put very plainly and simply, the ego's modus operandi was the antithesis of that spirit.

I could now see how Santiago had met the physical manifestation of the **material** half of his soul at the end of The Alchemist in the form of the leader of the refugees of the tribal wars. This man had led Santiago's beating, and in this beating the shepherd boy's **mystical** half had endured a direct encounter with the shadow of the **material** half of his own soul.

In other words, he had encountered his controlling ego, personified by the tribal leader, who had then MANIFESTED it for the shepherd with his own sadistically cruel behaviour towards him. However, right in the midst of this life-threatening situation Santiago had then suddenly realised, even if only subconsciously, that his treasure was actually something he had up until this very instant completely ignored – his own inner precious and sacred life.

With this he had been able to immediately abandon his quest for the material treasure he had so longed for, and in that moment the **material** half of his soul – the leader of the refugees – had then 'manifested' Santiago's true treasure for him. He recounted his own dream to the shepherd - A DREAM OF TREASURE BURIED IN A RUIN IN SOUTHERN SPAIN.

SANTIAGO'S VERY OWN HOME.

This archetypal pattern – and it was more than obvious
that this was exactly what it was – had been precisely
what I had gone through here in Granada,
and also since my first visit to the healing mass back in February.

***

With all of these totally unexpected epiphanies for me, I suddenly experienced one more as I understood that the elusive reality which I had been unable to grasp until this very moment in Granada was the following. This truth was that it wasn't precisely that I had gone to places where my treasure WAS NOT. No, that hadn't been it, even though from February to June I had continuously felt this to be what I had done.

No, what had really occurred was that I had zealously and obsessively made journeys to various:

external manifestations
of the **material** inner half of my soul.

Each time this had happened, I had encountered the shadow of this half of me. And inevitably, that shadow was actually my encounters with my **material** ego which of course could never give me the spiritual treasure I so desperately desired. The Chi Kung session had highlighted this perfectly when, as I had found myself bogged down by its apparent sterility, I had suddenly sensed that the feminine intuitive energy of my soul had been absent from what was going on.

In fact this absence had also been the signature feature of what had happened when I had participated in the healing masses in February and March, and also when I had made my journey to *Calle Puerta del Mar* a few months later. I had gone to these metaphorical 'pyramids', unaware that the intuitive aspect of my soul wouldn't be present, and so a metaphorical 'beating' was my 'reward'.

This meant that on each occasion I had experienced the METAPHORICAL CUPBOARD OF MY SOUL TO BE BARE, but then paradoxically this alerted me:

TO WHAT AND WHERE MY TREASURE REALLY WAS.

As I sat at my table amidst the to-and-fro of a normal Saturday lunchtime at the end of May, I can only say that I was completely overcome with emotion regarding these realisations. But, surprisingly, even more light came flooding in. Instantly, I could see the mistake I had made when I had walked to the church in Malaga at the beginning of the month after leaving *Calle Puerta del Mar*. The flyer for the Chi Kung weekend hadn't been my treasure as I had surmised, but a MANIFESTATION OF MY SHADOW.

It had entered the physical domain of my life because it had come INTO THE LIGHT of my consciousness, just like the shadow of unpainted wall in my living room back in September 2002. And now, with this same gift of hindsight, I could see that my treasure had actually been the unassuming plaque on the church wall in Malaga saying AVENIDA DE LA AURORA.

That was the very same AURORA to whom I had
given birth in my dream of April 2000.

Although, as far as signs went, the plaque in Malaga had been extraordinary, I could now also comprehend that the invisible realm had never intended it to signal the end of my journey, but rather a new and much deeper phase. Oh, my God, oh my God was all I found myself saying. These revelations were truly incredible!!! However, now the only question which immediately filled my mind at this very moment was how on earth had it been possible for me to have been so blind? ALL OF THIS WAS SO OBVIOUS!

***

With each of these connections and insights coming my way I also suddenly saw something else. In an instant of total clarity I now found myself understanding exactly what had happened to me in Paris back in 1996.

At the time I had concluded that the faeces and urine in the psychomagical act Alejandro had prescribed me had been symbolic of DEATH – THE UNIVERSAL SHADOW OF MAN. However, sitting on the terrace of the cafeteria in Granada, I suddenly understood another meaning of the act. Yes, it was true that the faeces and urine were symbols of death, but they were also symbolic of EVERYTHING THAT WAS COMPLETLEY AND UTTERLY 'SHITTY' ABOUT ME. They were the lousy, selfish, egocentric side of my personality. When I had droned on and on about my past in Alejandro's study, with his active collusion, I had experienced this ego aspect of myself.

In Alejandro's summer house in Paris I had metaphorically experienced myself 'covered with my own shit', and it was only when I had felt utterly sick and tired of it all that I had been able to accept being 'washed clean' of it. That inner epiphany, or change in consciousness, had been my moment of SPIRITUAL REBIRTH - the rebirth of my soul, and therefore the consequent rebirth of my spirit.

MY GOD, MY GOD, MY GOD, I THOUGHT TO MYSELF,
I HAVE FINALLY SOLVED THE RIDDLE
OF
THE ALCHEMIST!!!!

These eight-and-a-half years of questing had not been in vain, despite all the times I had felt so lost and desperate. Paulo's fable had turned out to be much, much deeper than I had ever imagined. My incessant searching and questioning had revealed the truth. It was a shepherd's unconscious desire for an encounter with:

THE SHADOW OF THE OTHER HALF OF HIS SOUL.

Only by being willing to submit himself to that encounter - that is to say to endure the beating led by the leader of the refugees – had be been able to achieve spiritual rebirth and the finding of his inner treasure. **(See figs. 1 and 2.)** Then, following on from this thought, a question immediately came into my mind. Was it perhaps in some way possible that each one of us was born WITH A DOMINANT HALF to our souls?

Could it be that some of us, like Santiago, would have our **mystical** half playing the dominant role in our lives, whilst others would be like the leader of the refugees, with the **material** half leading the way? In either case, it seemed that each half was inexorably searching for the other.

Figure 1.

The two halves of the soul

I stared back at the church on the opposite side of the road. How could it be at all possible that I was living out this extraordinary supernatural adventure, with all these incredible insights coming to me, as I sat munching my way through tapas on an ordinary Saturday in May?

But, just as I imagined that I had understood absolutely everything I could possibly understand, and that my mind was incapable of showing me anything else, another huge insight came to me as I went over these thoughts. In a sudden flash I knew and understood the metaphysical heart of Paulo Coelho's tale. All of this meant that:

THE ALCHEMIST WAS THE STORY OF
MAN'S SEARCH FOR REDEMPTION!

Now, what on earth do I mean when
I use the word redemption?

Well, it seems to me that life here on our planet is one great longing in each and every one of us to find the light of our spirits. Subconsciously, we desire nothing else than to live from this transcendental truth buried deep inside our souls. It is the very place which we sense to be our true home — where all of the love we need to feel and share resides.

Figure 2

The two halves in the alchemist

However, what I had come to understand about human nature at this point on my journey was that our **material** selves always try to sabotage this quest. Redemption is thus the process by which any spiritual seeker has to be willing to confront his/her own shadow - the **material** half of the soul, and KNOW IT, FEEL IT, AND EXPERIENCE IT WHOLLY FOR WHAT IT IS. This act means that the shadow is no longer denied, projected outside oneself, camouflaged, rationalised, hidden or ignored BUT FACED FULL ON.

This action brings it out from the dark of the unconscious,
and into conscious awareness which, in a nutshell, is
THE PROCESS OF REDEMPTION.

***

Sitting alone in a quiet street in Granada, I was being shown that Paulo Coelho's The Alchemist was an archetypal tale of Man's search for this REDEMPTION OF THE SHADOW. Furthermore, I could now see that this was the only route to spiritual rebirth for each and every one of us. The only way of finding our inner light was to face and redeem - bring into the light of consciousness - our inner darkness.

With all of these insights flooding through me as a result of this journey to Granada, I felt wave after wave of stunned euphoria wash over me, and my whole world changing all around me. Then quite spontaneously, I remembered that The Alchemist was not entirely Paulo Coelho's tale. His fable had been inspired by a story he had read in the centuries-old book The 1001 Nights, also known as The Arabian Nights.

Was it possible that the archetypal pattern of this ancient tale was in fact as old as we humans were? Was it part of what Paulo called the **Soul of the World**, and what Jung had named the collective unconscious?

There in Granada I felt myself to be inside the timeless mystery of who we were as a species. This seemed to be starting to turn into a journey about discovering a vital truth concerning what it actually meant to be human, and I can only say that I felt completely and utterly aghast about exactly where I had come to!

Turning away from these adrenalin-filled insights, I breathed out deeply several times in order to recover some kind of sense of normality. Then, hoping that I might have returned somewhat to the so-called 'real world', I posed myself another more pressing question. Where might I now be on my soul quest?

As I sat alone at my table on the terrace of the Cafeteria Siglo 21 I knew that I still wasn't at the end of my journeying. I had a hunch that there was still just one more place — ONE MORE EGYPT — to which I was meant to travel. It was somewhere I had thought of visiting a few years earlier, but I had never managed to get there. Now I was filled with the overwhelming feeling that this was most definitely my next port of call. Would it prove to be the very last encounter with my shadow? I certainly hoped so, but I still wasn't sure.

This odyssey had lasted so long, and had constantly taught me that I needed to submit myself to it without reservations or preconceived ideas. It appeared that God wanted a pilgrim who was willing to relinquish all aspirations and desires TO CONTROL the journey. The Deity was only interested in someone who would do it His Way — so, could I be that pilgrim? After eight-an-a-half years of questing I had burned all my bridges, and there was definitely no going back. Obviously I couldn't stay where I was, floating in the middle of my personal ocean with no landfall in sight, and thus forward was the only direction open to me.

I knew with total certainty that I was MORE THAN WILLING - of that I had no doubt - but to be very honest as yet I had absolutely no idea if I WOULD BE ABLE. Only more courage and leaps of faith would give me the answers to the unknown lying ahead of me — the future beckoned.

14

THE SEA OF THE UNCONSCIOUS

Never fear shadows – they always mean there is light shining somewhere.

JONATHAN SANTOS

IF Granada, six hundred and thirty metres above sea level was the place the universe had chosen to reveal the underlying meaning of The Alchemist to me, then the real practical work would begin in a place almost at sea level. This was the Costa de la Luz - The Coast of Light - on the southwest coast of Spain, overlooking the mysterious Atlantic Ocean. I was totally unaware that this was to be my Everest Base Camp because, as with every moment on this journey, the invisible realm was programmed to protect me from knowing the true nature of the trials which lay ahead of me.

A week after my return from Granada I went off to the aforementioned coast, and to Almacete. This was the place with the church which I had spent several years wanting to see. Somehow my intuition had always known that destiny would bring me here, and now, with everything that I had learned on the terrace of the Cafeteria Siglo 21, I was under no illusions:

Almacete was another journey
to
the 'pyramids' of Egypt.

Here was where, once more, I would be able to encounter the shadow of the **material** half of my soul and so paradoxically discover my inner treasure or light.

I arrived in a heightened state of anticipation because this was possibly the last of my symbolic Egypts; the place where my final soul rebirth was about to take place. With that heady and intoxicating prospect in sight, my inner child bubbled over with excitement for what was to come. After a long and tiring bus ride via Seville, I finally checked into a comfortable hotel near the beach, and spent the first evening just getting used to my new surroundings. The next day, I took a short bus ride into Almacete, and as I had foreseen on other occasions, I found myself yet again encountering the **material** half of my soul.

Wandering around the town, it wasn't in the least bit surprising that, true to the archetypal pattern I had discovered in Granada, I couldn't find any glimmer of my treasure. After a few hours of nothingness I knew it was time to locate Almacete's church, as twice I had found the outer manifestation of my treasure when I had gone in search of a church. Would this tantalizingly be THIRD AND FINAL TIME LUCKY?

The building was easy enough to locate, and surprised me with its beauty, but disappointingly I couldn't see anything on or near it which I could interpret as a MANIFESTATION of my treasure - even though I looked long and hard for quite a while. From my experience in Granada I knew that the church was not necessarily the only place which could give me a manifestation of my inner treasure and so, with this in mind, I turned my back on the building and walked away very slowly.

I was aware that all my senses were on red alert to spot anything unusual, but paradoxically I found that I didn't need this level of attentiveness. This was because the first manifestation I had been hoping for appeared within seconds of me beginning my walk. A young boy in a crowd making its way to the church casually past me, and emblazoned on the front of his T-shirt were the words CAE LA NOCHE. In English, this means NIGHT FALLS.

My heart stopped, and my subconscious mind instantly knew what this meant, even though my conscious mind had begun to scramble in desperation to undo what had just occurred. *No, my mind said, he didn't really walk past you. You've just imagined it.* However, that deep part of us which knows absolutely everything had instantly registered the meaning of this calamity. This was clearly a manifestation of my shadow, but it also signalled something else, and immediately I knew what it was. I was now entering:

THE DARK NIGHT OF THE SOUL.

Nevertheless, before I could even assimilate this enormous realization, less than a few seconds after seeing the boy and his T-shirt, the manifestation of my treasure suddenly appeared in the form of a beautiful Irish Red Setter dog.

As I mentioned earlier in this story, when I had first come to Andalusia I had been the proud owner of not one, but two beautiful Red Setters. This particular dog looked more or less identical to one of them, but the sudden MANIFESTATION of the dog was of no comfort to me whatsoever. The overwhelming reality I was staring at was that I was being told by the invisible realm that I was now about to enter the darkest and most frightening recesses of my dearly beloved soul.

If one can ever conclude that some things in life really, well and truly stink, and I mean STINK, then this was one of those 'apocalyptic' moments. Suddenly, looking at myself with a huge degree of objectivity, I felt as if I were staring at one of the most naive persons on our planet.

Somehow, I had obviously thought that I could go WHERE ANGELS FEAR TO TREAD, hopping and skipping in search of my soul like some kind of Little Miss Red Riding Hood. Despite everything I had learnt up until this point of my quest, it had never occurred to me that sooner or later I would have to encounter life's NASTIES - the really big terrors and demonic experiences that make great horror movie fodder. Well, now I knew with blood-curdling clarity just exactly what kind of journey I had thrown myself into.

The invisible realm had 'graciously' decided that my blinkers needed removing, and that this was the ideal time to show me THE TERMS AND CONDITIONS OF THE CONTRACT!

***

What exactly is
The Dark Night of the Soul?

This metaphor for aspects of the spiritual quest originated from a poem written by St. John of the Cross (1542 to 1591), a Spanish Carmelite monk and mystic. St. John's understanding of The Dark Night was that the spiritual seeker or mystic passes through a period of trials and agony when his/her soul is purified, or purged of its sensual elements. St. John saw this time as being in many ways similar to the agonies and trials suffered by Christ in his flesh before his crucifixion.

In modern times The Dark Night of the Soul has become a metaphor for many types of spiritual trials endured by seekers. It can denote a massive encounter with the ego self, a period of despair and loss of faith, a feeling of having been completely abandoned by God, or simply a loss of connection with anything spiritual in one's life. What kind of Dark Night was being signalled to me in Almacete?

Back then in June 2003 the true understanding of what type of Dark Night I was about to endure was only revealed to me three years later, at the end of 2006. With hindsight, that revelation showed me that my journey to Almacete had been my symbolic entrance into the THE SEA OF MY UNCONSCIOUS - exactly what had been signalled in Malaga at the beginning of May 2003 in *Calle Puerta del Mar*. There at sea level, and overlooking the Atlantic Ocean, I had started to climb from the bottom of my soul's pyramid-shaped 'iceberg' to where it EMERGED from beneath the WATERS OF THE UNCONSCIOUS into the 'light' of day or CONSCIOUSNESS.

However, this climb had only been possible because I had been willing to encounter all the UNCONSCIOUS aspects of the **material** half of my soul. Perhaps 'willing' is not really the right word, because the truth was that I was so committed to this quest, that choice never came into it.

In June 2003, none of this knowledge which surfaced for me in 2006 formed any part of my understanding of my supernatural quest. Up until the summer of 2003 I had only been learning about and encountering *the conscious part of my shadow,* in the form of my ego and sexual passions, but suddenly the MONSTERS lurking within the watery deep of my unconscious mind would come and say HELLO!

In this 'sub-aquatic Egypt', encounters with the shadow of the **material** half of my soul would be much more terrifying and challenging than anything I had experienced earlier in the comparatively 'benign' world of my conscious mind. However, as was so typical of this journey, that day in Almacete I was totally unaware of any kind of 'climb' ahead of me as I walked back to the bus stop to return to the hotel.

Nevertheless, despite my ignorance, the fact that the Dark Night had suddenly popped into my head on seeing the boy and his T-shirt quite literally terrified me. Of course, I had received prior warning of this when I had discovered the shadow of unpainted wall in my apartment back in 2002, and realised that the subconscious was the seat of so much horror. But now, I had absolutely no idea what horrendous experiences awaited me.

This new, deep-seated terror I felt only served to make me want to bury my head and heart firmly into the deepest metaphorical sand I could find. Thus it was that hours later, at dinner that evening in the hotel, my conscious mind was still valiantly engaged in rationalising the T-shirt incident.

> You need time to think Karen. You're not an expert at interpreting these manifestations. Give it time. You'll probably see more clearly when you get back home.

However, the invisible realm was only too aware of its agenda for me, and that night when I went to bed, an inexplicable dread began to well up inside me. This certainly wasn't normal anxiety or fear because it seemed to emanate from somewhere within the very depths of my being.

The hours passed and then the dread took on overtones of paranoia and sleep was nowhere in sight. Around 4:30 a.m. I had had enough. I couldn't lie in the bed any longer enduring this terror, so I dressed myself and went out into the street outside the hotel to try and walk myself back to normality. I wandered around in the dark for about two hours until finally I was able to return to the hotel feeling vaguely myself once again - apart from a sensation of total exhaustion.

Never in my entire life have I ever left a hotel more eagerly or gratefully than I did the following day when I said goodbye to Almacete in the early afternoon. I arrived back at my apartment in the evening and collapsed straight onto my bed, instantly falling soundly asleep. There were no more horrific sensations of high-voltage angst and paranoia, and luckily the next few days saw me return to normal. I felt completely calm and sane and it seemed that I had panicked unnecessarily whilst in Almacete — at least this was what I desperately wanted to believe! Surely, that terrible night in the hotel room had probably just been some kind of a one-off aberration.

***

Once back inside the walls of my comforting home, my thoughts now turned away from the nightmare I had just experienced, and focused yet again on my dream of buying a piece of land and putting a wooden house on it. I hadn't given any energy to this utopian vision since the somewhat disastrous viewing of the north-facing hillside back in January, but for some seemingly inexplicable reason the dream had decided to come back into my consciousness with a force and passion that completely surprised me. What I didn't realise at the time was that my soul quest was starting to build up momentum.

My journeys to the various symbolic 'Egypts' in the last four-and-a half months had quickened my spirit, and this was the reason the dream of the land with the wooden house had returned to inhabit all of my waking hours. About a week after my return from Almacete this obsessive idea suddenly transformed itself into a brainwave inside my head. I realised with mounting euphoria that I didn't have to wait another year or two to make my dream a reality because I was the complete owner of the apartment in which I lived.

My parents had given me the money to buy it outright, and so all I had to do was sell the apartment, pay off my bank loan, and then I would have the rest of the money available to buy the land. I couldn't understand why I hadn't thought of this before - it was barely rocket science, to say the least!

The next day I mentioned that I wanted to sell the apartment to my neighbour, and within less than twenty-four hours she knocked on my door to tell me that the owner of the small supermarket opposite our block had indicated to her that he wanted to buy it.

Arturo came to see me two days later, and after a little wrangling over the price we shook hands on a deal. Then, ten days later we met at the notary's office to exchange the deeds to the property and finalise the sale. Incredibly, within only twenty days of my return from

Almacete I had sold the apartment, and for me that could only mean one thing - the invisible realm had made everything happen!

There was no doubt in my mind that it wanted me to go ahead with OUR SHARED PLANS, and so my thoughts now began to coalesce around where this mystical piece of land gripping my imagination could be.

When I had been in Granada at the end of May, after leaving the Cafeteria Siglo 21, I had meandered back to the hotel where I was staying and en route had passed an estate agency with photographs of a new development of villas in one of the windows. I had stopped to look and discovered that they were being built on a part of the Granadinian coastline with a spectacular mountain backdrop. However, what had really been eye-catching were the prices of the properties. They were substantially lower than any of the prices in the area where I lived, and this told me that the land prices would also be much lower than in my own locality.

After shaking hands with Arturo in June, I began to speculate as to whether or not I should go and investigate this area with a view to this being the site of my dreamt-of plot and a future retreat. And so, once the sale of my apartment had been completed towards the end of June, I stopped all my wondering and decided to visit the location. Thankfully I had been free of anxiety or any signs of paranoia since my return from Almacete, and this bolstered my confidence that everything was essentially in order. Perhaps the premonition that The Dark Night was just around the corner had simply been a symptom of my hyper-sensitivity.

Arturo was kind enough to allow me to stay in the apartment until the end of the first week of July, even though it was no longer mine, and this allowed for the possibility of a quick trip up to the Granada coastline. Such amazing serendipity would then still give me time to return, pack up my things and leave the apartment empty.

***

On the last weekend of June I made my way to Malaga to catch a local bus to the Granadinian town of Peralta. The vehicle that arrived at the bus depot to take us passengers there was fairly dilapidated and covered in several layers of dust and grime. It had clearly been the latest thing in transportation in the early seventies, but now it just looked like a quaint reminder of a bygone era. I walked to the front of the bus, and placed myself in front of the steps ready to board this charabanc. But, before I had even raised my foot to mount the first step, an intuitive flash hit me:

My God, Karen, we're off to the pyramids again!
Your heavenly piece of land won't be there, you idiot.
This is The Alchemist all over again!

In that split second I had a chance to turn around and walk away from the vehicle because I knew exactly what awaited me. I would be going to 'Egypt' yet again - to the **material** half of my soul - and, of course, I wouldn't be finding any treasure there. Like all the other journeys since February, this encounter with the shadow of the **material** half of me would administer its metaphorical 'beating', and then paradoxically bring me into contact with my true treasure — in other words, my sacred inner light.

Now, dear friend, allow me if you will to digress slightly at this point. I have repeatedly spoken of these metaphorical journeys to Egypt as being encounters with THE SHADOW OF THE MATERIAL HALF OF MY SOUL but in actual fact this statement is somewhat misleading. From the start of my attempt to decipher The Alchemist my definition of the shadow had been that it appeared *not to be a part* of the **material** half of the soul, but THE WHOLE OF THE MATERIAL HALF.

To put it another way,
I believed that shadow and matter seemed to be
one and the same.

It was true that my understanding of the Beauty and the Beast fairy-tale had given me a different view of the composition of the **material** half of the soul. There, I had realised that the character of the Beast embodied both MATTER AND SPIRIT- beast and prince. Nevertheless, at this point in my quest, my hypothesis concerning The Alchemist did not mirror the insight I had achieved with this fairy-tale.

For me, in Paulo's fable the **material** half of Santiago's soul, and my own, were at this stage of the odyssey ONE HUNDRED PER CENT matter or shadow. So, why then have I been using the phrase THE SHADOW OF THE MATERIAL HALF OF MY SOUL?

The answer to this is that the phrase is a deliberate hint on my part of the incompleteness of my understanding. Three years further along on my journey in 2006 I would effectively be given the insight that divine light – Spirit - was also a part of the **material** half of our souls. This light was of course Paracelsus' Lumen Naturae apparently 'imprisoned' in nature, which only the alchemy of love could 'liberate'.

Our inner 'Beast' was both shadow and Spirit, and for this reason the phrase allows me to suggest that a more complete picture awaited me at another point in the future. Secondly, dear friend, I need to clarify my particular definition of the shadow. The one I use in this story is not the usual definition you will find in most psychological writings, but very much my own. This is because my odyssey is the story of a search for:

an Absolute Reality - the Reality of the Spirit

When I studied the sciences at school and university I learnt about the concepts of THE ABOSLUTE and THE RELATIVE. These concepts also apply to the metaphysical world; in fact, THEY ARE METAPHYSICS.

Spirit is absolute because it is non-material, and hence immutable or unvarying truth. However, the ego, and all other aspects of our material selves, are relative because they are material, and therefore very much subject to variation. They can only ever aspire to be *an approximation* of the truth, but never the truth itself. So for me, the 'ego and co', whether expressing themselves positively or negatively, are fundamentally the shadow of the Spirit. In other words, they are not the light of what we call the absolute truth.

You will have to excuse my pun dear reader
when I say that this truly is
THE NATURE OF THE BEAST!
There, I mention the word 'beast' yet again.

Although it was the Beauty and the Beast fairy-tale which had originally enabled me to identify the two halves of the soul, naming them the **mystical** and the **material**, I had still failed to understand the connection, if any, of this fairy-tale to the meaning of The Alchemist. I was to discover that missing piece of understanding further along on my quest. Surprisingly, it would turn out that Beauty and the Beast wasn't, as one might have supposed, another version of Paulo Coelho's fable.

Rather, the fairy-tale is actually the story of what happens AFTER The Alchemist – that is to say AFTER Santiago finds his treasure. As such, it could be accurately subtitled THE ALCHEMIST – PART TWO. I will give an analysis and explanation of what I mean by this in one of the last chapters of this book.

***

Now, let us return to the bus station in Malaga. My foot hovered in mid-air as I hesitated about whether or not I should step into the bus, but in a split second my subconscious mind placed my foot on the first step. I knew I wouldn't find any treasure in Peralta, but somehow a weird kind of logic was telling me that I was supposed to make this journey.

Within less than 24 hours of my arrival in the town, the invisible realm obligingly confirmed my more than well-founded suspicion and produced a sign to show me that I had been right about going to 'Egypt' once again.

It was inside the weekend magazine of one of Spain's national newspapers which I bought on the Saturday out of sheer agonising boredom. The front cover was a picture of the Egyptian Queen Nefertiti, and the article was about a British Egyptologist, Joann Fletcher, who had just identified one of three mummies found in 1898 as being that of Nefertiti. And so it was that, just as I had suspected, I spent yet another weekend in the wrong place - this most definitely wasn't Shangri-La where I would find my piece of land for the wooden house.

The arid, almost desert like landscape surrounding me, with the furnace-like intensity of the summer heat reflecting off scorching earth and boulders immediately prompted the realisation that the land I so yearned for wasn't here – YES, THIS WAS MY SHADOW ALL OVER AGAIN - but awaited me in the foothills of the sierra where I lived. And, this meant only one thing, as it had done so before - I needed to get back home as quickly as possible in order to find it.

Once again, it seemed that my treasure was not SOMEWHERE OVER THE RAINBOW where the grass repeatedly promised to look so much greener, but always far, far closer to hand.

With this predictable outcome to what I had instinctively known would be yet another Egypt, one question now began to torture the deepest recesses of my heart: how much longer would I need before these 'beatings' finally produced a complete and definitive rebirth of my soul? Typically, no answer came.

Thus, instead of staying in Peralta for four days desperately scouring the dust-covered hills and mountainside for my piece of Heaven on Earth, I cut my stay down to two, and with great relief boarded the bus at the end of the weekend. On my return home I quickly packed up my belongings, placing some items into storage, and left my sold apartment on July 4 - American Independence Day.

I moved into a caravan I had decided to rent at a local campsite overlooking the beach in Salveira because this seemed the best and cheapest possible accommodation option available to me as I began what I imagined would now be the REAL SEARCH for my illusive piece of land. The invisible realm, however, smiled down serenely on me, probably with a degree of compassionate amusement, recognising that I was a lot further away from my cherished goal than I could have possibly imagined.

As my very human self settled into the campsite and began ARRANGING the few belongings I had brought with me in an attempt to adapt them to a completely new environment, greater forces on the metaphysical plane were engaged in their own ARRANGEMENTS, because they and only they could know that a quite different fate awaited me.

15

C.G. JUNG AND THE ALCHEMIST

**No matter how dark life becomes, it is because
you have been brave enough to say
'no'
to the status quo.**

ANON

WITH my mind set on that life-changing search for a piece of land, and a fervent prayer that I truly was within sight of the final rebirth of my soul, I turned to this new phase of my journey with yet more high hopes and naïve enthusiasm. But, instead the invisible realm decided that now was the perfect time for me to be plunged deep into the terrors of:

The Dark Night of the Soul.

The T-shirt sign which had appeared before my eyes in Almacete had been WAITING IN THE WINGS to keep its appointment with me, even though almost a month had passed since I had seen it. Once I had settled into the campsite The Dark Night which ensued began to take me through all the horrors I had experienced with the dental anaesthetic back in 1993, and also an awful lot more. For three long weeks my intuition prompted me to follow 'signs', all of which led me forward onto yet more 'journeys' to metaphorical Egypts, and as I did so I found myself battling the worst my subconscious could throw at me.

At sea level in the campsite I experienced panic attacks, the desire to throw myself in front of speeding cars, and an apparently overwhelming urge to stab myself in the eyes with kitchen knives. Then, following a sign, I moved out of the campsite and further up into the sierra into the luxurious embrace of a 5-Star hotel, but this changed absolutely nothing for me. During that short stay, I experienced several moments when I had to leave barely-begun meals on their plates in the hotel restaurant as I found myself overwhelmed by feelings that I was about to have an enormous epileptic seizure.

Finally, this period ended with a truly soul-crushing incident. I had left the hotel, deciding to seek some kind of refuge even higher up the sierra – the signs were still guiding me all the way - and so that incident manifested in the form of an uncontrollable impulse in the middle of the night to throw myself off the first floor balcony of a holiday apartment I had just rented in Campana.

With this truly awful last episode, I made a third and final hasty departure and rushed down the mountain in a taxi to the first cheap two-star hostel I could find in Salveira. I had unwittingly but curiously travelled in a complete circle, from sea to mountain top, and then back down to sea level again! Nevertheless, as I did so, it was far from lost on me that by slowly creeping up from sea level and the caravan, travelling *higher and higher,* until nearly reaching the top of the sierra in Campana, simultaneously I seemed to have experienced *deeper and deeper* encounters with the fear and terror buried inside my subconscious mind. Yes, that was it! I had once again performed THE TWO JOURNEYS I had spoken about earlier in Chapter 12, when I described my journey to Malaga.

These were the OUTER and the INNER journeys which always occurred simultaneously. It wasn't in the least bit surprising therefore that the most terrifying encounter - the desire to completely destroy myself – had taken place OUTWARDLY at the highest point of this climb – in other words the apartment balcony in Campana – and also INWARDLY in the deepest part of my subconscious.

***

Now, lying on my hostel bed in Salveira, listening to the noise coming from the square and park on the opposite side of the road,

I felt extremely fragile and ill. This really did feel like the end of my quest; no 'beatings' could ever be worse than what I had just gone through alone inside that apartment in Campana. Perhaps this final trial of suffering had been the Hell my subconscious mind had first introduced me to back in the dream of December 1994. If the deepest and most treacherous aspects of inner darkness were what I had been asked to face and redeem as part of my destiny in life, then THIS SURELY HAD BEEN IT! I was utterly shattered by the events of the last three weeks.

Of course, all of this had been predicted for me earlier on in my quest. The journey to *Calle Puerta del Mar* had symbolically forewarned me of an imminent encounter with the 'terrors of the deep', just as my paranoia had in Almacete. Both 'journeys to Egypt' had been preparing me for the moment when I would enter the metaphorical SEA OF MY UNCONSCIOUS — and true to the specific symbolic language of the invisible realm, it had all begun in Salveira's campsite at SEA LEVEL.

In effect, in three distinct stages I had started to experience the part of the shadow of the **material** half of my soul which was 'submerged' in this area of my mind.

Over the period of three weeks, just as my intuition seemed to have sensed at the time, I had journeyed from the base of my 'iceberg' soul submerged under water to the point where the unconscious meets the conscious — in other words THE SURFACE OF THE WATER. And once again, I had intuitively used the OUTSIDE WORLD to paradoxically produce the INNER JOURNEY I felt I was being asked to make.

**Dear reader, I cannot begin to explain to you just
how cataclysmically traumatic this encounter with
my subconscious had been.**

During those three weeks I had quite literally been on the edge of madness and death, and my mind and nerves had completely collapsed under the onslaught of this DARK NIGHT. Only a few days had elapsed since I had signed myself into the hostel, but everything was becoming one great, gigantic challenge. Now, terror and anxiety appeared to have taken up permanent residence in me as I panicked if I even did so much as peer out of the first floor window of my tiny room.

I still also felt the impulse to throw myself in front of oncoming cars when I was in the street, and continued to be unable to pick up a knife when I went to a local restaurant just around the corner from the hostel for fear of stabbing myself in the eyes with it. The only one thing I did with relative ease was to walk the few metres from the door of my abode to a bench in the adjacent park where I sat people-watching and taking in the scenery.

With the Dark Night faced in all its horrific cruelty, but somehow continuing to plague me, I quickly concluded, if only for my own sanity, that eight-and-a-half ' diabolically' intense, long years of an odyssey had come to an end and I needed to find some way of getting back to normality. As far as I was concerned the job was done. So how then was I going to find this illusive normality I asked myself, given just how extremely mentally ill I felt?

Lying in the grim surroundings of my hostel room, with the occasional cockroach for company, I decided that my situation was so bad that I would have to ask for help, and instinctively knew that this would have to come from The Almighty Himself. Of course, I more than understood that He/She or It wouldn't miraculously intervene in my life directly, but would work through the body of another human being, and the only person I could think of who might be 'up for the job' was my friend Justine.

'Coincidentally' I knew that she lived within walking distance of the square. Justine was an exceptionally faith-filled person, and although I wasn't particularly keen on her modern evangelical way of expressing her Christianity, she had a powerful brand of love for God all of her own.

***

My friend responded immediately to my call for help, and ran to my side to sit praying for me whilst I lay in my hostel bed in a state of utter emotional exhaustion. She didn't just ask the Holy Spirit to heal my mind, she positively ordered it to DO ITS STUFF, but nothing, and I mean absolutely nothing happened.

And so, the next couple of days were just the same for me as the ones before. I couldn't pick up a knife in the Chinese restaurant, and still wanted to throw myself in front of cars. Never one to give up too quickly, I phoned Justine again a few days later, still distraught and very worried for my sanity, and this time she brought reinforcements with her. We all met in the park. My friend appeared with two other Christians, and we made our way to a round table on the terrace of an outdoor café.

Lamely and in a terribly self-conscious way I explained to Justine's companions that I was on a spiritual path in search of my soul. That 'mission' had taken me to a campsite after the sale of my apartment because I had wanted to go in search of a piece of land on which to begin the seeds of a spiritual retreat. However, whilst still in the campsite I had received an angst-filled email from a friend in desperate need of money, and this unexpected turn of events had led to me completely changing the focus of my journey.

After some intense soul-searching, I decided to abandon my initial plan for the piece of land, and instead help my friend, and also other people who found themselves in dire financial straits. My friend's terrible plight spoke directly to my heart, and it seemed to be telling me that the invisible realm was looking for a much deeper spiritual response from me than the one I had so far been willing to offer. Thus it was that, in between battling through the Dark Night of the Soul, I had started to give my money away to strangers and friends in need.

Justine kept quiet whilst I 'blurted' all of this 'madness' out. Weeks earlier, when I had still been in the campsite, we had met in a local cafe and she had been the second person I had decided to assist financially - but only on the condition that no one should know that she had been one of my recipients of help. Now, I confessed to her friends that I was in a total mess, experiencing panic, terror and the desire to destroy myself in some way.

This godly couple listened attentively to what must have sounded totally bizarre to them. Their faces barely disguised a look that seemed to ask, 'are there really people in the world as insane as this one - giving all her money away? Fortunately, or unfortunately, I was living proof that there really are!

**

Once I had finished my weird tale, I could see that Justine's colleagues were now busy formulating a plan. They consulted my friend and decided that we would finish our soft drinks in the park, return to my room in the hostel, and then have another session with the Holy Spirit. The feeling was that with three people praying for me, there was bound to be a breakthrough.

Just before we were about to leave, I looked around at the four of us sitting at the round table. I noticed that Justine sat opposite me, as if we were some kind of human North and South, and the other two were at the other two cardinal points of this human compass. We formed a cross. Then quite suddenly, and with no preamble, it hit me:

This was the formation of the human soul!

All this time I had been working with the hypothesis that the soul was made up of two halves, but as I looked at the four of us I realised that it was actually formed of four quarters. But not just any old four quarters.

I suddenly remembered that Jung had introduced the idea of the human psyche having four functions capable of consciousness. Jung saw them as being arranged in pairs: **THINKING AND FEELING** were what he called the RATIONAL FUNCTIONS of the psyche, and **INTUITION AND SENSATION** were the IRRATIONAL FUNCTIONS.

According to Jung these functions formed a cross, and were the ways in which the psyche operated in the physical world. I had known now for quite a few years that I was a deeply intuitive person, and that in a sense this was my modus operandi. At that moment, as I looked at Justine opposite me, I knew without a doubt that she was the SENSATION end of our pairing, and so this made her other two friends *the* THINKING-FEELING axis of Jung's cross.

Here we were in the middle of a park, configuring what I felt was the basic structure of the human soul as we sat at a small round, plastic table, *and the only person who knew this was happening was me!* Then a final realisation came to me:

the **mystical** half of my soul was actually
the *intuition-sensation* half of Jung's cross,

and the **material** half of my soul was
the *thinking-feeling* axis.

Although we were sitting around the table in cross formation, I knew I could 'undo' that cross in my imagination, and place the two axes side by side. This would then produce the two halves of the soul within a circle: **mystical** and **material,** and their subdivisions - Jung's four quarters, two in each half. (See fig. 3)

Fig.3.

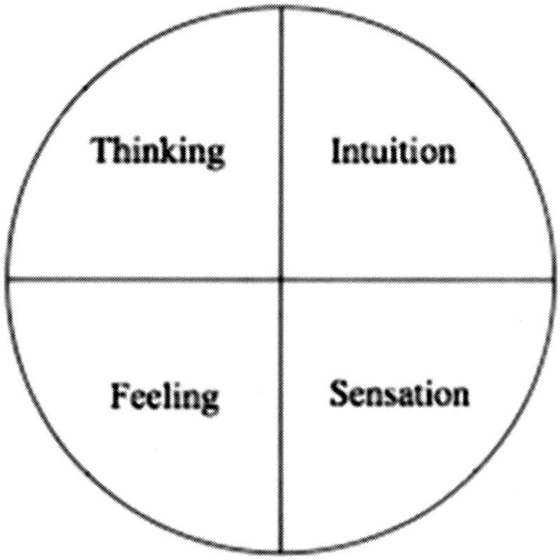

Thinking   Intuition

Feeling   Sensation

*The author's interpretation of
C.G. Jung's model of the
human soul*

***

Jung's theory of the four psychic functions related to the workings of the conscious aspect of the human psyche, but after everything

I had gone through, I was convinced that these four functions were also the fundamental organization of the totality of our souls.

His thinking was that all four functions existed within the one human psyche, but individuals varied according to which of these functions was dominant - or conscious - in them. This produced different personality types, with some people being intuitive whilst others were dominated by their thinking function. Others of course were either dominated by feeling or sensation, and because of this variation amongst people, no one person had all four functions in a state of complete balance within themselves.

Jung postulated that man's first task in life was to come to know himself, and this involved discovering those functions that were the non-dominant ones within his own psyche. He called the process by which a person gained command of all four functions, and so became 'rounded' and not skewed in any one direction INDIVIDUATION, and from my own journey I was beginning to sense that The Alchemist was possibly an archetype of THIS PROCESS OF INDIVIDUATION.

Although no one function was inherently more important than another, my intuition was beginning to suspect that there were actually two cardinal functions, or those that, in some way, could be regarded as MASTER FUNCTIONS.

And, as far as I was concerned, these just had to be
INTUITION AND THINKING.

For me, it now seemed quite obvious that if this were so, then the **mystical** and **material** divisions of the human soul I had coined for myself, and which had been personified in The Alchemist by Santiago and the leader of the refugees, were these two master functions.

So far my questing had always led me subconsciously to seek out encounters with the **material**, or thinking half of this duality within me, just as it had for Santiago. In so doing, both he and I had been experiencing the shadow of our non-dominant function. Bringing that shadow into the 'light' of consciousness, and therefore redeeming it, was thus in all probability our *journeys of individuation* in the Jungian sense.

***

After this revelation in the park, there could be no doubt in my mind that I had finally come to my journey's end.

I had been led to an understanding of the deep underlying meaning of my quest, and also the real meaning of The Alchemist – mission well and truly accomplished! The four of us left the park and returned to my room in the hostel, and as I lay motionless on the bed, my three helpers prayed their hearts out for the healing of my mind and soul. But, as with Justine's prayers a few days earlier, yet again, the following days proved that nothing supernatural had really happened.

In a way I was devastated by this outcome, but had the incredible consolation of what I had discovered in the park. All my attempts to unravel the story of The Alchemist, and the blind courage I had shown in journeying to so many MANIFESTATIONS of the **material** half of my soul had paid off. The invisible realm had always known that this final revelation of Jung's four functions had been waiting for me in a small, municipal park.

With these exciting revelations, there was also just one more fascinating detail which I had long since forgotten, but which now suddenly came into my head. I remembered back to my time inside Alejandro Jodorowsky's summer house in 1996, and how there had been FOUR of us sitting inside the building. With my new insights, that fact made complete and total sense. I could now see that it had never been an accident:

> James, Odette, Alejandro and I had been the material
> personifications of Jung's four functions!

I stayed in the hostel in Salveira for another two weeks, recovering some strength, and then moved into a rented house just behind the square. I imagined that this sumptuous accommodation was the reward I deserved for having completed such a gruelling and extremely painful quest. However, after a bout of continuing severe panic attacks in the echoing emptiness of this cavernous three-bedroom dwelling, a few months later I admitted defeat and found myself returning to my parents' house amongst the olive groves, and next to the hill where my mystical ruin stood.

In the tranquillity of this setting I slowly recovered from the ravages of the Dark Night with the help of some medication and visits to a local psychiatrist. That process lasted just under a year, and my patience through this period began to pay dividends fairly quickly. In March 2004, having rediscovered the 'normality' I had previously hoped for with Justine's prayers, and undaunted by the suffering I had endured, I boldly set out again to continue my life's path, still firmly believing that my spiritual odyssey had now truly come to an end. Oh, yes, naivety and lack of any hindsight are such wonderful things!

I therefore found myself eagerly planning a completely new direction as a newly-born AURORA. As normal functioning resumed I came up with the 'brainwave' that I could train as a primary school teacher in the U.K. To that end I persuaded a local English Primary School just outside Salviera to take me on as an unpaid teaching assistant, and then in June I journeyed to the south of England for an interview at a teacher training college.

My encounter, or rather confrontation, with the senior lecturer at this establishment was a totally unmitigated disaster. The rebel in me sensed that I was utterly incapable of fitting myself into this conventional, academic world. I could feel myself balking at the political correctness of the interviewer, and needless to say a few weeks later I received the news that no offer of a place had been made to me.

At the end of July 2004, utterly unwilling to accept defeat, I then decided to move onto Plan B. AURORA was calling to me, and I needed to follow the WINDS OF DESTINY, but I also realised only too painfully that this meant a definitive break with my beloved Andalusia, my dear, adored parents, and *'my ruin'* at the top of the hill. None of this was easy by any means, but my 'personal legend' seemed to be willing me forward.

And so, on August 27 I caught a flight to Galicia in the North of Spain to embark on a course I had found on the internet; to gain the qualification of Teacher of English as a Foreign Language.

***

On my arrival at the small town where the course was to be held, once again the rebel in me emerged and I decided to give this structured and hectic month of learning a miss. Nothing about it seemed to have anything to do with a newly-born AURORA – the light of my spirit – and so I allowed my soul to take wing. I certainly didn't require any of my long years of experience with signs to tell me where to go. That MAGNIFICENT FLIGHT saw me heading off to the famous pilgrimage town of Santiago de Compostela which I had spotted on a map - just a short bus journey away.

If I am really honest, dear friend, this RUSHING INTO THE UNKNOWN could only be described as highly exhilarating and intoxicating – a sort of spiritual bungee jumping, only with my feet firmly attached to the ground. Yes, of course, underneath it all there was fear, but to be meeting my fear and apprehension with what I imagined was boundless faith and enthusiasm felt like something out of an Indianna Jones movie – or was I perhaps a real-life Lara Croft?

After a very brief stay in Santiago, imbibing the romance and spirituality of its cathedral and historical streets, I determined that the only place which could guide me to my bright new future would be Madrid.

Here was where I had once lived with Alberto, and my intuition was signalling to me that the city was now drawing me to itself as I contemplated my brand new life as the fully reborn soul I had dreamed about becoming oh so many, many long and arduous years ago.

AURORA WOULD NOW CLAIM HER DESTINY!

16

THE TWO ROADS TO REDEMPTION

**In a world of duality, everything and everyone
has its equal but opposite, and like magnets each
is drawn to the other.**

ANON

MADRID was very much home-from-home for me since my time with Alberto, and yet again, as with every aspect of this odyssey it was no mere 'coincidence' that my intuition had taken me there.

Now that I was facing a great, unfathomable unknown, familiarity was vital for me. But equally familiarity wouldn't be enough. Realising full well that its protégée was teetering on the edge of yet another gigantic LEAP OF FAITH, the invisible realm seemed to understand that it needed to go into overdrive to watch over me, and I unconsciously responded in kind. Temporary accommodation whilst I pondered this next stage of my life was an urgent priority, and so a week after my arrival in the city the invisible directed me to a health food shop and its notice board.

There, pinned to the cork surface was the mobile telephone number of someone offering lodgings. 'Coincidentally' the first three numbers of this person's telephone were exactly the same as the first three numbers of my own mobile. Inwardly my spirit smiled as I thanked the universe for its help.

The number belonged to Sila, a Spanish lady around my own age, who worked as an English translator for a national charity.

We agreed to meet, and after a short interview in which both of us knew instinctively that we had clicked, she made me welcome in her atmospheric, soulful attic apartment a few minutes' walk from where I had lived with Alberto. Settled with a roof over my head, I now had time to aimlessly walk the streets, squares and parks of the city and think.

***

The journey of The Alchemist had come to an end after nearly ten years of blood sweat and tears, and I was justifiably proud of what I had achieved.

I had engaged with an invisible reality based solely on faith in my intuition and also my ability to recognise and interpret 'signs' - and I had been completely vindicated.

Through that process I had also made a second discovery, and this was that the invisible realm was in fact far more real than the visible world we lived in. To put it simply IT WAS THE SOURCE OF EVERYTHING VISIBLE. The ABSOLUTE created the RELATIVE, but they were somehow locked in some kind of magical dance together, each interacting with the other to create more.................more what? In that moment as my thoughts coalesced, I knew I had the answer. Paulo Coelho had been right in The Alchemist:

the mysterious 'dance' was about
love – DIVINE LOVE - the love that is our spirits.

When we dared to believe our hearts, the **Soul of the World** really did get better as he had said in the fable, and we moved ever closer to God's Light and Spirit. The darkness could not hold us prisoners; divine light was always calling us. And now that my quest was at its end, my conscious mind needed to grasp fully what I had learned about Paulo's iconic tale.

I knew that it was the story of man's subconscious search for the other half of his soul. By finding it he then encountered the shadow of the **material** half of himself, and in so doing redeemed it as he brought that shadow into the light of consciousness. This process of redemption was not just a sideshow to the fable, but THE VERY HEART OF THE STORY, and something no one seemed to realise – at least not anyone I had ever read on the internet who talked about The Alchemist.

The reason for this was that the heart of life itself is essentially paradoxical. The only way in which man's divine inner light can be revealed to him is through an encounter with his own darkness. But Paulo Coelho's archetypal myth didn't just contain one central paradox; it was also paradoxical in a second sense.

There was only one means by which the LUMEN DEI of the **material** half of the shepherd's soul could be accessed by his **mystical** half, even though it was actually within himself, and this was by searching for its physical manifestation in the outside world.

In other words, what was actually INSIDE every seeker could only be reached by an OUTER journey. Furthermore, just as the name of the road in which Alejandro Jodorowsky lived had suggested back in 1996, the quest for redemption was a journey towards LIBERATION; a journey where we 'broke' the chains of darkness within ourselves, and this would then allow Mankind to access a new, transcendent consciousness within itself. Of course this was the consciousness of **THE BIG DREAM** I spoke about in the preface to this book.

My thoughts also led me to suspect that the four functions of the soul, once liberated from their shadows, would be able to somehow fuse, and thus give birth to the number FIVE - a soul which was now metaphorically a five-pointed STAR. The medieval alchemists had tried to turn base metal into gold, and now I could see that my modern alchemical journey had been about turning my 'base' self into 'starlight' – THE LIGHT OF THE DIVINE!

Whilst staying in the holiday apartment I had briefly rented back in the summer of 2003, I had unwittingly come across a huge sign. I had picked up a book and found the following quotation by Nietzsche:

"He must have chaos within him, who would give birth to a dancing star."

With this final connection made, it seemed that I could now unequivocally conclude that all these years of blind faith in my intuition really had proved that intuition was the ROYAL ROAD by which anyone could discover the hidden language of the **Soul of the World,** and also the archetypal pattern governing Man's quest for transcendence.

***

As I continued to think about The Alchemist, more insights came to me. With astonishing clarity I now realised that the fable was structured in a singularly one-dimensional way. Santiago was always the hero of the story and the focus was always on HIS journey, HIS trials and lessons and finally, HIS reward for daring to follow his dream. However, my personal journey and the amazing discoveries I had made were showing me a deeper understanding of the fable than this. After all my own trials and lessons, I could see that there were actually:

TWO ROADS TO REDEMPTION
AND NOT ONE

Santiago was NOT THE ONLY protagonist of The Alchemist because it was fundamentally the tale of TWO QUESTS and TWO SEEKERS. The leader of the refugees who beat Santiago was every bit as much the protagonist of this iconic story as was the Andalusian shepherd.

In reality, they were each other's complement; in the same way that day only exists because we have night, or male is the complement of female. **Mystical** Santiago followed his heart in search of his **material** leader of the refugees, but equally the **material** leader's spirit had also been in search of **mystical** Santiago. Their meeting in the desert sands was the culmination of two separate journeys undertaken by two separate figures for the sole purpose of each of them finding redemption and soul rebirth.

Seeing all of this so clearly, I now also understood that The Alchemist was not in any way a tale of Goodies and Baddies, or heroes and villains, as one might conclude from a superficial analysis of the book. Naturally, in concentrating exclusively on Santiago, the simplicity of Paulo Coelho's fable gives it its power to communicate directly with the human heart. Most myths and allegories use these simplified forms, but unfortunately, although their directness holds great appeal, they can also be somewhat misleading. Nevertheless, whether a myth or a fable, The Alchemist's deepest spiritual meaning is in reality the story of:

TWO PATHS TO REDEMPTION.

THE TWO HALVES OF THE ONE SOUL

From this awareness my intuition sensed that when Santiago had found his redemption and his inner light, the leader of the refugees was also paradoxically 'rewarded' with the key to that very same redemption. However, Paulo's story ends before we ever find out whether he experiences it or not.

So, finally, there you have it, dear friend:

> The journey of THE ALCHEMIST was one in which
> the two physical personifications of the opposite
> halves of the soul went in search of each other
> in order to encounter their shared shadow.

My insights were truly astonishing me. This apparently simple 'fictional' tale had taken 'little old me' on:

THE LONGEST TREASURE HUNT OF MY LIFE!!!

***

With all the 'cosmic' pieces of my spiritual puzzle seemingly finally in place, I now turned my energy and focus towards the tantalising prospect of my new life. There was now no need to engage in any further analysis of the past; I was finally free, *utterly free* to spend almost a month in Madrid in search of that life. Nothing could be rushed because I needed to be absolutely certain that any new step into the unknown would be revealed, as it had always been, by my intuition - and as ever accompanied by the appropriate 'signs'.

AURORA WAS HERE — yes I could now shout these words out loud to the universe, as long as I was somewhere where no one would be able to hear me — AURORA WAS HERE, and her destiny was at last the mystery I would be able to uncover.

I rested in Sila's apartment, and used my time to wander both in the city and in my mind. One hot, sultry afternoon I headed to one of my favourite bookshops in search of signs and my new direction. As usual, I aimed for the esoteric new age section of the shop, hoping to find inspiration for this new beginning. On one of the display cabinets my eyes caught sight of the name of an author I had read before - Brian Weiss.

This was the American psychiatrist who had pioneered the development of Past Life Regression Therapy in the U.S.A. I had read his first book: **MANY LIVES, MANY MASTERS** about five years earlier and had felt very excited and challenged by his work. But, for some peculiar reason I hadn't taken what I had read any further. Standing in the bookshop I decided to buy the Spanish translation of the same book and re-examine his thesis.

A few days later I finished the book and sensed that I hadn't been so inspired in years. The time that had elapsed between my first reading of Brian Weiss' story of his patient Catherine, and her encounter with her past lives, and this second reading had only served to make the account even more powerful. Then, quite suddenly the realisation came to me in an instant: AURORA HAD FINALLY HIT UPON HER FUTURE!

I was enthralled and excited. Once again I found myself in the grip of a real-life Eureka moment, just as I had all those years ago in 1995 when I had picked up Alejandro Jodorowsky's book in the bookshop in Salveira. **MANY LIVES, MANY MASTERS** was groundbreaking work in the field of healing, and I was now convinced that my new life could be that of a Past Life Regression Therapist. I already had a degree in psychology, and so this would probably make any training as a therapist shorter for me than for someone coming into the field from a non-psychological background.

With these thoughts running around in my head, the next step seemed almost blindingly obvious to me. I would need to train in my mother tongue, and this would therefore mean returning to England. That was it - decision made! I would leave Madrid and head for my homeland to live and study near a reputable therapist. Once I had decided on this new direction, in what I have to say was less than the blink of an eye, I started to act on it immediately.

With so much zealous drive inside me, events moved very quickly indeed. Almost instantly I phoned my parents to let them know about my plans, and then the following week I set about booking myself a flight to London. The month I had spent in Madrid had allowed me to find this new path in a completely intuitive way, and because of this approach, I had managed to avoid any abrupt or emotionally violent end to my time in Spain. Of course, I was bereft to be leaving this country which had been my home for more than sixteen years, but I knew that the future was calling me and nothing in life stands still.

***

On Sunday, October 3, Sila graciously accompanied me on the Madrid metro to Barajas Airport. In the airport building she was able to come with me as far as a gate with a large door-shaped metal detector. From this point onwards I would be on my way to a new life and have left my beloved 'Espana' for good.

Sila and I struggled to say goodbye to each other. We had forged a sisterly friendship together in the short time we had known each other, and we found ourselves awkwardly stalling for time before the inevitable parting. 'Coincidentally', we were not the only people doing this. A small group of a mother and father was also immersed in exactly the same process with their son. He looked to be around seventeen years old and I suspected on his way to study English.

His parents were visibly upset that he was going, and yet they were all trying to be brave and upbeat about the separation. I noticed that the boy was holding a book in his left hand, and after saying my farewells to Sila, I tilted my head slightly to be able to read the title of the book. I was astonished, and yet not astonished, as the title came into view:

THE ALCHEMIST!!!

Inwardly, I smiled the widest of all possible smiles, marvelling at the invisible realm's incredible timing!!! Even after almost ten years on my path, I still didn't understand how these 'apparent' COINCIDENCES happened.

The boy walked through the metal detector and then I followed him. It occurred to me that we might possibly be taking the same flight to London.

How amazing to be given a sign mere seconds before leaving Spain that my journey had well and truly come to its end!!! No one knew that I had spent almost ten years living out this story. It had been the secret journey of my spirit in search of soul rebirth, and here in the airport our synchronistic universe had wanted to speak to me through this sign in a stranger's hand.

The invisible realm loved me — that was what everything had been all about - and just wanted to tell me that no matter how lonely, terrified and abandoned I had felt in these last years, victory came to those who persisted in their dreams. I HAD FOUND MY TREASURE AT LAST!!!

PART II: 'COMING HOME'

A Guardian of Light is not a saint, but someone who keeps the light of Divine Love burning inside, even in the midst of their own darkness.

Karen Williams

17

LOVE AND YOU WILL FIND

**Darkness cannot drive out darkness; only light
can do that.**

MARTIN LUTHER KING JR

ON Monday, October 4, I sat in my brother's house near London
staring at two telephone numbers. They were for two past life
regression therapists I had found on the internet whilst staying
with Sila. I had chosen them from a number of therapists listed
as living in the south of England, but for very different reasons.
The man's curriculum had greatly impressed me; he seemed an
experienced and dedicated professional. I chose the woman for her
name – PENNY.

This looked to be a message straight from the invisible realm
as she had exactly the same name as Penelope in the Greek myth
of Ulysses and Penelope. Once more, the appearance of such a
meaningful sign was just something I couldn't ignore. Now that I was
back on English soil, where I would live depended entirely on which
of these two therapists I decided to work with. I picked up my mobile
phone and dialled the first number which belonged to the male
therapist. I can't remember now if I spoke to him, or a secretary, but
either way I was informed that there was no possibility of seeing him
as he was fully booked for months ahead.

Next I tried Penny's number and was thankful that someone
answered the phone. It was Penny herself, and she confirmed
that yes she was a Regression Therapist, and that she had space
available to see me. I immediately felt incredibly relieved to hear this

as I was reluctant to go back onto the Internet and start searching all over again.

My second question was to find out where she was located in the south of England. The name of the town I had seen on the website had rung no bells with me, and I was eager to know where I would be putting down roots and making my home. She gave me the name of the village and county in which she lived, but I still hadn't any clear idea of where she was. To give me a better idea of the location, she told me that she wasn't too far away from a large coastal resort town called Ambleton.

"Ambleton!" I shrieked in disbelief! "Did you say **AMBLETON?**"

Gently, she confirmed that she had. My God, I thought, feeling panic rising up inside me - this can't be happening. The very town I had lived in for ten months back in 1995 and 1996 as I had waited to make the journey to Paris for my fateful meeting with Alejandro Jodorowsky! In a split second I was just about to thank Penny politely for her time, but inform her that I wanted to be in a different part of the country, when I suddenly blurted out a confession: "My God, I used to live in Ambleton and I hated it. THIS MUST BE FATE!"

I heard these last four words echoing inside my mind, knowing full well that I was experienced enough by now to understand that they had come directly from my subconscious mind. I also felt foolish for having been so openly honest about hating Ambleton, and quickly tried to rectify the situation. I could sense total confusion coming from Penny's end of the line. My conscious mind had registered my flash of insight concerning the word FATE, and I knew I couldn't run away from this. A decisive and confident decision was needed —A TRUE LEAP OF FAITH!

And so I immediately apologised to Penny for my outburst and said that I was delighted that she would be able to see me. I finished off our 'conversation' by saying that I would ring her within a week now that I knew where she was. Thus it was that just over twenty-four hours later, through my faith in coincidences and signs, I found myself stepping off the train in Ambleton after an absence of eight years and seven months.

That day in October I had no idea I was embarking on the very last part of my spiritual quest - the section of my pyramid-shaped 'iceberg' which was above water, and, therefore in the area of conscious awareness. Instead, I continued to assume that my odyssey was finally over, and within days of settling into new accommodation, I took myself off to a local village for my all-important meeting with Penny.

Dear, unsuspecting Penny could never have lived up to my expectations of what I hoped from her as a therapist, given that my model of what a Past Life Regression Therapist should be was Brian Weiss himself. The dream of undergoing this therapy and then training to become one was shattered after seeing her. Reality and expectations quite simply did not coincide. I returned to my attic room in my new home sensing that there wasn't a clear path open to me in this area. My intuition was telling me that at this precise moment in time, Past Life Regression therapy was not the road I was supposed to go down.

***

To enter into a detailed description of what happened to me in these last years of my journey here in England would be virtually impossible. In all honesty that account would probably require another separate book all of its own. Instead I have decided to highlight the major events during this time, and also the revelations that came to me through them. They enabled me to find and put together the final pieces of this transcendental, cosmic jigsaw puzzle I had been living out since 1995.

THE COMPLETE MYSTERY OF THE ALCHEMIST WOULD FINALLY BE SOLVED!

One factor which was overridingly significant for my first year in Ambleton was that by the time I arrived there I had virtually no money to speak of. My idealistic determination to change our world and help my fellow man, which had prompted me to start giving my money away back in the summer of 2003, meant that fifteen months later I had only one thousand three hundred Euros left to my name. I naively hoped to start a brand new life with this paltry sum which I carried around in a purse tucked into an inside pocket of my winter coat.

Given that when I moved into a shared house eight days after my arrival, and had to pay a deposit and a month's rent in advance, I was obviously functioning more on fantasy than reality. That reality would bite much sooner than I expected, so that only a few weeks later, by mid-December, my world would start to fall apart.

A second defining factor that shook me out of complacent dreaming in that first year was the collapse of a Master Plan I had elaborated for myself in Madrid. In the last week before my departure from Spain I had gone onto Paulo Coelho's website and 'accidentally' discovered that he would be giving a talk in Holland in November. The admission price for the conference was a symbolic amount of a mere two Euros, and I could book my ticket online.

I was ecstatic when I found this information, and instantly concluded that fate was offering me the chance to fulfil the dream I had nurtured since the letter I had sent to Brazil in 2002:

a meeting between The Alchemist's author and
the 'real-life' Santiago,
who was me!

My plan was to fly to Holland and ask Paulo for help - financial help. I would write a letter telling him of how I had dared to do something quite exceptional when I had decided to give away my money to help people in need. I knew for certain that he would be moved by what I had done, and would offer to help me in the short term. Once we had established respect and trust on both sides, I could then tell him how for ten years I had lived out the story of The Alchemist, and in doing so had discovered its true meaning!

With this heady, idealistic dream in my heart I spent the last of my pitiful sum of money on a plane ticket to Holland, and set off in search of my 'mentor'. As you may have already guessed, dear reader, nothing happened quite in the way I had hoped. Paulo was gracious and friendly - I think he even liked me when we met - but on my return from Holland there was just a polite and warm email of thanks from him in the inbox of my emails, and nothing more. I had obviously come across as a complete and utter oddball, and so therefore he made no offer of financial help, or any hint of a future possible meeting between us.

That was the defining disaster I naively hadn't seen coming, and the moment when my personal metaphorical SHIT HIT THE FAN -so to speak. By Christmas I found myself almost penniless, with no money to pay the next month's rent, and it was now glaringly obvious to me as to what had *really been going on* since my arrival in England.

I had spectacularly misread the sign at Madrid Airport when I had seen the boy holding a copy of The Alchemist! That moment hadn't been the universe signalling to me that my journey had ended. Oh, no, no, no, it was actually THE VERY OPPOSITE! You idiot, Karen, I rebuked myself as I sat in my room in a complete state of misery, that was the invisible realm telling you that you had more of this journey to complete, and that's exactly WHY YOU ARE HERE!

***

Devastation is not too strong a word to describe what I experienced after this revelation. I couldn't believe that God, Spirit, the universe, or whatever word one used to describe the ruling force, could be so cruel and heartless with me. But whether or not I could assimilate and accept this new reality, the fact was that I had to face it, and heroically I eventually did.

For almost ten long years I bit the bullet and accepted the cards fate had dealt me. I cried oceans of tears, but managed to go from a state of near total breakdown to one in which I embraced the challenges before me in true wounded warrior spirit. During the start of those long years there were times when I journeyed almost weekly to the **material** half of my soul, and received 'beatings' from people, places, friends, acquaintances, and even loved ones.

I got into debt, moved home seven times, worked in an assortment of jobs, and then became very ill – both physically, mentally and emotionally. But finally, yes finally, I DID FIND MY TREASURE!

However, along with this almost disastrous beginning to my life in my motherland, I also received an incredible miracle at the very start of this final phase. A month after I moved into the shared house, a ruggedly handsome gentleman also moved in. The moment I set eyes on J I knew I was standing face-to-face with my soul mate. This man was nothing less than the prince of princes I had dreamed about since my childhood. Here was my other half; my love of loves; my light – MY EVERYTHING - I was completely and utterly smitten!!!

My spirit was correct about this sudden KNOWING, but failed to inform me that I was also staring at a double-edged sword. Yes, it was totally true that J was my light, but that was only half of the story. Unknown to me at this point, he was also my shadow – in other words what at this stage of my journey I understood to be the **material** half of my soul.

This would mean that over the next four years and more the two of us would find ourselves dancing together the DANCE OF REDEMPTION. Time and time again we would metaphorically meet in the *'desert sands in the shadow of the pyramids'* and re-enact the end of The Alchemist. The universe had VERY SPECIFICALLY brought us together right at the end of this journey precisely because WE WERE EACH OTHER'S HALF!!!

***

Though my first year in Ambleton saw me in a deep state of emotional collapse, it brought me two very important revelations concerning the real meaning of Paulo's fable. As always, these revelations came in the form of flashes of insight as I continued with my practise of living from my intuition. Each moment of every day was important, and only my intuition could connect me with the wisdom and knowledge of my spirit buried and hidden deep within the unconscious part of my soul.

The first realisation concerned the true motive for why I had decided to give all my money away. The surface explanation was simple and clear: I had wanted another powerful, transcendental dream to fuel my journey in search of soul rebirth. As a child I had always been an idealist, and the idea of turning the rules of an unjust world upside down to help those who were the victims of injustice was a powerful motivating force for me. But in Ambleton I began to see a far deeper reason for my crusading zeal.

I realised that by having given my money away, and leaving myself with next to nothing, I had recreated the same situation for myself as Santiago had faced at the beginning of his odyssey when on his arrival in Tangiers he had been robbed of all his money. My intuition had somehow connected with a profound metaphysical imperative within this archetypal myth, and that imperative was that this journey could only be undertaken if the seeker no longer had any control over their destiny.

Without money, both Santiago and I could not manipulate or control the quest with our egos. Instead we were completely dependent on God, Spirit, and the universe for direction and support. Ultimately this invisible realm would have full control of the details of how our journeys evolved.

The second revelation about this soul quest came to me through one of Paulo's books. When I had been in Spain I had read his work in Spanish, but now that I was in England I decided to re-read some of the books in my own mother tongue. The first one I read was his work **THE PILGRIMAGE**. In it Paulo narrates the metaphysical journey he made as he walked the famous Camino de Santiago in 1986 in search of an enigmatic sword.

I found the book difficult in places, but one particular section stood out for me as if it were screaming a message to me from the hilltops. This part was near the beginning of the book, where Paulo describes an encounter with a Catholic monk called Father Jordi. They meet shortly after Paulo sets out from the French Pyrenees to walk the Camino Frances. The monk reveals to Paulo certain esoteric facts concerning the nature of some ancient 'roads' walked by pilgrims, and then tells him that the pilgrimage routes are analogous to the four suits of a deck of cards.

The Camino de Santiago is the Road of the Spades, and if successfully completed, confers power to the spiritual seeker. The priest goes on to mention two other ancient pilgrimage routes, each with their own special metaphysical qualities. Lastly, before the two men part, Paulo reminds Father Jordi that he hasn't mentioned one final 'road' - THE ROAD OF THE DIAMONDS. It is then that Father Jordi says the following:

> **'Exactly. That's the secret road. If you take it**
> **someday, you won't be helped by anybo**dy.
> **For now, let us leave that one aside'.**
> **(The Pilgrimage: Paulo Coelho.)**

When I read these words, I instantly knew what *The Road of the Diamonds* was. It was the archetypal myth which I had lived out for ten years and was still living out here in England. As far as I was concerned Paulo Coelho's The Alchemist WAS THIS ROAD. What an extraordinary revelation!

Apart from these two crucial insights right at the beginning of the conscious phase of my quest, probably the single most important revelation of my whole journey came to me in September 2006, towards the end of my second year in Ambleton. It was certainly the missing piece in my understanding of The Alchemist, and as usual the invisible realm gave me absolutely no warning of what it was about to show me. I was to encounter the **material** half of my soul yet again, even though my conscious mind had been working busily to persuade me that my 'beatings' were now well and truly over.

***

The revelation came when I managed to get a permanent job in a local care home for the elderly. I was being trained to empty catheters, wash bodies, hoist residents in and out of their beds, and all the other tasks a care assistant was expected to perform.

I started the work with high hopes and high ideals, but my enthusiasm quickly evaporated when a quite different reality began to dawn on me. Each shift revealed just how little quality time I could give to these elderly people who were drawing ever closer to the end of their lives. I rushed from one task to the next, barely catching my breath, and never having any time to sit down for a break and a welcome cup of tea. Conversations with residents came down to sound bites, and often I was forced to wash someone and put them to bed at breakneck speed in order to be able to go on to the next person.

After three weeks of this I had had enough. No one was benefiting from this way of working. I was stressed and exhausted, and deeply distressed when I had to rush my handling of a resident. The most heart-breaking aspect of the work was seeing how lonely and abandoned most of the elderly people felt. In short, all of this was more than I could stand.

One day, at the end of a shift, I took stock of the situation and decided to hand in my resignation. I knew that once again I had come to a symbolic Egypt and was meeting the shadow of THE **MATERIAL** HALF OF MY SOUL. I didn't exactly understand *what aspect* of my shadow I was encountering, but I was determined not to continue receiving this 'beating'. There was no treasure here and my journey would obviously continue somewhere else.

The resignation interview I had with the owner of the home a few days later revealed an enormous amount to me about the fundamental spiritual values underlying The Alchemist, and what actually made it a tale of redemption. I had to keep extremely cool and level-headed at the interview as it was clear that my character was going to be stripped and reviled because for the owner I was nothing less than a 'traitor'.

I had shown the unbelievable 'audacity' to walk away from these elderly residents. After my grilling was over, and I had managed to stand my ground, even though at one point I had almost lost my temper.

> I realised that this was the moment when, yet again, I had abandoned my quest for the **'false treasure'** I had been 'digging for', and had found my true inner treasure.

However, the most important element of this process of metaphorically 'walking away' from what could bring no rewards of love, peace, compassion, and truth - all the characteristics of true spiritual light - was that I had managed to do it in a spirit of peace and non-violence. And Santiago had done EXACTLY THE SAME at the end of The Alchemist.

He had not abandoned his quest for his treasure by turning around and, in an act of revenge, beating the leader of the refugees in return. No, he hadn't sought the gratification of any feelings of anger and hatred. Instead he had quite simply abandoned the quest in peace. Of course it was true that he had shouted out the confession of his dream to the men who had beaten him, but there was no violence in this act.

His words to the leader of the refugees expressed the agonizing pain he had felt from the beating, and conveyed to the man that his whole attitude was one of resignation and acceptance. It was this which made his actions redemptive. He refused to fight his encounter with darkness with more darkness and my own experience with the many metaphorical 'beatings' I had endured over the years confirmed this for me. I had always endeavoured never to allow myself to respond to my suffering with revenge, rage and hatred. I had disciplined myself to either endure, or 'walk away' in peace.

Of course, I wasn't by any means 'Miss Perfect', and there had been a few times on my journey when I had failed to completely embody these spiritual values. However, I never allowed my 'failures' to be as big as they could have been had I not had the awareness of the spiritual dimension of what was happening to me.

The resignation interview was testing and fraught with the possibility of failure, but I managed to hang on to a peaceful outcome, and in doing so, found my redemption. The interview taught me that *The Road of the Diamonds* was fundamentally a road of peace and wisdom, and that these led to the inner treasure of transcendent love. But the biggest revelation of all from this short period at the care home still awaited me, and came in my final week at the home as I worked out my notice before leaving.

Edith was the elderly resident who gave it to me.

***

A few days before I was due to finish, the home had organised a social entertainment evening for the residents. This was something I knew I was *dreading*. In the artificial environment of the home, where denial seemed to reign supreme, this kind of event could only spell disaster. Rather than cheering the residents up and giving them a break from the monotony of a routine characterised by loneliness, isolation and boredom, evenings such as these risked highlighting just how awful their situation truly was.

Sure enough, that is exactly what happened. Edith began to show signs of distress at the end of the 'festivities' and this manifested itself in her state of dementia becoming more exaggerated than normal. I spotted her pain and made my way over to her wheelchair determined to calm her down. I decided that the first thing I needed to do would be to distract her by taking her to her room. The ride in itself might bring her some relief from the distress she was feeling.

As I took hold of the wheelchair, another elderly resident shook her head ruefully, and said, "You're wasting your time, you know; it won't make any difference."

By the time I got Edith to her room, she seemed to have improved, and my next thought was to spend some time chatting with her. She needed that very personal one-to-one contact, even if she was unable to communicate with me because of the dementia. I sat on the floor so that I would be in a totally non-threatening position for her; I wanted her to be able to look down on me, rather than me looking down on her. I can't remember how our conversation started because I simply let Edith say whatever came to her.

Quite suddenly she started talking about her brother and it wasn't clear to me if this was something recent or belonged to the distant past. To get some idea of where Edith was in her mind I asked her where she was with her brother and it was then that the miracle happened.

"Oh, we're in our house in South Wimbledon," she said nonchalantly.

I couldn't believe my ears. I was born and brought up in the London suburb of WIMBLEDON, and had gone to school near SOUTH WIMBLEDON. Edith had given me something spectacular with which to be able to connect with her - somewhere both of us knew very well indeed. Instantly I realised that we were back in Edith's childhood or girlhood, and I immediately told her that I had been born in Wimbledon and had also lived there as a girl.

"Did you used to go to the baths in South Wimbledon, Edith?" I asked.

This was a swimming pool I had attended regularly in my early twenties, but which had originally been a public bathing house where people went for a weekly bath if they didn't have one in their own home. Edith's face brightened and she started to smile as she told me that she remembered the baths, and used to go there as a young girl.

Our conversation continued for a good ten minutes as memories of her early years spilled out and soothed her emotions. In a way all I had been expected to do was sit and listen as she reminisced. Eventually, another member of staff came to collect me as there was medication to dispense, and residents waiting to be prepared for bed. Reluctantly, I left Edith and went off to perform my duties, but this miracle stayed with me.

I had followed my heart in wanting to help this lady, even though the whole situation had seemed hopeless, and the invisible realm had shown me that my heart had been beating to a UNIVERSAL PULSE which connects each and everyone one of us.

THE PULSE OF SPIRIT.

Days later, after I had left the home, I went back over this extraordinary incident to try and understand it. And that was when the revelation came to me:

the material half of the soul was not all shadow.
There was light, divine light there too!

Although working in this care home had been yet another journey to the shadow of the **material** half of my soul, and yet another 'beating', this half of the soul had also 'magically' revealed its own light. The cupboard wasn't 'bare' after all because dear Edith had shown me that.

For a few years now I had understood that the places we call HOME are really symbolic of where we experience our inner home. We are all familiar with the phrase 'home is where the heart is', and I knew that the true meaning of this was that deep inside our hearts we have a special and unique 'home' that is our soul. In that inner sanctum we find our spirit - the light of God within us, or what I have been calling THE LIGHT OF DIVINE LOVE.

Edith had been able TO 'GO HOME' with me that night – and experience her own spiritual light - as I sat on the floor listening to her because we had shared the same physical home of our childhoods - Wimbledon. But, Wimbledon had only been a sign; one lovingly crafted by the invisible realm in order to show me that the two of us had in actual fact shared OUR INNER HOMES - *the inner spiritual light our souls.*

Now, with this new understanding of what had really happened between Edith and me, I suddenly found myself understanding perhaps one of the most 'invisible' aspects of Paulo Coelho's fable - one which I have never, ever seen revealed anywhere in print by anyone. I now knew precisely why Santiago had told the leader of the refugees that he had dreamt of finding treasure buried near the Pyramids of Egypt.

THERE REALLY WAS TREASURE IN EGYPT!

This was not a clever twist to the end of Paulo's fable in order to make it work as a neat little fairy-tale. Oh, no. Santiago had brought the message of the existence of that treasure to the leader of the refugees because that treasure was, of course, THE LEADER'S INNER LIGHT!

These two protagonists of the story were each messengers carrying the treasure of the other half! **Mystical** Santiago had carried the leader's treasure to him, and the **material** leader had carried Santiago's treasure to him when he had recounted his own dream of treasure buried in a ruin in southern Spain. And here, without even expecting such a revelation, the care home and Edith had incredibly and astonishingly shown me this missing piece of the puzzle.

What had been for so very long a story of JUST ONE HALF OF THE SOUL'S SPIRITUAL LIGHT WAS FINALLY COMPLETE. The **material** half of our souls was:

BOTH SHADOW AND LIGHT

just as the Beast had shown me in the Beauty and the Beast fairy-tale. Edith's great gift had been to show me that GOD'S SPIRIT WAS EVERYWHERE. Even in the midst of great darkness, nothing could obscure the fact that:

EVERYTHING HAD LIGHT!

It appeared that enduring 'beatings' was the only way to redeem the darkness obscuring that light, and this would then somehow allow the light to shine forth. Again, the metaphor of liberation came into my mind. THE ALCHEMIST WAS THE ARCHETYPE OF THAT ROAD TO LIBERATION!!!

So, with this extraordinary, new revelation of two sources of light coming from two separate halves of the soul, I now asked myself the old, familiar question — was this really the end of my journeying? The invisible realm either couldn't or didn't seem to want to answer this question for me at that very moment because no huge, transcendental signs or intuitions emerged for me.

Instead, an unknown remained implacably on my horizon. It appeared that, as before, I would be expected to rely on yet more patience and perseverance. These were the keys — the taskmasters of my soul quest. I only hoped that as they demanded metaphorical blood from me, I would be sufficiently equipped with these qualities to see my quest followed through to its very end. My goal of soul rebirth simply wasn't optional; this journey had now become a truly life-or-death endeavour.

18

TWO HALVES MAKE A WHOLE

"That which you offer turns to gold. That which you hold back turns to coal."

GURUMAYI CHIDVILASANANDA

As I had just discovered, Egypt possessed Treasure.

THE Alchemist was the tale of two halves; two halves each subconciously in search of the other for the sole purpose of redeeming their shared shadow, and thus paradoxically finding their spiritual light. Edith had been the physical personification of the **material** half of my soul, and because I had been willing to abandon my search for the treasure my ego had so desperately wanted, the truth was revealed to me in all its glory.

In this chapter, dear reader, I now feel the time has come to share a very important insight with you. In a sense I am moving us forward on this journey to April 2012 when I sat writing what I thought were the very last chapters of TREASURE: New Edition II. At the beginning of April 2012, in the middle of that work, I quite spontaneously found myself writing something other than the new chapters. I began to flesh out an account which I had quite mysteriously begun 'channelling' just over a year earlier.

It was a new ending to Paulo Coelho's
The Alchemist.

The Soul of the World seemed to want to tell me how the odyssey had ended for the leader of the refugees in Paulo's book.

The care home had shown me THE OTHER HALF OF THIS ODYSSEY: in other words that the leader in The Alchemist was also in possession of spiritual light.

Just like Edith, he was also a personification of the **material** half of the soul – but in this instance, the **material** half of the shepherd Santiago's soul. He was therefore the custodian of both Santiago's shadow and also his Lumen Naturae. However, in Paulo's tale the leader never discovers his personal treasure because his role is confined to being exclusively that of the instrument by which Santiago finds his own redemption and treasure. Nevertheless, as my hands pressed down on the keyboard of my computer in April 2012 I found myself telling the leader's story.

Suddenly, filled with contrition and remorse for his treatment of the shepherd boy, the leader returns to the dune where he had met Santiago, and there finds gold, silver, and precious jewels in another hole only metres away from the hole where the shepherd had been digging. I wrote every word down with next to no effort, and at an amazing speed, sensing that I was now giving form to what had been given to me earlier as a priceless gift from the collective unconscious of Mankind.

When I had finished writing this ending to Paulo's The Alchemist, the only task remaining was to give the leader of the refugees a name, and so I went onto the internet in search of Arabic names. I struggled for some time through long lists, desperately wanting something of great symbolic significance for this *'forgotten man'*. Finally, after a fairly extensive search I managed to find exactly what I was looking for.

The other 'hero' of The Alchemist would be called Anwar – because in Arabic Anwar means LIGHT! And so, dear reader, here is his half of the story; the half which makes THE WHOLE OF THE ALCHEMIST COMPLETE.

THE CHANNELLED ENDING TO ANWAR'S JOURNEY

Anwar sat by the camp fire with his companions and watched. His friends tossed the piece of gold they had found on Santiago to one another and mocked the skinny boy they had met on the dune. These men were Anwar's friends, but tonight they seemed like childish adolescents.

Anwar's head began to hurt, and so he made his excuses and retired to his tent. His eyes closed and again the dune appeared before him. He could not forget that they had found this stranger at the very place where he had experienced his recurrent dream of finding treasure buried under the roots of a sycamore tree inside a ruined church in the fields of Spain.

The boy had also told them about a dream. He said that he had twice dreamt of finding treasure near the Pyramids of Egypt. A coincidence? Anwar didn't believe in coincidences. His father had died at the age of twenty nine, and yet here Anwar was, still alive at the age of thirty four. He rolled over onto his side, determined to fall asleep, but that sleep was not to be had. The skinny boy's words would not leave him.

As the last of Anwar's companions found their own tents for the night, Anwar rose in the dark, mounted his horse and rode back to the dune overlooking the pyramids. The dawn light was just breaking when he arrived at the hole in the dune where they had found Santiago.

Anwar felt foolish, yet somehow sensed that he had been compelled to return to this place. The hole was still in shadow, but there was just enough light by which he could roughly see its depth. He jumped down into it and stood stock still. Suddenly a memory flashed into Anwar's mind.

He was sitting at his father's market stall, and he could hear the words his father was saying to him: "Anwar son, life is not what we think it is. Look at that man there. I don't know him at all, he is a stranger. But, give a stranger bread Anwar and you will never go hungry."

"...........give a stranger bread Anwar," the words echoed in his mind. Why now, after so many years, did his father seem to be standing with him inside a hole overlooking the pyramids? His heart was pierced by an unexpected pain. He and his cohorts hadn't given the strange, skinny boy bread; instead they had beaten him to within an inch of his life.

And then Anwar had told him his own ridiculous dream of a treasure buried in Spain. Well, the boy had deserved it, he reasoned to himself. There had been something very irritating about him. Anwar hadn't liked the fanatical expression on his face when he had grabbed hold of him and they had stared at each other for only the briefest of moments.

But, just immediately after this thought, quite mysteriously it was followed by the sound of a woman's voice inside Anwar's head: "When you are ready......" It was Amira, the Egyptian fortune teller! To his surprise, unexpectedly obeying instincts he had long ago learned to control and ignore, Anwar prodded the ground under his feet with his sword, and then knelt down to see what he had found. He pulled a piece of cloth from the end of the sword, and when he rose the dawn light revealed that it was a blood-stained shred of Santiago's shirt. Anwar flung the cloth out of the hole in disgust.

He continued his prodding for a few more minutes, but the hole was just the same old hole they had left behind the day before when the boy had confessed to his stupid recurrent dream. Anwar hauled himself out of this man-made tomb, and gazed out at the pink light falling on the pyramids. "Dreams, stupid dreams," he cursed out loud to himself.

"Where are my dreams? They left me the day my father died, that's what happened to them." Unlike the stranger, he wasn't so foolish as to believe in his own stupid recurrent dream. Aimlessly, he found himself walking over to where the ragged cloth lay. He had tossed it further than he had imagined. Using the tip of his sword, he hooked the rag, and flicked it away for a second time.

To his shock and surprise, he saw a scarab beetle lying on the sand where the cloth had been, and then suddenly Santiago's words about his dream of treasure at the pyramids of Egypt flooded Anwar's mind yet again. He knew that in Egypt the scarab was a symbol of rebirth. Was this why he had left his companions snoring in their tents? Was this why he had returned to the dune?

Was this why suddenly, and without warning, his father seemed to have come to be with him? Was it time to become a man, instead of the power-hungry person he had enjoyed being for so very long? Was that what the beetle was telling him? Yet again, the pain returned to Anwar's heart and he felt warm, salty tears slowly trickle down his cheeks.

"Damn", he muttered, "damn." He could not understand what was happening, but deep inside his soul he knew this moment to be sacred. Slowly he inhaled the cold, dry desert air, and placed the end of his sword into the golden sand. Then gently he traced a large circle around the spot where the beetle lay. To complete the ritual, he stabbed the ground in the centre of the circle close to the scarab beetle's body.

Suddenly, without warning, Anwar's sword and almost half of his arm disappeared into the sand as it gave way under the force of his blow. Now on his knees instead of standing on the ground, Anwar found himself staring into a deep cavernous hole in the dune. But unlike the hole he had just left behind, this one was shiny. The light blinding his eyes was silver and gold, and it shone from jewelled necklaces, rings, cups and vases tangled together in a heap at the bottom.

No words came from Anwar's lips; not even his breath moistened the dry desert air. Time seemed to have completely vanished from the face of the Earth. Only one sound filled the void both inside and outside his head; a voice he had once loved more deeply than life itself: "................give a stranger bread Anwar and you will never go hungry."

19

DIVINE ALCHEMY

When the heart weeps for what it has lost, the spirit laughs for what it has found.

Sufi teaching

NOW, let us return to my journey. After the revelation in the care home in the autumn of 2006, as each week passed I hoped with all my heart that the grand finale of my quest was just one more 'beating' away. But 2007 rolled around, and passed off much in the same way as 2006. Week in and week out I encountered the shadow of the **material** half of my soul in people, places and situations, and there now really seemed to be no end to what felt like a prison sentence of sorts.

In response to a long letter I sent to Paulo Coelho in October 2006, where I gave him yet more information concerning what I had learned about The Alchemist, he emailed me to say that he would be interested in meeting me again. The most convenient date was sometime in April 2007 because he was scheduled to be in London at that time. For me this was the perfect location as it would require only a simple train journey up to the capital. But when April arrived Paulo never contacted me. Disappointment is an understatement for what I felt.

Paulo had enthusiastically used his blog to share a true story I had sent him just before Christmas 2006, and now only a few months later he had either forgotten about me, or decided to ignore me. Something had changed, but I didn't know what that *something* was. In an attempt to understand this apparent 'mystery' I sat down for a good, in-depth conversation with my Higher Self.

Yes, this was a terrible blow I told myself, but perhaps not a totally incomprehensible one. On my many forays onto the internet I had discovered that Paulo had legions of fans but also many critics, amongst whom were a few hardnosed individuals who really HATED HIS WORK WITH A PASSION. How could he possibly be certain that the oddball who had appeared from nowhere in Holland in 2004 wasn't one of his many foes?

***

By now, I was entering my thirteenth year of this never-ending quest, and I really couldn't understand what more the universe required of me. A welcome break from the stress and strain of it all came at the beginning of September 2007 when my mother paid for me to visit her and my father in Andalusia. I hadn't been back since a brief stay during the Christmas of 2005, twenty months earlier. Now, for ten days I returned to my beloved Andalusia and could see that *'my ruin'* was still standing at the top of the hill, even though the hill itself had been bought by a property developer and was being cut open to make way for the building of luxury villas.

In January 2008, four months later, I would be given a huge sign by the invisible realm as to where exactly I was on my journey to the summit of my personal Everest, but it would take me more than two months, and another visit to Andalusia, in order to be able to interpret it.

A month-and-a-half after my return from Spain, at the beginning of November 2007, and after just over a year of unemployment, I managed to secure a permanent job as a health care assistant in a local hospital. I underwent a three-week training course and then started work on one of the rehabilitation wards. Most of the patients were very elderly and had quite severely restricted mobility. A large percentage had problems with incontinence, and this meant a lot of cleaning away of faeces and changing of incontinence pads. The morning shifts involved head-to-toe washing of patients, and then the rest of the time was spent with visits to the toilet, bringing out commodes and more changing of pads.

I truly put my heart and soul into the work, but once again, just as in the care home, I found that I wasn't happy. I gave the best of myself as far as I could to the patients, but invariably there was always a huge conflict between attention to detail with them and the time constraints of the shifts. I had already felt very stressed when I began the job, and at the end of December I came down with a particularly bad flu virus. Terrified that I would lose the job, I began a pattern of spending two days in bed and then one day at work, two at home, one at work. This went on for more than three weeks and still there was no improvement in my health.

One afternoon towards the middle of January I was coming to the end of my shift when I spotted a patient in need of help. I was still suffering from the flu virus and desperately wanted to go home, but decided to make one last effort to find out what she needed. It turned out that it was a magazine by her bedside table, and she wondered if I might be able to bring it to her. I walked over to the bed and picked up the magazine. And that was when I saw the sign. Lying propped on the bed was a cute little brown teddy bear, and around his neck was a label. In bold red letters it announced the following:

'Aurora – Gift of Smiles'

I knew instantly that the invisible realm was giving me this all-important sign, however in my state of fatigue, and feeling as ill as I did, I couldn't really understand what the message was. That was one of my last days at the hospital, because a few days later the flu symptoms became worse and I found myself permanently confined to bed.

***

At the beginning of February most of the infection had cleared up except for a persistent chesty cough, but I was feeling an exhaustion that wouldn't leave me. In a last ditch attempt to get myself well enough to return to work, I booked myself for a long weekend at a retreat. My plan was to be in a place of utter peace and quiet so that I could rest and prepare myself for a resumption of normal activity.

However, as usual with my quest, this wasn't what happened. Once at the retreat the exhaustion worsened and I was barely able to do anything at all. Nevertheless, this 'grinding to a halt' allowed a great gift to come my way when on the second day I booked a session with the spiritual counsellor at the centre. It was Imogen who greeted me warmly and took me off to a room where we could talk in private. After barely five minutes with this young woman, I immediately sensed that she was an unconventional person, and so felt confident enough to open up about just how ill I was and how stressed I felt in my new job.

Again, it wasn't long before my intuition told me that here was someone to whom I could confess a little of the spiritual journey I had been on. And so, without going into great detail, I explained to Imogen how I had been living out the story of The Alchemist, and how this had involved years of repeatedly encountering my own inner darkness. Imogen listened and nodded as if understanding what I was saying, and then told me that she had studied shamanism and other religions before returning to her Christian faith.

"You've been living symbolically, Karen," she said with total authority.

Although I knew this wasn't quite correct — simply because symbols and physical manifestations are not exactly the same thing - her statement told me that Imogen had a deep knowledge of, and was more than familiar with, this area of spiritual seeking.

After nearly an hour with this highly intelligent and intensely compassionate person, I had unburdened myself of a considerable amount of emotional tension, been able to share just a portion of my quest, and come to the decision that I wouldn't return to the job at the hospital. Imogen had taken me out of some of the darkness of my isolation and pain, and allowed me to confess to someone - a person who understood - a little of what I was all about.

The next day my precious confidante came looking for me just to check on how I was doing, and was disappointed to see me slumped in a chair, tucked away inside a quiet alcove. The truth was that I was feeling even more exhausted than I had the day before. Imogen had clearly underestimated the level of stress I had been carrying, and I hadn't really given her a complete picture of just what I had been through.

As a final parting gift Imogen quite spontaneously and unexpectedly stepped out of her conventional role, of counsellor, and for a brief moment took on the mantle of a shaman. She extended her arm towards me, took hold of my hand in hers, and gripping it with the strength and force of a primitive warrior, pulled me out of the chair towards her.

"Karen, I pull you out of the darkness and into the light," she said.

Instinctively I knew that, although this was a symbolic ritual my friend had just performed, it was also one that went far beyond mere symbolism. It was something which entered the invisible psychic and spiritual realms. I had no physical sensation that she had brought me into any kind of light, but that wasn't in the least bit important. The fact was that Imogen had engaged with the unseen world of spirit, and I was honoured and deeply moved that she had decided to step out of her role and meet me on this level.

With a few tears on my part, we said our heart-felt goodbyes to each other knowing that we had been able to communicate something of our hidden spiritual selves to one another. That I sadly realised was a rare privilege under so-called 'normal circumstances' – ordinary life simply didn't usually allow for such things to manifest between individuals.

The next day I left the retreat, and returned to my rented room in a suburb of Ambleton. I then sat down and wearily accepted the fact that I needed to write a letter of resignation to the hospital.

***

After this episode, even though I had experienced enormous relief and comfort from my encounter with Imogen, my health continued to deteriorate. I coughed incessantly for hours at night, and again for at least an hour each morning when I woke up. The exhaustion worsened and I was able to do next to nothing. Each day I spent hours in bed, just lying with my eyes shut, unable to sleep, but equally incapable of getting up to do anything. But worst of all, I had started to experience the return of panic attacks.

Towards the middle of February I felt so ill that I decided to speak to my mother on the phone. I made no mention of the panic, but focussed on my intense feelings of exhaustion. She explained to me that she had just seen a new doctor for a problem with her blood pressure, and told me that he had a fantastic, state-of-the-art, diagnostic machine which was able to see inside the body without making any incisions of any kind. There and then we agreed that I should go over to Spain and have a consultation with the doctor to see if I had anything seriously wrong with me.

And, so it was that on February 26 I flew out to Malaga, completely unaware that in fact my spirit had other, far more transcendental reasons for taking me there.

I decided to stay for around ten days, because my mother's eighty-second birthday was on March 4, followed by my parents' Diamond Wedding Anniversary on the fifth. I saw the doctor and his machine the very next day after I had arrived when he hooked me up to his mysterious contraption, and sat behind me, twiddling various knobs and taking readings. After about twenty minutes he released me from the wires, and took me into his consulting room to give me the good news - there was fundamentally nothing wrong with me. He felt that the return of the panic attacks was probably due to what he considered my obsessive nature.

He recommended some medication and that I pursue Neuro-Linguistic Programming as a therapy. This would help me overcome the impulses for self-harm which had originated with the cocaine-based dental anaesthetic back in 1993, and would also deal with my accentuated tendency to obsess. Needless to say, I didn't quite agree with his assessment, but conscious of just how lucky I had been to have this examination, I promised to take up his advice.

My fatigue continued after the consultation, and I spent my mother's birthday and my parents' wedding anniversary in bed. However, the real spiritual purpose of my visit started to reveal itself when a truly 'cosmic' sign appeared as if from 'out of the blue'. A few days before my parents' Diamond wedding anniversary my father had handed me a local magazine, and inside it I found a large colour advertisement for a jewellers. This shop seemed to be selling every conceivable shape and size of diamond. Suddenly, the truth dawned on me:

the advertisement was no 'coincidence'.
It was there, shouting out at me that I had finally arrived at
the end of The Road of the Diamonds!!!

I was stunned by this revelation. If this were true then I knew that the only way of finding out for sure was if I were to journey to the top of the mountain where this shop was located. That would mean going up to Campana, the village just below the mountain's summit. This had all the echoes of what I had done back in 2003 when I had decided to climb six hundred and thirty metres above sea level up to Granada in my attempt to find my treasure. This time, however, victory seemed much closer to hand, and I sensed the magic in the sign I had received.

I was not, and had never been, in search of the glittering light of precious jewels, but the subtle, invisible light of spirit, and so the jewellery shop was not my true destination. Instead, I knew I needed to head for Campana's church. My treasure had manifested before when I had gone in search of churches, and my intuition told me that this pattern would repeat itself again in Campana. I decided I had to do this before any return to England was possible.

***

Thus it was that nine days after arriving I had enough strength to go out for a short walk and at the same time embark on a two stage process ordained by my intuition. The first part entailed a long overdue visit to *'my ruin'*. When I had arrived in Andalusia on the twenty-sixth, I had looked out of the car window in the direction of the ruin and saw that it was no longer there at the top of the hill. The development of villas had progressed considerably since I had been here five-and-a-half months earlier, and its romantic outline had now been removed from the landscape forever.

That Thursday, March 6, I walked to the base of the hill and climbed up past the unfinished new villas now sitting where the fennel-covered terraces had once been. I was determined to say a last farewell to the place which had been my holy spot; the place where my journey had begun so many years earlier. I managed to climb over some metal scaffolding poles to finally reach the top of the hill and the remains of the ruin. The broken walls had completely disappeared, and now all that was left was the flat cement floor of the building.

As well as the demolition of *'my ruin'*, the energy here had also somehow changed. The otherworldly feeling of peace and soulfulness had gone. The mystical sensation of being closer to God had also disappeared. As I stood on the cement floor looking out onto the glittering Mediterranean Sea stretching to the horizon, even this view had lost its transcendental beauty.

It was then that the thought suddenly came to me that the ruin had been demolished because the universe had known that my journey had come to an end.

Tears started to roll down my face as I stood there alone, unable, or perhaps not wanting, to take in this reality. I knew unequivocally that this was the truth, and now it seemed more than obvious as to why I had returned here to Andalusia. It really had had nothing to do with seeing the doctor, but was actually about this - standing here on the remains of *'my ruin'*, and feeling my grief. The invisible realm was harmony and precision itself, and knew that my journey had to end where it had begun. I had travelled in a circle in search of treasure, and now, like all circular journeys, I was back where I had started.

My spirit had been in search of my spirit - the inner light of the divine within me - and God was showing me that I had found it. I picked up two small stones lying on the cement floor, knowing that they had once been part of the broken walls of the ruin. I rubbed their rough surfaces with my fingers, remembering the many times I had come to this place in order to find myself.

I promised the universe that one day soon I would give these stones to Paulo Coelho. Then he too would be able to hold them in his hands and know for sure that there really had been a ruin on a hill in Andalusia, and that I really was Santiago. Life was as magical and amazing as he had said it was in The Alchemist. He had predicted the future through the book, and I hoped that fate would one day very soon allow me to tell him my whole, incredible story in person.

I closed my eyes and thanked God through my tears for this extraordinary, supernatural odyssey, and then to show Him that I was willing to live from my inner light, I recited the Lord's Prayer out loud to the wind. The Divine Creator's Will needed to be at the centre of my life, and not my own. SPIRIT WAS KING.

'As he was about to climb yet another dune, his heart whispered, be aware of the place where you are brought to tears. That's where I am, and that's where your treasure is.'

THE ALCHEMIST, PAULO COELHO

***

My next stop, and the second stage of this intuitive process, was of course Campana and its church. The following day I took the bus up to the village in search of my SPIRITUAL DIAMOND.

I headed in the direction of the church which stood within the walls of an old ruined Moorish fortress, and had spectacular views over the Mediterranean Sea below. Here I was, ready to find the physical manifestation of my spirit - the treasure I had set out in search of thirteen long years ago - and I didn't know what was going to happen, or what exactly it would be.

I entered the darkness of the church and instinctively sensed that I had to make my way to the main altar. But I also sensed that I wasn't supposed to do this in a hurry. With that in mind, I started at the entrance to the church and decided to walk slowly around the edge of the nave. As I did so, I passed life-size statues of Jesus and Mary ensconced in dimly-lit alcoves, and all the time I was aware that this was an incredible appointment with destiny and that I needed to approach it with the awe and humility it deserved. Finally, I arrived at the front of the nave and the main altar. This was the place my intuition told me where I would find my DIAMOND.

I was astonished and overwhelmed by what met my eyes. I could not have predicted in a million years what I saw before me. On one of the steps leading up to the altar lay a green piece of card. It was resting on the step and had obviously been left there after a service; probably one for the village children. On the green card was written a Spanish word in thick, black felt-tip pen. It said 'LUZ' – THE SPANISH WORD LIGHT!!!

Here I was, using only my faith in the signs that came to me, and I had climbed a mountain road to come to this church because I knew that I would find my diamond here. And now I was staring at it right in front of me:

LIGHT, DIVINE LIGHT!

My God, I thought in utter shock and amazement, what I had searched for over so many years was now a reality, lying on an altar step of the village church in Campana. My soul had finally been reborn!

***

Back in my room in Ambleton three days later I had a lot to think about. I needed not just to understand that my journey had ended, but I needed to completely comprehend HOW IT HAD ENDED. My thoughts went back to the teddy bear at the hospital in January, and the label saying **'Aurora - Gift of Smiles'**. Then there was Imogen at the retreat pulling me out of the darkness and into the light, my parents' Diamond Wedding Anniversary in March, and my tears where my beloved ruin had once stood. And, finally, the journey to Campana where I had found the light I had spent so many endless years searching for.

But there was also one more detail I had overlooked - the date on which I had boarded the plane in England and flown out to Malaga. It had been February 26. On exactly the same date twelve years earlier I had taken the Eurostar train from London to Paris to fulfil my dream of seeing Alejandro Jodorowsky. I put all these pieces together, and came up with the final picture of this puzzle.

Alejandro had been right with his psychomagical act all those twelve long years ago. Soul rebirth was only possible if I was prepared to face the SHITTY side of myself and life in general - my shadow in other words - and that was exactly what I had done by working in the hospital. Each shift had seen me working intimately with the darkness in life. I had spent most of my hours cleaning excrement off people's bodies, holding bed pans under bottoms and tending to people who were experiencing pain and the disabilities of old age.

Two patients had died on the ward whilst I was there. But, despite all of this darkness, I had also made a very important discovery. Even though I had felt no vocation for the work, I had brought compassion and love to my daily tasks. The teddy bear had been the invisible realm's sign to me to tell me that AURORA had been born one winter's day as I had forced myself to make just that little bit of extra effort to help a patient whilst feeling very ill myself.

The full rebirthing process then ended in the retreat a few weeks later, when Imogen, in her role of shamanic midwife to my soul, had pulled me out of the darkness and into the light. Nevertheless, in spite of all of these events, the journey had required one final stage of me, even though it was true that I had just given birth to my inner light and had reached what I thought was the summit of my personal Everest.

The invisible realm had wanted me to return to where the whole quest had started back in Andalusia because: what I had found at the 'summit' of MY CONSCIOUS MIND I had also needed to find at the 'summit' of MY SUBCONSCIOUS MIND. England was symbolic of the conscious aspect of my soul, and the unconscious aspect was to be found in Andalusia. And so it was that I had climbed the mountain road up to Campana to find this very same light!

As I looked at this final picture I had pieced together, I could only gape in awe at the timing and precision of the invisible realm. How could I have ever imagined finding a physical manifestation of the spiritual light I had unconsciously gone in search of some thirteen years earlier at the top of the very same mountain where this whole odyssey had begun!

If I had ever doubted that I had thrown myself into a cosmic mystery back in 1995, then this uncertainty had been completely eradicated by this astonishing finale to my quest. No greater proof existed; my heart knew this truth.

Love will always make manifest your hidden treasure.

Anon.

20

FEAR OR FAITH (BEING A PILGRIM)

**Amazing Grace, how sweet the sound, that
saved a wretch like me.........**

OLD ENGLISH HYMN

AMAZING! Incredible! I should have been utterly ecstatic with this extraordinary ending to a journey of passionate blind faith and determination, but I wasn't.

I was ill, very ill, and continued to be more or less bedridden for another two months after my return from Andalusia. In those months 'beatings' started to reappear again sporadically, and now I found myself completely baffled and mystified – if not desperate! I knew I had found my inner light both at the retreat with Imogen, and then on the altar step in the church in Campana, and so then why, oh why on earth were these 'beatings' continuing? No answer materialised. Unknown to me, the invisible realm decided that I would have to wait more than another two years in order to understand the motive for all of this.

2008 remained a year of continuing poor health, but in June I summoned up enough strength, from God only knows where, in order to be able to travel to the famous pilgrimage site of Santiago de Compostela in northern Spain. The reason for this sudden NEW MISSION was that I had gone onto the internet in May and received an astonishingly 'cosmic' sign. On Paulo Coelho's website he announced that in June he would be visiting this iconic town. Santiago de Compostela was somewhere I simply couldn't ignore, even though I desperately wanted to.

As a sign, this destination had a very special significance for me on many levels. It had been Paulo's goal in 1986 when he had walked The Camino Frances in search of his enigmatic sword, and it was also one of the places I had travelled to back in 2004 before going to Madrid, and where I had experienced a surprisingly supernatural event. On that first visit almost four years earlier magic had been both metaphorically, and literally IN THE AIR as I had found myself flying from Malaga to Madrid on a plane called LA GUATEMALA.

A few days later, and another flight later, I had stood at the base of one of the huge towers of the cathedral in Santiago de Compostela and realised that I was staring up at the clock tower I had dreamt about seven years earlier. That dream, as you may remember dear friend, took place in GUATEMALA.

However, this time in 2008 my mission in Santiago wasn't 'tourism' but to meet and talk to Paulo Coelho. Stoically, I accepted that there seemed to be just a TEENSY WEENSY little bit left of this journey to complete before I would finally be given my treasure. This new challenge was immense for me, for not only was I unwell, but I was also running out of money. I was fully aware that if I went ahead with this trip I would return to Ambleton more or less penniless. There would only be money for July's rent, and no one to borrow from in August.

Once again, my odyssey seemed to be asking me for an ALL-OR-NOTHING response. Spending money I didn't really have on a flight to Santiago would be either a complete and utter act of madness on my part, or an inspired LEAP OF FAITH. My head would never, but never have sent me on this outwardly 'crazy mission', but my intuition positively screamed a powerful and unequivocal message to me:

DO THIS KAREN, AND YOU WILL BE
REWARDED WITH YOUR TREASURE!

***

TWO PILGRIMS MEET

In the middle of May, a few weeks prior to boarding a flight for northern Spain I decided to hand-write a small book for my 'guru'. The time had come for Paulo to know in as much detail as possible how I believed that his fable The Alchemist had happened to me in real life. But, there was also another motive for my book, one which had magically appeared when I had gone onto Paulo's website. It was yet another truly 'cosmic' sign as I made plans for my next 'adventure'.

On Paulo's site he informed his fans that his visit to Santiago would be in order for a street in the city to be named after him, and in several emails given out by the Santiago Tourist Office the general public was told that the plaque bearing his name would be screwed to a wall in the aforementioned street and be called: **RUA PAULO COELHO – PAULO COELHO ROAD.**

However, as soon as I read this information, little old me suddenly knew something much MORE. This was a SIGN, and a truly enormous one gifted to me from the invisible realm; one which instantly jogged my memory taking me back to 1996. Then, in February of that year Alejandro Jodorowsky had predicted that after my rebirth I would have to go OUT INTO A STREET and find a machine which printed identity cards. By inputting my data into the machine, I would be rewarded with a card showing my new name and new profession. Now, as I processed this latest information in May 2008, I understood instinctively that as far as the interpretation of signs went, dear friend, this wasn't what one might call rocket science.

PAULO COELHO AND KAREN WILIAMS
IN
SANTIAGO DE COMPOSTELA.

The street sign **RUA PAULO COELHO** was quite obviously the symbolic equivalent of the identity card which Alejandro had predicted for me twelve years earlier, and the obvious connection between these two seemingly separate events was that both the identity card and the plaque bearing Paulo's name were to be found OUTSIDE IN A STREET!

But, there was more than this to what was going on. Instinctively I realised that this extraordinary SIGN also pointed to the fact that Alejandro's prediction had applied to Paulo as well.

For a long time I had concluded that I wasn't the only human being living out the story of The Alchemist. My intuition had constantly prompted me with the information that it was more than likely that Paulo Coelho was also engaged in living out the fable he himself had created. This meant that the universe had decided long ago that Paulo and I would meet in Santiago in order to complete our separate journeys of The Alchemist – our individual ROAD OF THE DIAMONDS.

I spent several days analysing this sign, and finally arrived at a firm and decisive interpretation. Although Alejandro had told me that my identity card would show my NEW name and NEW profession, I sensed that this wasn't exactly accurate. All through my years of questing I had been constantly reminded that spiritual rebirth was essentially an INNER PROCESS. Knowing this, I decided that both my identity card and Paulo's Street name would show our old existing names – but they would now be 'clothed' in a NEW LIGHT. However, when it came to our 'old professions' these now truly would be infused with NEW LIGHT.

So it was that I used everything I had learned up until this moment, and made the decision to dare to go 'out on a limb' with an audacious prediction.

Even though I knew that the Santiago Tourist Office had said that Paulo's street would be called RUA PAULO COELHO, Alejandro's prediction had told me that Paulo's 'identity card' would have to include his profession, and so I therefore boldly used my handwritten book to make a 'cosmic' statement of truth. Right at the end of my account of how The Alchemist had happened to me in real life I proclaimed to my 'guru' that his street name would NOT BE:

RUA PAULO COELHO,
but:

RUA PAULO COELHO
PEREGRINO.
In English this translates as:

RUA PAULO COELHO
PILGRIM

Of course, I knew that Paulo had been a writer for many years, but I felt that his true profession – and mine too - had always been that of SPIRITUAL PILGRIM, and so for this reason I made my choice of this term for his street name.

***

Thus it was that on Monday June 23, Paulo and I did meet, right in the very heart of Santiago, only metres away from its famous cathedral. Surrounded by pilgrims ending their epic journeys in the main square, I gifted him my handwritten book together with my cosmic prediction.

Paulo graciously accepted the little book, recognising me from our first encounter in The Hague in 2004. He even invited me to join his group as they headed for Santiago de Compostela's town hall and a meeting with the mayor. About twenty minutes later I found myself standing on a balcony with some of Paulo's group staring at the magnificent cathedral whilst our 'hero' attended to local dignitaries and the press. Buzzing with adrenalin as I was, I could feel my blood sugar levels start to fall and so closed my eyes briefly to remove myself from the hustle and bustle surrounding Santiago's famous guest.

Suddenly, with my attention removed from the visual world around me, my ears began to pick up the strains of a musical instrument being played in the distance. I could hear the most beautiful sound in the world coming from the side of the cathedral where a man stood playing the Galician pipes. The melody was the haunting sound of the English hymn:

AMAZING GRACE.

At that very moment I had absolutely no idea that it was a prophetic message for me from the invisible realm; a message to let me know that my trip to Santiago, and the days after it would quite literally *be showered with that grace*. As my part of that spiritual contract, all I had to do was to continue with faith in my signs

In the afternoon I rested on my bed in a pilgrim hostel and then returned to Paulo's group in order to participate in the inauguration of his street. This was my moment of reckoning; the moment when I would discover whether my 'cosmic prediction' had been right or wrong. Alejandro Jodorowsky's 'identity card' would be the plaque bearing Paulo's name and profession, and would be the definitive proof that both Paulo and I had been engaged in a supernatural journey – the journey of THE ALCHEMIST.

Everything happened very, very quickly. A large group of us arrived at the street as Paulo stood in front of the plaque which was covered by a small velvet curtain. The mayor of Santiago paid a short tribute to our man, and then Paulo pulled a cord to reveal the honour which the city had bestowed upon him The curtain fell away, and there we all were staring at it.

RUA DE PAULO COELHO
ESCRITOR
RUA DE PAULO COELHO
WRITER.

Inside myself I was jubilant. I had been right!!!
There for all the world to see was:

PAULO'S NAME AND PROFESSION.

Yes, of course I instantly understood that I had been wrong in thinking that it would say 'PILGRIM'. That had been little old esoteric me being somewhat pedantic with my absolute truths. Instead it said 'WRITER', but fundamentally Alejandro's prediction made twelve years earlier had been vindicated! For me, this could only signify one thing:

Both Paulo and I seemed to finally be at the true end of
THE ROAD OF THE DIAMONDS.

RUA DE PAULO COELHO ESCRITOR.

Image courtesy of Marcos Leite

Although Paulo's name looked down on all of us from the side of a newly-built family home, in my imagination I saw another plaque HIDDEN BEHIND HIS. On it was written the name:

RUA DE KAREN WILLIAMS
ESCRITORA
(WRITER)

I had brought my hand-written book to Santiago for my 'guru', but it most certainly wasn't the first book I had ever written in my life. In fact I had been writing since the age of fourteen – poems, essays, diaries, reflections and articles - but I had never tried to publish any of them. Now, just as Alejandro Jodorowsky had said, I had my very own 'identity card', albeit an invisible one - and my endless questing had finally come to an end.

***

After this utterly supernatural ending to my quest I stayed in Santiago for another two days, just resting on my hostel bed and befriending the lady sleeping in the bed next to mine in the communal dormitory. Hansje was a feisty, down-to-earth, charismatic Dutch lady in her early sixties.

She told me that one night she had seen a television documentary about the Aids epidemic in South Africa on dutch T.V. and had decided there and then to cycle all the way from Holland to Santiago to raise money for this cause. Her story was beautiful and very moving, and a living testimony to the fact that every single one of us is spiritually powerful in our own individual way. As Hansje shared with me, I too shared some of my personal story of spiritual journeying with her – each of us pilgrims wanting to do something to make our world a more loving place.

On the morning of my departure, this beautiful lady and I said our sad farewell, and as we did so she pressed a small bundle of papers into my hand and wished me luck. When I arrived at a café in the centre of Santiago to buy a tea before boarding the bus to the airport, I unclenched my fist and saw that Hansje had given me a rolled up wad of notes totalling a hundred Euros!!!! Yet again that AMAZING GRACE I had heard as I stood on a balcony of Santiago's Town Hall was accompanying me on this all-or-nothing journey. Although I knew that a hundred Euros wouldn't solve my financial problems, it was more than enough to keep my fear and panic at bay.

However, right there and then what I didn't realize was that this supernatural grace would transform itself into a full-blown miracle; a miracle awaiting me on my return to Ambleton - and all because I had dared to risk everything in going to SANTIAGO DE COMPOSTELA!!!

Nevertheless, temporarily at least, I was crushed by huge disappointment when I found myself back in my tiny room in England and opened up my emails excitedly only to discover that Paulo had emailed me his thanks, but gave me no offer of any meeting between us at a later date. Of course my devastation was trauma-inducing to put it mildly, but by now I had finally come to accept that Paulo occupied a unique position in public life.

As I have already said, his fame has meant that he attracts both fans and foes. Given that I had suddenly popped up from seemingly nowhere, claiming that a book he had written twenty years earlier had predicted my own spiritual quest, was it not entirely probable that in his eyes I could be viewed as a potential 'wolf in sheep's clothing', pretending to be an ally rather than an enemy? Reluctantly I conceded to myself that this was more than likely. However, despite my apparent failure in Santiago, the miracle I had never anticipated manifested for me a few weeks after my return. Astonishingly, I was gifted:

A PROPER HOME, WITH ITS OWN FRONT DOOR!

Less than thirty six hours after flying back to England news of its availability suddenly 'turned up' as if from nowhere, and I knew instinctively that yet again this had been NO COINCIDENCE. J phoned me on the day after my arrival, and excitedly explained how he had met Connie at the Quaker Meeting House's Strawberry Tea. He and I had attended the Quakers two years earlier, and Connie was one of the chief Quakers. She had always had a soft spot for me, and at the tea party she had asked J to tell me with great urgency that a studio apartment had suddenly become available in a block of apartments run by a charity.

Looking at these facts, there seemed to be only one conclusion: the apartment had specifically manifested because I HAD TAKEN MY INNER LIGHT TO SANTIAGO. Whilst in the pilgrim town I had given a completely impromptu speech of thanks to my 'hero' in front of some of his fans. In it I had talked about just how much HOPE his books had given to his readers and:

> this was the light I had brought to Paulo,
> and which he had also gifted to us all with his writing.

Not only that, but I had received one more amazing sign from the invisible realm whilst there. The plaque announcing the road named after Paulo had been attached to the side wall of a *soon-to-be-occupied brand new family home,* and I knew full well that homes were the invisible realm's symbol of the human soul. My question to the universe was then whether or not this empty studio apartment, being also a home, was actually THE MANIFESTATION OF MY TREASURE - The treasure of treasures I had so longed for? The answer came swiftly into my mind – yes it most certainly was.

Naturally, I had always been hoping for something far more rarefied and '*cosmic*' than an apartment – in other words a meeting and collaboration on the writing of a book with Paulo Coelho. But obedience to a Higher Power had been the core discipline throughout my quest, and I wasn't about to let me ego change the rules right now.

At this point I have to say that it never dawned on me at the time that the appearance of the apartment represented the moment when an important physical manifestation of my 'treasure' WAS RETURNED TO ME. The apartment in Salveira, bought for me with the Divine Love of my parents, and which I had 'apparently thrown away' so readily, along with the money acquired from its sale back in 2003, was being RESTORED TO ME! Now it was MANIFESTING once again, but this time in the shape of the studio apartment in Ambleton.

> An almost insane leap of faith based on my own
> personal interpretation of signs had magically and
> serendipitously worked 'cosmic magic' in my life!

On August 1, 2008, I moved into this magnificent accommodation and could comfort myself with the knowledge that my days of renting small rooms in shared houses or being some money-grabbing landlord's tenant had finally come to an end. I was now in the metaphorical arms of a charity which offered cheap rents to people in need, and if this wasn't treasure, then I didn't know what was.

***

However, even though I could now revel in the reality of my own home, 2009 began promising absolutely no change in my journey. 'Beatings' continued from people who were the outer manifestations of the shadow of the **material** half of my soul, and there seemed to be no hint on the horizon of an imminent end.

What I didn't understand at the time was that, even though I had found my inner light in Campana's church in March, and had thus become a CARRIER of spiritual light rather than a SEEKER of it, there were still aspects of my shadow which I had not identified or reckoned with. This meant that in Santiago de Compostela I had brought both light and shadow to my encounter with Paulo Coelho.

I had 'gifted' him a seemingly innocuous little, hand-written book, but that work had in fact been penned by my controlling ego mind – my seemingly indomitable thinking function or shadow. That shadow had been my ego's desperation, and I can assure you dear reader, utter desperation to forge an alliance with my 'guru'. Unadulterated fear lurking in the background, as well as hope, had been at the core of my actions, and so it was more than inevitable that the continuation of 'beatings' was a very clear signal to me that a total VICTORY over my shadow hadn't as yet been 'won'.

That victory would start to manifest in November 2010. However, at the beginning of 2009 I found myself still facing a totally incomprehensible unknown.

21

THE KABBALISTIC TREE OF LIFE

**Look more closely at the ordinary and you will
discover the extraordinary.**

ANON

EVERYTHING started in February 2009 when I came across a sign which sent me off on a last ditch attempt to meet Paulo Coelho once again. This was to be one of the first among many other signs from the universe telling me that there was still JUST A LITTLE MORE TO DO. This sign brought me to London on Monday March 2, and to the inside of the foyer of The Royal Dorchester Hotel, staring at the receptionist standing behind his desk.

It was a minor miracle that I was here at all. A few weeks earlier I had gone onto Paulo's website and seen that he would be attending a money-raising forum in London in aid of third world charitable projects. That sign seemed to have a special message for me. Longing for resolution, I decided that it was the invisible realm telling me that both our journeys were finally coming to an end, and that there was no better place for this to happen than in the city where I had grown up - MY HOMETOWN.

On Friday, February 27 I felt too exhausted and unwell to make the journey to London, and so made the shorter trip to my local post office to send a package to Paulo. In it I had put my worn and dusty shoes and the two stones I had picked up from the floor of *'my ruin'* back at the beginning of March 2008.

For me, the shoes had come to THE END OF THEIR ROAD. I had bought them in the spring of 2003, and they had taken me to many places and many beatings. I hadn't cleaned them in all those years, and they were impregnated with the dust and grime of every 'Egypt' I had reached. The stones were also a symbol of journey's end. I placed them in a small jewellery box I had found in a local charity shop. The lid was decorated with the head of an ancient Egyptian Queen. I felt I couldn't express my message any more clearly or eloquently than with these two objects.

On the morning of Monday March 2, quite inexplicably I felt a window of energy open for me. I was exhausted but I knew I had just enough strength to be able to make the train journey up to London and back. Sensing that this was once again the invisible realm urging me on to fulfil an appointment with destiny, I dressed myself and headed off to the mainline train station. Of course, I knew instinctively that I was once more going to:

a modern symbolic manifestation of the Pyramids of Egypt,
but I was completely unaware
of
JUST HOW RIGHT I WAS.

***

The invisible realm decided to communicate this fact to me in an extremely unlikely place – within the depths of the London Underground system. On my arrival in the capital, I followed the escalators down two deep tunnels in order to get to the platform which would take me to the Park Lane area of the city. As I made my way onto the platform, full of thoughts of a meeting with Paulo Coelho, the figure of a woman suddenly appeared in front of me, and walked very slowly past my line of sight.

The incredible thing was that I recognised her! It was Samia, my Egyptian friend and fellow student, with whom I had studied psychology back in the 80's. I hadn't seen her in the flesh for TWENTY-SEVEN-AND-A HALF YEARS!!! I called out my friend's name, and as luck would have it Samia recognised me too!

Now, dear reader, do you believe in the power of intuition and the manifestation of signs? Samia and her family are the only Egyptians I know, or have ever known, in my entire life, and so the fact that it was she who walked past me is even more miraculous. Yes, I was well and truly 'going to the Pyramids' for what I hoped would be the very last time.

We talked at high speed as adrenalin coursed through each of our bodies. Fate ordained that we would 'coincidentally' both be travelling in the direction of Park Lane, and so we were able to catch up a little on each other's lives in the few minutes during which we occupied the same train compartment. As the train slowed on its approach to my station we quickly exchanged phone numbers, promised to ring each other, and then it was time for me to leave for another connection to Park Lane. But now, let me return to The Royal Dorchester Hotel foyer where I stood looking a little like orphan Annie a mere twenty minutes later.

I moved forward towards the reception desk, wearing the best friendly smile I could possibly muster. I was hoping I would look normal and relaxed, but needless to say, I didn't. The receptionist surveyed me with a trained eye experienced in discriminating between the 'important' and the 'not-so-important' people of this world. I didn't like the look on his face.

I began addressing him by saying that I knew the author Paulo Coelho was staying at the hotel. I also knew this because he was participating in the forum scheduled for the next day. I wondered if the receptionist would be so kind as to ring Mr. Coelho's room because I had sent him a package on the Friday, and wanted to know if he had received it.

"Does Mr. Coelho KNOW YOU" the receptionist asked in that aggressively polite tone that went with his steely stare?

At this point I crumbled, realising full well that I had lost the battle. I could easily have changed gear and launched into a convincing act of how Paulo and I were actually friends, and that there really was NO PROBLEM. I wasn't some kind of groupie or twisted fan, hell-bent on seeing my hero, but I knew that this wasn't the spiritual way of doing things. The subterfuge would have only backfired on me emotionally and nothing good would have come of it.

"Yes, he does," I replied timidly, with deflation and defeat written all over my face. If this had been an arm wrestling contest, this canny receptionist would have won in less than two seconds flat.

"The concierge desk over there will let you know about the package," was his perfunctory reply, and then, turning his attention to some papers he had on the desk, his curt body language signalled that I was dismissed.

The concierge was not so brittle, and after examining his sheet of paper assured me that my package had arrived and that Mr. Coelho had received it. I thanked him as sincerely as I could and asked if I could leave an envelope with him, which I hoped could be forwarded to Paulo. Inside I had placed a candle and a birthday card: - MY SIMPLE SYMBOLS OF SOUL REBIRTH.

A few days later, I received a warm and friendly email from Paulo thanking me for everything he had received, but telling me that I now needed to continue my journey on my own. Once more, the pattern between us repeated itself, and there was no offer of any kind of meeting. The only conclusion I could come to was that it seemed that his nervousness regarding me was still intact. Of course I understood that my somewhat crazy behaviour didn't help, and perhaps being gifted an old pair of shoes only served to confirm his suspicion that I was some unhinged individual obsessed with destroying his reputation.

The invisible realm, however, didn't function in an emotional cauldron as I did, and always knew its cosmic plan for me far better than I. It had signalled that I needed to go up to London, *not to see Paulo,* but to undergo a vital rite of initiation. Taking my inner light to my HOMETOWN signified that I was now embarking on the final stage of my quest, and unknown to me, the penultimate ascent before my final ascent to Everest's summit.

London was part of the first week of what would be twenty-two weeks; twenty-two, symbolising the twenty-two major Arcanas of The Tarot deck, but also coincidentally, and equally significantly, another set of twenty-two I had never even contemplated. About a month before going to London I had made this important discovery. It was called:

The Kabbalistic Tree of Life.

A few weeks after my return from Santiago de Compostela in 2008 I had been emailed some photographs of Paulo and myself by bubbly, vivacious and determined Rosa. She, it was, who had pestered me to have my photograph taken with Paulo before we his fans had all boarded a bus taking us to the new road named in his honour. I subsequently learned that Rosa was not just any old fan, but had created the Paulo Coelho Galician fan club.

One of the photographs she had forwarded to me was intriguing - there seemed to be something supernatural about it, but at the time I couldn't identify what that supernatural element was. Nevertheless, a few weeks before the trip to London, in a flash of insight I HIT ON IT! Paulo and I stood side by side in the picture, and behind us was a tree, its foliage forming a crowning halo around each of our heads. The supernatural aspect was in the shape of that foliage.

As you can see in the photograph, there is a considerable difference in height between myself and Paulo, and yet mysteriously the foliage somehow 'allows' for this 'difference', crowning and following the contours of our heads with a remarkable degree of accuracy. I also then remembered that Paulo had placed a sycamore tree inside the old ruined church in Andalusia where Santiago had had his fateful dream for a second time.

It was under the roots of this tree where the shepherd boy had finally found his longed-for treasure. Suddenly, and without warning, the thought came to me that I was looking at THE KABBALISTIC TREE OF LIFE! This was something I had heard about on my spiritual travels, and which I knew belonged to an esoteric branch of the Judaic faith known as the Kabbalah. I went on the Internet to find out more.

One site described how The Kabbalistic Tree of Life was a model of the path taken by seekers in search of transcendence and God. There were four worlds in the tree, just like Jung's four functions, and ten spheres called sephiroths. But more importantly, these spheres were joined by twenty-two paths. For me it was not a coincidence that the photograph of Paulo and I had been taken in front of a tree.

Could it be that both of us had individually and separately climbed our own 'Kabbalistic Trees of Life' - the journey of The Alchemist - and had met in Santiago de Compostela almost at the end of that journey? I suspected that this might well be the truth, and so printed off a few copies of the photograph and included them in the package I sent to Paulo in London, together with my esoteric hypothesis.

However, in the coming months after my return from London I was to discover that I was only partially correct about the tree in Santiago. Those twenty-two paths of The Kabbalistic Tree of Life had not come to an end in that Spanish pilgrim town eight months earlier as Paulo and I had stood facing Rosa's camera. Oh, no, they awaited me once I had undergone the initiation rite in my beloved 'hometown' – YET MORE OF THIS QUEST LAY AHEAD.

The Kabbalistic Tree of Life, with its twenty-two paths and ten sephiroths.

22

SOUL CONNECTIONS

Connection is the supreme reality of our universe.

ANON

THIS dawning realisation came to me about nine weeks after my journey to The Royal Dorchester Hotel. By then, important insights were flooding into my mind, along with some very subtle 'beatings', and two of these amazing insights concerned the configuration of the human soul. One morning, I was gluing some photographs of myself into my diary when a question which had been lodged within my subconscious mind was answered. The photographs were a set of four - they were passport photographs - and as usual I knew there was no such thing as a COINCIDENCE.

Four identical shots of my head stared up at me from my diary, and suddenly I realised what I was looking at. This was a manifestation of the **material** half of my soul, but I had stupidly ignored a very important part of Jung's theory of psychological functions. I had been working on the basis of the existence of four functions which were neatly subdivided into two pairs - one pair for the **mystical** half of the soul, and the other for the **material** half. However, I had completely overlooked the fact that Jung had postulated that each function manifested itself in an EXTROVERT and also an INTROVERT form.

According to Jung this meant that there were eight different combinations of personality type, depending on which function was dominant in a particular person. For me, I could now see that each human soul had not just four functions, but FOUR TIMES TWO - in other words each function in a duplicate form. This meant that instead of seeing only two functions in each half of the soul, I was actually looking at the two functions expressed in their two identities - introvert and extrovert - and that made four manifestations, just like the photos I had stuck in my diary. **(See fig. 4.)**

Suddenly, I also now understood why there were eight pilgrimage routes to the famous pilgrim town of Santiago de Compostela. If there were eight expressions of Jung's functions in each of our souls, then Santiago was an outer physical manifestation of the archetypal organisation of the human soul. It was in effect a beautiful mandala with its eight roads representing the eight expressions. It wasn't surprising, therefore, that this town had been a place of pilgrimage for more than a thousand years, and that I had found myself there on two separate occasions.

Figure 4

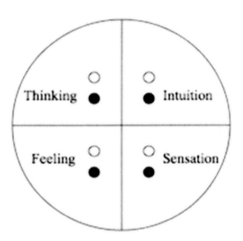

The introvert aspect (●) and extrovert aspect (○) of each of Jung's four functions give rise to eight possible combinations within the human soul.

***

By week ten of my ascent of The Kabbalistic Tree of Life, I realised that these last twenty-two weeks, which I felt corresponded to the twenty two paths of the tree, seemed to divide up into several distinct sections. In week ten I sensed that I was drawing to the end of the first twelve weeks, and ahead of me lay another six weeks, and then three weeks and finally the summit, which would be one week - or week twenty-two. Although I didn't really understand why the journey appeared to divide up so naturally in this way, it clearly gave me a pyramid-shaped ascent to what I concluded would be my final 'beating'.

However, it was the steady climb through week one to week twelve which revealed to me something quite unexpected and awesome. By the time I reached the end of week twelve on my birthday I had discovered that I had unwittingly lived out the reality of the tripartite organisation of my soul.

The amazing insight which came to me was that our souls were a trinity – MIND, BODY AND SPIRT - and each part of the trinity contained the eight expressions of Jung's psychological functions. How did the first twelve weeks of The Kabbalistic Tree of Life show me this? Well, the key was a desperate search for insight and understanding during those weeks, and as always, it was my intuition which gave me the answers. The vital understanding I needed came towards the end of those first twelve weeks.

I knew I was meeting the shadow of the **material** half of the soul each week because of the inevitable 'beatings' I continued to experience. And I also now saw that this half contained four expressions of Jung's thinking and feeling functions - two for each. But, by the end of the twelve weeks I could also see that I had had to go through THREE 'BEATINGS' for each expression - one beating per week over a three week period. This then explained simply and elegantly why the number of weeks of this initial part of the climb came to a total of twelve, (See fig. 5 - three times four is twelve.)

It was at this point of insight when I realised that these three weeks were not just a group of arbitrary weeks, but were in fact symbolic of one overwhelming reality - the trinity structure of the human soul:

Mind, Body and Spirit.

Fig 5.

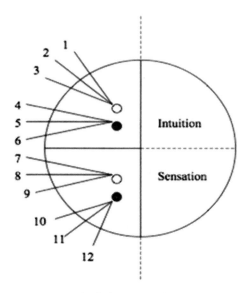

Each function is both
extraverted and introverted,
and each of these also
manifests as a trinity: mind,
body, and spirit.

For me these three 'components' corresponded to the Holy Trinity of my Christian faith: Spirit being Father, Mind being Son, and Body being The Holy Spirit. But, with my transcendental approach to everything, I also hoped that this trinity would be some kind of universal truth which I had somehow 'accidentally' uncovered. In late June my intuitive hunch was rewarded after reading a book called **THE ELEVEN: ELEVEN CODE** by Hilary Carter.

This lady wrote that certain esoteric schools of Yoga taught that there was not one heart chakra, but THREE. Wow, I thought to myself, that's another trinity! So, this 'truth' really is something universal. I had concluded long ago in the first few years of my quest that the soul was located in the heart, but the yogic three heart chakras now suggested something else. These chakras are located slightly to the right of the physical heart, but it doesn't require a massive leap of imagination to suppose that our physical organ is energetically connected to the energy fields of these yogic chakras — hence their names.

After identifying the trinity nature of our human soul through my twelve week ascent of the first part of The Kabbalistic Tree of Life, I immediately began to consider another idea. Was it at all possible that I had been wrong in thinking that the soul was located INSIDE the physical heart? It seemed that the chakras were suggesting that our soul was probably these three energy centres situated slightly to the right of our hearts. I mulled over this change in my hypothesising for quite some time, but never came to any clear conclusion.

However, either way, it was obvious that spiritual traditions separated from one another by centuries and continents all expressed fundamental truths buried deep within humanity's **Soul of the World**.

Once I had completed my twelve week ascent, and gained all the extraordinary insights which had come with it, my spirit lightened considerably. Only another ten weeks lay ahead of my incredible marathon quest, or so I thought, and just another ten more 'beatings' before soul rebirth at the summit of my personal Everest.

Those remaining weeks did divide up as my intuition had foreseen. Firstly, there were six weeks, ending with week eighteen and then another three weeks, ending in week twenty-one. And lastly, but not least, one week, being week twenty-two. My discoveries concerning the trinity nature of the soul didn't expand to this part of the journey, but it was obvious that six and three were both divisible by the number three, and week twenty-two, although being a single week, was possibly what Christian theology meant when it talked about the Holy Trinity also being THREE-IN-ONE.

***

Finally, my ascent of The Kabbalistic Tree of Life drew to a close in spectacular fashion with two completely miraculous and unexpected MANIFESTATIONS.

The first came about in week eighteen of that climb when I woke up one morning groggy and exhausted. After breakfasting and turning on the computer, I walked over to my lounge window to check on the weather, and as I gazed out of the window I saw a man and a woman standing outside looking lost and puzzled. I could see that neither of them was a resident of the block, so I opened the window to ask if they needed any help. "Are you lost?" I called out, trying to sound friendly.

The man replied quickly, saying that they weren't sure if they were in the right place.

"Is this where there used to be a maternity home?" he asked worriedly. I confirmed for him that it was. An old Victorian maternity home for unmarried mothers had been demolished in 1969, and the present block of apartments had been erected in its place. And it was at that very moment when the totally unexpected miracle occurred. "Oh," he said excitedly. "I was born here in 1964, and was then adopted."

BORN HERE!!!

My God, my subconscious mind instantly grasped what was happening. I was talking to the physical manifestation of my own birth – MY SOUL REBIRTH!!! The invisible realm had created yet another one of its synchronistic and miraculous encounters. How would I know for sure if or when my soul had been reborn? "Don't worry," said Mr God, smiling down on me with indulgent compassion, and knowing full well that I was in a complete and utter state of confusion: "I'll send along someone to TELL YOU. No problem!!!"

The second extraordinary manifestation came speedily on the heels of the first - the following week - in week nineteen. Since the trip to Santiago I had been corresponding with a young woman from Madeira who had been part of Paulo's group of fans.

Marisela was a joy. Brave and very sensitive, in June, a year after we had met in that iconic pilgrimage town, she emailed me to ask if I could meet her in London because she was coming to England on a short holiday. I emailed back to say that it wouldn't be possible because I was still suffering from extreme fatigue and exhaustion, but inexplicably in the email I casually mentioned that I lived in a seaside town on the south coast called Ambleton.

She replied to my email almost immediately to say that an amazing 'coincidence' was that she would be spending a few days staying with a friend in Ambleton, and so she would be able to see me anyway! There seemed to be some kind of steely determination on her part willing us to be able to see each other again. And so on July 2, my phone rang and it was Marisela. She wanted us to meet up for a coffee and chat.

"Where exactly in Ambleton are you?" I asked anxiously, because health-wise I wasn't in any shape to get on buses and travel to an outlying suburb of this large and sprawling town. Marisela gave me the name of the suburb where she was staying, and the 'coincidence' became even more extraordinary when it happened to be the very same suburb in which I lived. *She was quite literally a ten-minute walk away!*

I met Marisela and her friend Mariana at a local café, and we sat down, ordered our coffees, and began to go over the incredible way in which fate had brought her to my doorstep after an equally fateful but completely unplanned meeting in Santiago. It turned out that Marisela had been invited to a party in Paris a few months earlier in March by Paulo Coelho. It was a celebration Paulo organised every year to mark St. Joseph's day.

Mariana, who lived in the very same suburb of Ambleton as I, had 'coincidentally' gone onto Paulo's website and managed to secure a ticket for exactly the same event, and so the two of them had then met in the foyer of the hotel where they were staying in The City of Light. The meeting between them was made even easier because both were Portuguese speaking - Mariana was Brazilian and Marisela was from the Portuguese island of Madeira.

Meeting this young woman in Santiago de Compostela, and then the subsequent series of fateful 'coincidences' which had brought Marisela to a café in a busy street in Ambleton, minutes away from my apartment just a year later, was one of the most miraculous aspects of my entire odyssey.

Marisela offered me a gift from herself and Mariana to cheer me up and bolster my faith. It was a green candle of hope which they had placed in a decorative bag containing a get-well card for me. After an hour or so in the café, we all agreed that we would meet up again before Marisela was due to return to Madeira, and so I walked back to my apartment in a total daze — the invisible realm yet again produced its miraculous 'coincidences', and even after so many years of questing, I still didn't understand how they happened.

Once at home I put down the bag containing the candle, and pulled out the card from inside it. I read Marisela and Mariana's heartfelt wishes for a recovery in my health, and then I removed the candle and placed it on my bookshelf. After I had done this, I walked into my kitchen and was just about to consign the bag to the rubbish bin, when suddenly I stopped myself. My friend had gone to a lot of effort to present the candle to me in an attractive and eye-catching manner, and throwing the bag out without a second thought would have been a total act of ingratitude on my part. I picked up the bag and examined it.

There was a flower-shaped tag attached to one of the handles, obviously designed for writing messages to the recipient of the gift. I looked more closely at the tag and saw that neither Marisela nor Mariana had written anything for me. A little disappointed, I turned it over to appreciate the flower motif on the decorated side and that was a moment I shall never forget as long as I live.

My eyes nearly popped straight out of my head and my heart seemed to miss several beats as I took in what I saw before me. Right in the centre of the flower was something bright and hard, reflecting light. It was a perfectly formed little jewel. Astonishingly, it was A SMALL WHITE PLASTIC DIAMOND!!!

23

THE AGE OF SPIRIT

**Someday, after mastering the winds, the waves,
the tides and gravity,
we shall harness for God the energies of Love,
and then for a second time in the history of the
world, man will have discovered fire.**

PIERRE TEILHARD DE CHARDIN

YES, DEAR FRIEND, I KNOW IT WAS PLASTIC, BUT THAT WASN'T THE POINT!

IT was the invisible realm's language —the language of signs, the language of manifestations, AND THE LANGUAGE OF LOVE. Much like the man and woman who had appeared outside my window in search of an old maternity home, Marisela and Mariana had been divinely chosen messengers for me.

But the invisible realm always established a reciprocal relationship, and so I too had been a messenger for them. We were the opposite halves of each other's souls meeting in the dance of love, as our spirits subconsciously pushed us ever closer to the divine light within ourselves.

Naturally, my next assumption was that the invisible realm had chosen these two angels in order to tell me that I had completed THE ROAD OF THE DIAMONDS - or Redemption Road as I prefer to call it. On seeing the diamond that day I felt that nothing could be a more obvious message to me than this 'sign' to tell me that my odyssey was now well and truly over. However, was it? "Oh, no," I can hear you groan, dear reader, "I can't believe she is forcing me to read MORE! Why on earth did I ever decide to read this book in the first place?"

My heart-felt apologies dear friend – I fully understand how you feel - but as usual, nothing on this path was as straight forward as it seemed. Reality would again step in much sooner than I could have anticipated in order to demonstrate to me that once again I was premature in assuming that my quest had come to an end. But let us leave that for another chapter.

***

After the meeting with Marisela, another three weeks of 'beatings' followed, and yes finally I felt that I had reached the top of my personal spiritual Everest. The very last week involved not one but two final 'beatings', and their severity could be measured by the symbolic 'blood' they drew as they challenged me at the deepest possible level of my spirit.

The last 'beating' graphically illustrated this in that I was sternly urged, 'advised', or rather 'ordered' NOT TO WRITE THIS BOOK by a particular person. That encounter shook me to my very core. The full weight of the shadow of the **material** half of my soul came down on me from outside, and did its utmost to extinguish the divine light of truth and love within me. Nevertheless, despite this 'seismic blow', I managed to survive.

After all the drama of a fourteen-and-a-half year odyssey, what I took to be the last day of my epic journey seemed to end in a paradoxically serene and somewhat inconsequential way. It was Tuesday, July 28, and a few days earlier I had received a publicity flyer in the post from a company called EVEREST Ltd. Everest specialised in the installation of windows and the construction of glass conservatories. This was a company I remembered from my childhood days, however forty years on it had greatly expanded in size and scale.

My soul mate J had been living in new accommodation for the last eight months, but given the age of the building he was in, most of the windows now needed replacing, so I could think of no better way to mark the end of this enormous odyssey than by sending my OTHER HALF this sign regarding journey's end. That Tuesday afternoon I placed the Everest flyer in an envelope with a note for J, and walked the short distance from my apartment to the post box near the top of the hill where I lived.

I reached the box in a few minutes and surveyed the scene. It stood at a crossroads which neatly divided the surroundings into four segments. I couldn't help but be reminded of Jung's four functions of the soul as I looked out onto the intersecting roads. I took the letter out of my bag and slowly allowed myself to become fully aware of the moment. I was yet again in the role of messenger: Windows - light, Everest - mountain top. The signs were all magically there.

I dropped the envelope into the box, now completely convinced that I had reached the end of my extraordinary quest. Just like all climbers at the top of their mountains, I was planting a flag, but this paper missive wasn't a literal flag I had brought to this spot but a symbolic one. It was the 'flag' each of us carries to every one of our most cherished goals. It was a metaphorical tricolour symbolising the spirit of HOPE, FAITH AND LOVE - the transcendental trinity of our souls.

What else would make us willing to suffer and endure so many tests and trials along life's way?

'So that's it' I hear you dear reader sigh, 'after fourteen-and-a-half years, we now know what The Alchemist is all about!!!

'It is a journey of soul rebirth, which takes us up a huge metaphorical pyramid in search of the divine light of our spirits - the divine light of love.

'We find it, and are reborn only when we are willing to submit ourselves to a conscious confrontation with our own darkness.'

Through experiencing and bringing into consciousness — redeeming - what is dark inside ourselves, we find what is truly light'.

Yes, that's more or less it in a nutshell, except that what I thought were fourteen-and-a-half years of journeying would in fact turn into just over nineteen years. Standing by the post box that Tuesday July 28, 2009 I had absolutely no idea that the journey was very far from over. In Part III and BOOK III I will cover the very last unforeseen and unimagined 'curved balls' which this quest threw my way, and I will also analyse what else they revealed to me about this archetypal odyssey to which we all belong.

However, for now I wish to use this chapter in order to digress because I need to describe the most astonishing realisation which came to me just a few weeks after that memorable short walk to my local post box. It happened quite unexpectedly as I began the writing of the first edition of TREASURE in August 2009.

***

Everything started with an innocent search on the Internet for more information about The Kabbalistic Tree of Life, but before I knew where I was, I found myself in the Garden of Eden of the biblical Book of Genesis, reading about Adam and Eve and the two most famous trees in that garden. They were of course the Tree of the Knowledge of Good and Evil, and the Tree of Life. It was the first of the two that brought me my truly cosmic flash of insight and understanding.

As most of us know, these were the two trees prized above all the others in the biblical garden, but only one from which God had forbidden Adam and Eve to eat. They could have their fill of all the trees in Eden, including the Tree of Life, but could not eat from:

THE TREE OF THE KNOWLEDGE OF GOOD AND EVIL.

History was written when the serpent tempted Eve, and then Eve tempted Adam, and they both ate from this infamous tree. From that moment on this archetypal man and archetypal woman lost their direct connection with God, and were banished from the garden forever. Exiled from paradise, they were forced to endure all the sorrows and pain of mortal life — in other words the trials and agonies of being human. As I read about this tree, suddenly so many pieces of an unfinished jigsaw puzzle came together to give me an extraordinary insight. Suddenly I became aware of what was happening to all of us at the beginning of our twenty-first century.

For the last few years I had been reading different commentaries in books and newspapers concerning the imminent dawning of the so-called AGE OF AQUARIUS. This was to be a new age for Mankind which would herald a change in consciousness worldwide, and bring about a move towards peace, wisdom and greater love. Signs abounded everywhere indicating that Humanity was in desperate need of a NEW DAWN. The ecological crises all around our planet and global warming were only some of many portents pointing to an urgent need for change.

More and more people were connecting with an awareness that the industrial age, which has been the powerhouse of our modern era, was becoming totally unsustainable, both physically and morally. There was also talk in more esoteric circles concerning the supposed 'end' of the Mayan calendar in 2012. The pre-Columbian Maya Indians of Mesoamerica elaborated a system of time-tracking dating back to the sixth century B.C., and there were commentators claiming that it would finally come to an end on December 21, 2012.

Some individuals were apocalyptic in their interpretation of the Mayan calendar, feeling it would mark the demise of our physical world, but others were suggesting that it was somehow linked to the end of what astrologers called a two-thousand-year PISCEAN AGE and the dawning of the new two-thousand-year AGE OF AQUARIUS.

So, what does the Tree of the Knowledge of Good and Evil have to do with all of this?
My insight back in August 2009 was the following.

From the time its fruit was eaten by Adam and Eve, this infamous tree has defined Mankind. Even though the Genesis story is a religious myth, it is also an incredibly prescient and accurate one. It is the story of man's fall from grace and the beginning of sin, but what it really tells us is how our species became prisoner of something we call THE HUMAN CONDTION.

I mentioned the human condition earlier in this book in Chapter 8, but never explained what I meant by it. For me the human condition refers to the fact that man lost his direct UNCONSCIOUS CONNECTION with the divine and became conscious.

By eating the fruit of this tree, a choice was made to leave behind that unconscious relationship with God, and instead live and seek out the divine indirectly through knowledge. This was the new route of consciousness, and in taking it the human species evolved - but at a price. The price paid was that from the moment of Man's so-called 'fall' the left hemisphere of the brain became dominant over the right. Thinking would now rule over intuition; rationality over divine knowing, and thus THE HUMAN CONDITION WAS BORN.

To me it seems very obvious that consciousness was the inevitable next step on the ladder of evolution for Mankind, and so I don't consider that the eating from the tree of that consciousness was an act of pure rebellion by Adam and Eve. That is the conventional religious view of the Genesis myth, but I certainly don't believe it is the true SPIRITUAL meaning of the story.

Over many thousands of years both conscious halves of our brains would make incredible contributions to the development of our species, but as I have just said, it would always be the **material**, thinking left hemisphere — the knowledge-seeking part of us - which would seek to dominate or try to be 'in control'. So, dear friend, I believe I am beginning to make it clear as to where I am going with all of this — the dots are starting to join up.

The Alchemist is, as I have already stated, the story of these two halves of the human mind and soul. However, it is a story which concentrates almost exclusively on the **mystical** half of the soul — Santiago — and what happens to him BEFORE he reaches redemption. In other words in The Alchemist, the **mystical** half of the human soul is 'trapped' within the human condition. Although Paulo concentrates on Santiago, as I have already revealed, the 'beating' he receives from Anwar — the leader of the refugees — is the moment when both halves of the soul confront their shared shadow.

It is this confrontation which allows for redemption to occur, and because the fable is a universal allegory of transcendence, the consequence of this is that both Santiago AND Anwar experience the demise of the human condition within themselves.

The Lumen Dei present within the **mystical** half of the soul alerts Santiago to his ego-driven folly, and provides the route to redemption for both himself and Anwar. The consequence of this metaphysical encounter between the two men is the restoration of divine order within the soul. By this I mean that the Tree of the Knowledge of Good and Evil is defeated or 'destroyed', and the human soul is now able to return to a DIRECT RELATIONSHIP with the divine:

A RELATIONSHIP WHICH WAS UNCONSCIOUS
IN THE ORIGINAL GARDEN OF EDEN,

BUT IS NOW CONSCIOUS IN OUR MODERN WORLD.

However, let me set aside all of this for one moment, and go back to what I realised Mankind had created over a period of more than two thousand years as He made his ascent of the infamous Eden tree.

***

The downside of Mankind's search for God through knowledge has been that our species has created as much evil along the way as it has good; hence the name of the tree.

We have discovered every single piece of landmass on the planet, and every single ocean, but in the process we have massacred and destroyed countless indigenous tribes, and species of animals and plants. We have learned to fly, discovered penicillin, created antibiotics, laser surgery, x-ray machines, and found cures for many terrible diseases, but we have also built nuclear bombs, invented missiles that can travel down streets and turn corners, and unleashed germ warfare on innocent people all in the name of 'freedom'.

The **material** half of our souls is both light and shadow, and the shadow has perversely always wanted to be in charge. So, how does this connect with the AGE OF AQUARIUS and the story of Mankind's search for Redemption which I have shown to be the fable known worldwide as The Alchemist?

Well, we are now at the end of an evolutionary era. We are at the end of the Age of Pisces, and also simultaneously at the end of the Tree of the Knowledge of Good and Evil. Metaphorically, Man has eaten almost all of its fruits, and is now ready to move into the next evolutionary stage. Some say this is the much talked about AGE OF AQUARIUS, and that may be true. But for me it is what I like to call the *Age of Spirit*. As I have already hinted, in order for this age to begin the Tree of the Knowledge of Good and Evil must die.

By this I mean that the human condition needs to undergo a transformation, and for this to happen, the dominance of the thinking function of the **material** half of our collective soul must come to an end - just as it did at the very end of Paulo Coelho's The Alchemist. Mankind is poised on the edge of an internal evolutionary shift where the left hemisphere of the brain, which has tried to control us all for millennia, will now lose its dominance, and it is the right hemisphere, or the **mystical** half of the soul which will take over that role.

Intuition will no longer be the subservient function in the oppressive grip of rationality. Instead, these two will change places, and the thinking function will become aid and helper to wise, loving and peaceful intuition. So dear friend, if you have come to trust me through what you have read up until now, you may JUST be willing to 'buy into' my hypothesising, but you may also be wondering why am I so certain of everything I am saying here? Well, the simple answer to that question is TIMING.

The ends of eras always bring forth certain iconic works which help us to understand the greater spiritual forces shaping our lives at that particular moment in time. These can be scientific discoveries, works of art, mass consciousness movements, music, political change, and, yes – BOOKS!

The Alchemist has been that iconic book revealing
to all of us where we stand right now.

The very end of the era of the Tree of the Knowledge of Good and Evil has been taking place over the last fifty years. As humanity has found itself reaching the summit of this tree, it is therefore no great surprise that Paulo's book emerged, and in the language of symbols faithfully mirrored the process by which we have all been making that ascent.

This apparently simple allegory about a search for treasure is the path we as a species have been treading in order to ascend to the top of the Tree of the Knowledge of Good and Evil. Paulo's account of a shepherd boy's unconscious journey in search of redemption is the story of the last two thousand years of all of us – the now dying AGE OF PISCES.

As I have just outlined, we have lived for slightly over two millennia with the 'apparent' dominance of the thinking function of the collective human soul. Humanity's shadow has APPEARED TO BE KING, and over the course of countless centuries the process of redemption has had millions of Santiagos willing to journey to the **material** half of the collective soul.

These individuals, like the protagonist of The Alchemist, have been prepared to endure a 'beating' from the shadow of the **material** half of the human condition in order to bring us collectively into the light of divine consciousness – THE LIGHT OF LOVE. This has been the archetypal pattern Humanity has been wedded to for more than two thousand years as it has endeavoured to realise **THE BIG DREAM** written into its spiritual DNA.

Some of these 'beatings' have led to martyrdom and death for the carriers of the **mystical** half of our souls because the truth is that real life, unlike fables and fairy-tales, can be brutal, cruel and painful in the extreme.

***

Probably the most famous of all the REDEEMING MYSTICS in history has been the figure of Jesus Christ. In a sense, with his martyrdom on a cross the invisible spiritual realm had decided that He would be the agent to usher in the so-called PISCEAN AGE, which for me has been the Age of Redemption. He was the precursor to all those heroic individuals – the millions of Santiagos - who later willingly took the worst of the 'beatings' assigned to us as a human race as we went in search of the light of our spirits.

> The collective unconscious of our species has been defined
> and driven by this redemptive imperative ever since
> this Man/God obeyed his own Personal Legend.

My book is not about establishing whether or not Christ was or wasn't the actual Son of God, and I say that very deliberately dear reader. It is important every once in a while to shake things up a bit because we humans just love to waste time arguing over beliefs. Our egos, typically wishing to control life, attach far more importance to WHAT we believe rather than to WHO we are. And if ever there was a mystic who wanted to change all of that, then it was Christ.

But, in the final analysis, our modern world is now full enough as it is with religious fundamentalism from all the main monotheistic religious faiths. Each fights to convince us that they alone are the 'true way', but seen from the vantage point of the end of a spiritual evolutionary age, it becomes obvious that this fundamentalism is also a direct consequence of the negative aspects of the Tree of the Knowledge of Good and Evil.

> It is Christ's ACTIONS that count on the metaphysical plane,
> and not what we decide to call Him with our limited,
> rational human minds.

His ushering in of redemption two thousand years ago as the next route for the spiritual evolution of Mankind has meant that we have all been living out the story of THE ALCHEMIST. Every single person on the planet, whether Jew, Gentile, Muslim, Christian, Seik, Hindu, Zoroastrian, Agnostic, Atheist and all others has been living inside the current of a mighty metaphorical river, moving inexorably year by year, and century by century in the direction of redemption.

Some of us have made this journey as Santiago, and others have found themselves assigned the role of Anwars - the leader of the refugees. Some of us have made conscious journeys, and others unconscious ones, but ALL OF US, without exception, have kept divine appointments with the other halves of our souls in order to bring about redemption and soul rebirth for the human race. Is it any wonder, therefore, that Paulo's book became a worldwide phenomenon, selling more than 65 million copies all around the globe?

That was the collective 'nerve' he touched in each of us, and which he wondered about in his interview with THE METRO newspaper back in 2012.

***

ARCHETYPAL PYRAMIDS

As I stated in the preface to this new edition of TREASURE, and have reiterated here, the archetype of redemption which is at the heart of Paulo Coelho's fable is part of the spiritual DNA of each and every one of us. The universe's **BIG DREAM** of Divine Love for humanity has been calling each and every one of us to her, and we now stand on the threshold of being able to make that **BIG DREAM** a reality.

A graphic illustration of what I am saying here had actually turned up in my life six years earlier, well before I had managed to piece together this metaphysical agenda for our species. It was 2003, and I remember Alberto faxing me a short story he had written. Unfortunately, I have lost the fax, but I do remember the gist of this wonderful tale. In it Alberto told the story of a society of beings who lived on the bottom of a lake.

They were content enough in this environment, but knew that each time they looked upwards they could see light dancing on the surface of the water above them. This light was intriguing and mysterious, and it wasn't long before they knew collectively that they had to find out what it was. Thus began years of these beings constructing a giant pyramid with their own bodies in order that they would be able to reach the surface of the water of the lake.

One by one, all of the pyramids collapsed, but each time this happened, they became more knowledgeable about how to stand on each other's shoulders, and how many individuals they needed on each level. Finally, the time came when they managed to form a pyramid which almost broke through the surface of the water, and at this point they all realised that they needed just one more individual to climb to the very top of the pyramid, and finally pass through into the mysterious light.

After so many years of making pyramids, in order to ensure guaranteed success they chose the lightest youngster amongst their community. Their wisdom paid off and one glorious day this youngster climbed up through all the levels of the pyramid made up of his fellow beings. He reached its summit, and broke through the water to experience the light of the NEW WORLD for the very first time.

When Alberto penned this tale, which I know sprung directly from the deepest part of his subconscious mind, he had no idea that he had inadvertently given me a gift of one of the most important pieces of the puzzle I was working on. But, it was only six years later, as I made my search on the internet for information about The Kabbalistic Tree of Life, that his visual metaphor suddenly came alive.

I suddenly realised that back in 2003, he had unknowingly told me the story of ALL OF US - the journey we have all been making for more than two thousand years. This was The Pyramid of Redemption. However, it is only now, at the beginning of the third millennium A. D. that collectively we have been able to find not just one, but many 'youngsters' amongst us, 'LIGHT ENOUGH' to make the final ascent and metaphorically 'break through' into the light.

One of those 'youngsters' in Alberto's tale is me but obviously I need to qualify this statement. I would never be so arrogant and smug as to assert that I am THE YOUNGSTER of Alberto's fable. I know instinctively that this end-of-an-era is throwing up many individuals who are now finding themselves breaking through into the light of Spirit. More importantly, what I have been trying to show here is that, if the new Age of Spirit is dawning, it is because ALL OF US, CONSCIOUSLY OR SUBCONSCIOUSLY, have been striving to create Alberto's Pyramid of Redemption. We have stood on each other's shoulders, and the wonderful news is that we have done it:

WE HAVE FOUND THE LIGHT!!!

Later in this book I will go on with my exposition of how I see each of us entering the new *Age of Spirit,* however before I do so I will continue with my account of the last years of this odyssey in the upcoming Part III, and BOOK III sections of TREASURE.

***

However, just before we move forward, I need to digress slightly and cover one or two details which I have avoided clarifying. The first concerns the nature of the **mystical** half of the soul.

At no time in the telling of my tale have I mentioned whether or not this half of the soul has its own shadow. Till now I have only spoken of the **mystical** half as being the part of us in search of an encounter with the shadow of our **material** halves. But, as one might expect, the **mystical** half of the soul also has a shadow.

Because the two halves of the soul exist within the incarnation of a physical body, the shadow is an inevitable part of that physicality. However, there is a fundamental difference between the shadows of the two different halves of the soul. The **material** half of us oscillates constantly between its own light and shadow, and it is the shadow that ends up trying to predominate in almost all situations. On the other hand, the **mystical** half is not controlled by its shadow. Intuition dominates, and the shadow spends most of its time relegated to the position of passenger in the metaphorical car of this half of the soul. It was this 'car' I discovered inside me in Chapter 8.

Because of the qualitatively different relationship that **mystical** Santiago in The Alchemist has with his shadow in this half of his soul, he is able to access his LUMEN DEI, and so bring Divine Light to himself and also to the leader of the refugees when they meet on a dune overlooking the Pyramids of Egypt. It allows the shepherd boy to undergo his epiphany, his 'aha moment', and thus free himself of the 'prison' the **material** half of his soul is determined to create for him.

The second issue which I have somewhat *'glossed over'* in my book is the subject of trees. In Chapter 21 I talked about the last twenty-two weeks of my journey being a climb up through The Kabbalistic

Tree of Life, and now I am introducing the Tree of the Knowledge of Good and Evil, and also the Tree of Life, so which of these trees are we really dealing with here?

Many scholars suggest that the Tree of Life is also The Kabbalistic Tree of Life. As I have already said, in London I began a twenty-two week climb up through what I believed to be the Kabbalistic Tree of Life. Is it therefore at all possible that when Man, instead of eating directly from the Tree of Life, chose to break the divine rules by becoming enmeshed in the fruits of the Tree of the Knowledge of Good and Evil, He was then forced into a more difficult and complex relationship with Eden's Tree of Life?

Could this then have meant that this tree would become the Kabbalistic Tree of Life?

If this were the case, was humanity now obliged to metaphorically **'climb'** up it in order to evolve?

Another idea that comes to me is that it may be that the structure of The Kabbalistic Tree of Life is actually that of the Tree of the Knowledge of Good and Evil, but no one has ever thought of it in that way - not even the Kabbalists. I hope you can see that hypothesising, even though it may not provide a definite answer, can be fun! Nevertheless, regardless of where the truth really lies, and despite all these seemingly unanswerable questions, for me THE BIG PICTURE of humanity's spiritual search for rebirth and transcendence is the best model I can come up with.

*****

For me, I believe that we have spent the last two thousand years eating the last fruits of the Tree of the Knowledge of Good and Evil, and working on redeeming its shadow so that we can come into a much closer relationship with the divine - with our own spirits. This means, as I stated earlier, that we are now once more poised to be in a direct relationship with God, and hence once again in a direct relationship with the Tree of Life.

However, what I came to understand several years after all these insights had flooded into my consciousness back in 2009, was that this wonderful return to Eden WOULD NOT SUDDENLY HAPPEN to the human race at the end of 2012 - and more specifically on December 21, 2012 as so many 'experts' had predicted.

Just as redemption hadn't been instantaneous when Christ died on the cross two thousand years earlier, but had involved a laborious, incremental journey up through a metaphorical pyramid, then the new *Age of Spirit* would also take time, and be a step-by-step change in humanity's consciousness. However, now as I look back on 2012 with the benefit of hindsight, I can see very clearly *what was happening* to each of us at the end of that 'cosmic 'year'.

An inner metaphysical QUANTUM LEAP took place for the whole of Humanity, and that 'leap' was the activation within each human soul of the invisible energy of Spirit. Like the youngster who reached the top of Alberto's PYRAMID OF REDEMPTION, from the end of 2012 we have begun to 'break through' into the light of our Spirit. Or to put another way, we now stand at the historical moment of:

OUR COSMIC INITIATION INTO
THE
NEW AGE OF SPIRIT.

However, how long we will have to wait before there are real discernable changes in our collective soul is a question I cannot answer. With war still raging in Iraq and Syria, and I.S. still wreaking devastation in the lives of people around the world – all manifestations of the very pinnacle of our Pyramid of Redemption or the top of the Tree of the Knowledge of Good and Evil – I suspect that it may well be several decades before humanity's inner light starts to manifest as a substantive flame within our global consciousness.

Nevertheless, CONSCIOUSNESS and the wisdom it brings, is ABSOLUTELY EVERYTHING in our global 'battles' with our own *universal shadow*. And despite this somewhat pessimistic, but probably more than realistic view of our future a NEW DAWN for humanity truly has begun!

PART III: THE SUMMIT

There will come a time when you
believe that everything is finished.
That will be the beginning.

Louis L'Amour

24

TWISTS AND TURNS

Pure logic is the ruin of the spirit

ANTOINE DE ST EXUPERY

AT the beginning of August 2009 I was more than ready to begin writing my book. Certain that my quest was at last over, I opened up my Word document and typed the first sentence onto its page. However, over the coming weeks, as the writing progressed, it became clear to me *all over again* that I had been wrong in thinking that my epic had finally come to a close.

Almost immediately the creation of the book started to reveal itself as being part of yet more encounters with the shadow of the **material** half of my soul, and the inevitable 'beatings' which came with them. Only, this time, I was now no longer having to journey to people and places which were the external manifestations of the **material** half of me. Instead, everything was happening INSIDE ME. Santiago and the leader of the refugees – the physical personifications of the two halves of my soul - were finding themselves directly face-to-face with each other within the inner sanctum of my soul.

Day in and day out, the text on the computer screen became a faithful OUTER MANIFESTATION of the results of the umpteen INNER ENCOUNTERS between these two halves of me.

The journey had quite clearly entered a completely new phase.

Of course, this inner 'leader of the refugees' was my controlling thinking function – or in other words my individual, personal Anwar or inner Beast. Throughout the writing of TREASURE it 'beat' me mercilessly by administering various types of mental torture. These took the form of an obsessive perfectionism over the book, a complete inability to switch off my thoughts, both day and night, and finally an indescribable mental tension and fear concerning the quality of what I had written. But despite all of this, I was eventually able to free the spiritual light – Paracelsus' Lumen Naturae - 'imprisoned' in the **material** half of me as it offered up its inner light after each 'beating'. This came in the form of the book's chapters, and after months of insomnia, exhaustion, high anxiety, and stress-induced physical pains and malaises – all symptoms of my 'beatings'- the book was finally done!

***

During those pain-filled months of writing, I had constantly faced one continuous and intractable dilemma: because 'beatings' were still manifesting for me, when could I say that this journey had truly ended, and what would I tell you the reader?

The foundation stone of my testimony had been complete honesty, and I knew that without this my story would lack all credibility. Fortunately, as I submitted my manuscript to the publisher on December 21, 2009, I was rewarded with a final insight which resolved my dilemma, and soothed my troubled conscience. The insight was that the quest had been exactly like my wooden Russian doll – my Matroyshka. That doll was a perfect metaphor for this odyssey. It had been a gift to me from my Russian grandmother, and as a child when I used to open the large outermost doll, there would be another identical, but smaller doll inside.

Repeating this action once again with the second doll meant that another doll would emerge, until finally, after five or six of these 'openings', the tiny, innermost doll would make her appearance. For me, it was obvious that the journey had followed this very same pattern.

It had constantly supplied me with numerous APPARENT ENDINGS, all of which had been soul rebirths in their own right, and each rebirth had in fact signified an important staging post along the way. Of course, some had been more significant than others, and represented real quantum leaps into a new phase of the odyssey, but now with this latest insight, the writing process seemed completely intelligible and consistent with everything that had gone on before.

It appeared to me to have heralded the very final 'opening' - or rebirth – of the last tiny little doll of my quest, and with this seemingly logical conclusion a quiet sense of satisfaction came over me. Relieved, and far less stressed, I happily dispatched my manuscript to the publisher and breathed deeply and freely for the first time in a very long while.

But, nearly ten months later on October 15, 2010 my sigh was not one of relief from my turmoil, but one of pure exhaustion and pain. I sat at my desk with my head in my hands and glanced up at the picture on the wall in front of me. It was a photograph of the Great Pyramids of Giza in Egypt. A month earlier J had found the picture propped up against a rubbish bin outside in the street, just a few yards away from the letter box I had used to post him the flyer in July 2009. He knew it was a sign, and had delivered it to my door.

Nevertheless, despite the unexpected appearance of these iconic pyramids, I was still receiving beatings almost a year after completing the writing of TREASURE, and that afternoon of October 15 I had endured a particularly subtle and painful one. To all intents and purposes, it was so bad that my mind could only assume that it was the very last of my trials. Gazing up at the pyramids, standing majestically in the desert sands, seemed to confirm my intuition. But, yet again, if I had thought that these ancient stone 'mountains' were the definitive sign of journey's end, then I was very much mistaken.

Much, much more of this odyssey lay ahead of me. On that autumn day in 2010, slumped over my desk and barely able to raise my head, my overwhelming concern and priority was not WHEN my questing had ended, but the fact that my mind, body and spirit were in a state far beyond what one could call exhaustion. I was in desperate – *and I mean absolutely desperate* - need of rest and respite, but where on earth was it going to come from? Stuck in my apartment, with no money and no help, my bed was my only refuge in all of this.

Briefly, a thought flashed through my mind that falling into a temporary coma might be a solution to my feelings of total collapse, but as usual the invisible realm was 'on my case' and would surprise me, as only it knew how. Spirit hadn't finished with me by any means.

25

LOSING CONTROL

**Step 1: We admitted we were powerless over......,
that our lives had become unmanageable.**

THE 12-STEP PROGRAMME FOR RECOVERY

AS ever, those plans were surprising and quite simply completely unpredictable. October 2010 saw me filling in an application form to secure two weeks of charitably-funded convalescence in a Christian retreat. J had been given information about Willow Lodge by a friend at the beginning of the month, and he had felt that it might be exactly what I needed.

On the day I travelled to the retreat in the first week of November I was still convinced that my odyssey had come to an end. I was sure that the lodge would be the place where my soul would begin the recovery process after so many years of cosmic 'beatings'. However, as my train arrived at Waterloo Station in London, the universe surprised me with a huge sign regarding a completely different agenda.

I was due to catch a connecting train from Waterloo which would take me to the nearest town to Willow Lodge, but as I stepped out onto the platform on my arrival, and slowly walked towards the exit gates, I raised my head and found myself looking at the most dramatic and astonishing image. This was probably the largest physical sign I have ever received in my life. Straddling two platforms, and hanging above the exit barriers was a huge advertisement for holidays in Egypt!

It was a photograph of the ruins in Luxor. At one corner of the billboard a young woman was gazing in wonder at the ruins, and right in the centre of the image were the following words:

"The stones spoke to me"
EGYPT
where it all begins.

I stood stock still on the station platform, completely dumbfounded, and just stared and stared at the image and these words. It was as if this sign were shouting at me - laughing and winking with amusement - that I had not even anticipated that it would be there. Yet again, Egypt had returned to the centre of my life, and my exhausted spirit immediately registered the fact that I was OFF TO THE PYRAMIDS ONE MORE TIME!

It was obvious that the sign was telling me that I hadn't yet reached the top of the Tree of the Knowledge of Good and Evil as I had surmised only less than a month earlier. "The stones spoke to me," I muttered to myself. Even though it was now glaringly certain that I was on my way to another 'beating', would that be the only thing awaiting me at the retreat? I was beginning to sense something slightly different this time. It seemed that once again I was receiving a sign which was somehow signalling a totally new phase of the quest.

Would the stones of Willow Lodge finally give me my treasure? And why was the billboard saying, "where it all begins?" I felt confused, to say the least. However, despite these anxieties and questions surfacing in my mind, one thing reassured me: the appearance of the sign itself. It was more than generous of the invisible realm to have given me this information at the half way point of my train journey. This meant that I was being allowed to readjust, regroup and prepare myself for perhaps the grand finale to my spiritual quest.

***

After the second leg of the journey, to my utter astonishment, another 'cosmic' sign manifested, apparently as if from nowhere. As I sat in the back of a taxi travelling from the train station to the lodge, I could see that we were following behind an Everest windows van, with the image of the summit of MOUNT EVEREST facing me from the rear of the van. If the sign at Waterloo had left me mesmerized, then this double whammy was way beyond belief!

Despite the invisible realm's implacable determination to communicate with me, what was more than obvious was that I was in the worst possible shape, both emotionally and physically, to make a final climb to the summit of my spiritual Everest. However, the invisible realm seemed to want to ignore my emotions, apparently understanding my capacities far better than I did myself. It had a highly personalized agenda for me, and my 'ascent' would begin almost as soon as I had arrived at the retreat.

Barely five minutes after stepping into the lodge, the 'stones' of the advertisement I had seen at Waterloo Station made their totally unexpected appearance. As I was shown to my tiny room at Willow Lodge, the door opened and revealed this next cosmic sign. Walking past it into the room I could see that it was a photograph of a stone chapel. As soon as the nurse and doctor attending me had made their departure, I made a speedy beeline towards the image in order to examine it more closely.

Yes, it was a stone chapel, and the most self-evident thing about it was that it had just been newly restored. I was able to distinguish where the original ruined walls had been, and where the new stones had been placed. The amazing thing about the chapel was that it also bore an uncanny resemblance to *'my ruin'* in Andalusia. Although it looked slightly bigger, it was exactly the same shape. Even the stones were extremely reminiscent of the stones I had so loved at my sacred, mystical site.

Within seconds I had made the connection between this photograph and the sign in London. Yes, the stones WERE SPEAKING to me! This restored stone chapel somewhere in the English countryside was telling me that *'my ruin'* back in Andalusia was now, on some metaphysical level, once more whole. Although, it had been physically demolished in the winter of 2007, its spirit seemed to have a twin here in England, and that twin had somehow made its way to Willow Lodge in the form of the photograph.

My intuition then instantly moved forward along the same metaphysical line of thought, and I knew without any doubt that the specific message of this visual image was that:

the inner 'ruin of my soul', complete with my inner shadow,
was about
to be redeemed and 'restored'.

The photograph held out the promise that my battered soul would in some way be brought BACK TO LIFE! However, before the light of rebirth could manifest, I knew only too well that I was inevitably going to be asked to encounter my shadow once again - the shadow of the **material** half of my soul.. But, before I launch into the details of that encounter, I need to qualify what is to come.

As I think I have already shown in this book, absolutely nothing and no one in life is either black or white, and so it was with the lodge. During my stay I met many guests for whom their experience there turned out to be a 'little piece of Heaven on Earth'. I myself received the blessing of finally officially being diagnosed with Chronic Fatigue Syndrome, after so many years of unexplained exhaustion and fatigue.

Those others I encountered were treated by dedicated and compassionate professionals, and came away renewed, comforted and in the majority cases HEALED in some way. Nevertheless, in this very same environment, despite my more than welcome diagnosis, the invisible realm had decided that I was to fulfil a very different purpose and agenda.

***

The external manifestation of the shadow of the **material** half of my soul turned out to be the Christian Orthodoxy of Willow Lodge. Over the next few days the 'darkness' I began to observe at the lodge was that of a place which, though it had originally been founded on a living, vibrant faith, now had all the feel of a worn-out piece of furniture. Spirit seemed to be buried under layers of dogma and organization, and intuition wasn't exactly the first word which sprung to mind.

However, in my case there was one notable exception to what I was experiencing — the head counsellor at the lodge. Robin was the prince within this particular Beast. It was he who on our second meeting, after reading a short photocopied extract from the manuscript of my book, quite unexpectedly stuck out his compassionate and brave neck and made the following pronouncement:

"It seems to me Karen that you are what one would call a mystic."

Mere nanoseconds after he had made this extraordinary statement, something deep within my soul instantly became whole. I knew full well that in all probability he was totally unaware of the incredible nature of the gift he had just given me, but, by uttering this apparently innocent, little word — MYSTIC— he had thrown open the doors of a prison I had inhabited for a very long time.

I was now fifty two years old, and in many ways a person with absolutely no comprehensible identity in the outside world, yet in the space of a few seconds he had given me one. *I knew,* and in one way or another *had always known* that I was a mystic — but nobody else on the planet did. This kind of inability to communicate one's true identity to other human beings produces a very special kind of loneliness, almost akin to a sort of deep, unremitting agony.

However, in a quiet therapy room on my third day at the lodge, Robin inadvertently laid the first pivotal foundation stone of a newly-restored Karen, and the longed-for rebirth of my soul! Nevertheless, despite this wonderful encounter with spiritual light from deeply compassionate Robin, as the days of my stay at the lodge continued to progress, more experiences of 'darkness' seemed to await me.

The most significant one came at the healing mass I attended at the end of my first week. It took place in the specially-built healing chapel at the retreat. That afternoon, a group of us sat scattered inside this magnificent building, all harbouring one desperate, wordless longing – the desire to be healed of our individual woes. What transpired during the course of the mass was like being thrown the dry, hard husk of a stale piece of bread.

There was a lot of formality, ritual and theatre throughout the service, and perhaps because of this, my innermost feelings started to tell me that something was wrong. It didn't seem as if God's Spirit were hovering within our midst. I tried desperately to fill myself with optimism and thoughts of the supernatural power of the Almighty, but when each of us was ushered forward to the altar, and the chaplain finally placed her hands on my head, was it really the Holy Spirit producing the tingling sensation on my scalp? I didn't think so.

And so, an hour later, as I lay prostrate on my bed in my tiny room, I knew in my heart that ABSOLUTELY NOTHING HAD HAPPENED.

However, an inner fire made up of despair, hope and denial is something extremely hard to put out, and that deep knowing still hadn't crystallised into a 'done deal' in the depths of my hurting heart. Thus it was that five days later, with my soul still gripped by a desperate need for the Almighty's blessing, I took myself off to yet another healing mass in the lodge's chapel.

This time I was surprised to see that all the pews had been moved to face in a different direction. I sat down beside Rob and Tom who were two other guests staying at the retreat. We waited a few minutes in quiet and humble expectation as a group of chaplains assembled in front of us, and then the service began. Again, there was a new element to the mass. Not only were we all now at ninety degrees to the main altar, but the proceedings were being initiated and led by a young woman with long, blonde, cascading hair.

As I listened to her words, I could hear the strident, confident tone of voice I had heard in so many preachers when I had attended the evangelical fellowship in Spain. Sitting next to Rob and Tom, who were both following the service from their wheelchairs, her self-assured, upbeat voice positively GRATED on my spirit. After so many years on this spiritual path, it took a fleeting half second for me to realise exactly what 'Little Miss Glamour Chaplain's' appearance meant.

With her immaculately made-up face, she had all the lustre and shine of the NEW KID ON THE BLOCK. The stuffy, dry Christian orthodoxy I had been experiencing during my stay here was now opening its doors to something much more bold, brash and sensuous – ITS ZEALOUS, EVANGELICAL COUSINS. Sitting in my pew, I instantly understood that I was witnessing the logical next stage of the Anglican church's final ascent to the summit of the Tree of the Knowledge of Good and Evil.

It was nearing that summit, just as I was, but again like me, it hadn't quite met with and redeemed the last aspects of its shadow. Suddenly depression and despair engulfed me completely. I stared at the back of Rob's wheelchair, berating myself for not having understood the lesson I had been given at the first healing mass five days earlier.

Then, out of the blue, in a magical moment of insight as I was in the middle of singing our first hymn, the light 'dawned' for me. I instantly KNEW the true reason for my coming to Willow Lodge. My hand rested on Tom's back, supporting him whilst he made a supreme effort to stand and shakily for a brief thirty seconds sing his heart out to his beloved Maker.

Then as the team of healers started to make their way to the guests, most of whom like Rob and Tom were slightly disabled or confined to wheelchairs, a small voice inside me whispered a very short and concise message:

SHIT HAPPENS, KAREN, SHIT HAPPENS.

***

I could now see the truth with extraordinary clarity: none of us would ever escape the fact that life was regretfully an imperfect, broken and unpredictable affair. From cradle to grave, its shadow was with us, and that was the overwhelming reality of being born into a human, **material** form. Rob, Tom and I had come here with our own personal brokenness, and in this mass God seemed to be telling me that this was a cosmic rite of passage for me and my two friends.

The three of us had lived life, and had experienced our fair share of blessings and disasters, and now we had been brought here in order to see THE BIG PICTURE of our lives. We would need to accept what fate had handed us. Rob would not leave his wheelchair, neither would Tom, and I would not be miraculously 'zapped' by the Holy Spirit, and suddenly find myself free of Chronic Fatigue Syndrome. Then quite suddenly, as I sat slumped in the pew, an even deeper insight into what I was experiencing came to me.

It concerned the true nature of the 'beating' I had journeyed here to receive. Along with my physical luggage and inner light, I had also brought my own personal concoction of hubris — my shadow-to Willow Lodge. That cocktail had been my forceful ego and its controlling thinking function; alias my inner leader of the refugees.

This was that part of me which insisted on CONTROLLING life, and wanted a sure-fire, guaranteed 'healing-on-demand' from the all-powerful Divine Source. Just as Santiago had so desperately wanted the treasure buried in Egypt for himself, AND ONLY FOR HIMSELF, my tenacious ego had brought me here for a supernatural 'zapping' from the Holy Spirit - and for me, NOTHING LESS WOULD DO!

With this extraordinary revelation of truth, now the invisible realm was showing me exactly where I was on my journey of spiritual awakening. Paulo Coelho's hero Santiago and I were both:

CHILDREN OF THE AGE OF REDEMPTION.

This meant that the shadow within each of us had
believed that we could CONTROL our destinies
with the sheer force of our wills.

Yes, it was true that our actions came from the deepest desires of our hearts. But as I had learned over the years, our souls, whether inside or near our physical hearts, also contained darkness, and this needed to be redeemed before the gift of light could be found.

When I had come to Willow Lodge I had shared my light with Robin, and also the doctor who had given me my diagnosis of Chronic Fatigue Syndrome. Both had wisely been able to see it, but what I hadn't realised was that the dry, thinking-based orthodoxy of the lodge which so repelled me, was simply an outer manifestation of my own inner Beast. So, despite having brought light to the retreat, my shadow's unconscious desire *to control* had also been present, and had met with Christianity's shadow's unconscious desire to CONTROL.

***

This deep realisation in the chapel was now turning into a genuine quantum leap for me in the process of soul rebirth. At the beginning of my stay, despite the change in the nature of the quality of the signs I had been given, with all my heart I wanted to assume that this journey to Egypt would be like all the others I had experienced. I would encounter an external manifestation of the shadow of the **material** half of my soul, identify it as such, feel its 'beating', and then turn around and metaphorically 'walk away' from it just as I had done in the past.

But, the experience with Rob and Tom was transforming itself into a much more intimate and life-changing encounter than any of my previous 'beatings'. At Willow Lodge, God was metaphorically rubbing my nose into the very core of my own personal shit — because only He knew just how high the spiritual stakes were. There was nothing relatively cosy or comfortable about what I was being shown; nothing from which I could mentally 'detach' with ease.

The complete abandonment of control was what God wanted.

Surrender and acceptance were at the heart of what I and my companions were being asked to do. Our healings were all about the act of TURNING AWAY from our inner Beasts and TURNING TOWARD our inner princes and princesses. In other words we were being asked to:

'LET GO AND LET GOD'.

Once I had assimilated what I was being shown, I breathed in my defeat, taking on board that loss of control, and also the awareness of my personal hubris. I acknowledged my shadow for what it was, and breathed out my acceptance of a Reality and Power far greater than myself. These were two of the most significant breaths I have ever taken in my entire life. Then, leaving Rob and Tom with their respective healers, I walked up to mine, knowing that I now faced yet another one of the invisible realm's great, unfathomable unknowns.

I knew I wouldn't be asking for a healing as I had hoped when I first came to the mass. The *give me, give me* Karen had died on the wooden pew on which she had sat just a few moments ago. Perhaps the Almighty had a purpose and plan for me which I had totally overlooked., and so in genuine humility I sat in front of my healer, and sobbing quietly, asked if God might be so good as to show me what that purpose was.

***

Two days later, there was yet another healing mass in the chapel, but this time I decided to give it a miss. Instead, that evening I lay on my bed fully aware that I had experienced soul rebirth once again, but also aware that this time I was being asked to make a radical change of direction. As I lay there, I remembered that on November 26, 2004 I had knocked on J's door to say goodbye before leaving for my first encounter with Paulo Coelho in Holland. J had handed me a card on which he had written the following quotation:

**Peace comes when I unclench the fist that clings
to my vision of the future.**

Anon.

As I had stood in the hallway reading the words, I remember having felt myself become distinctly irritated. I barely knew J then as he had only just recently moved into the shared house, and I sensed a controlling energy behind his seemingly '*magnanimous*' gesture. The message had also irritated me. What nonsense, I had thought to myself, it was precisely my gutsy CLINGING to a vision of what I was searching for which was, at that very instant, taking me off to Holland to reap my reward for nearly ten years of blood, sweat and tears!

Now, as I went over this memory in my room at Willow Lodge, I could see that what had really happened that morning in 2004 had been an encounter between two control freaks – J and me. The supreme irony of the situation was that in trying to exert some kind of control over me, J had used a quotation which was an exhortation to the very opposite – A COMPLETE ABANDONMENT OF THE DESIRE TO CONTROL!

Equally, in my desire not to be told 'what to do or think' by a person I barely knew, I had been completely incapable of understanding the meaning of what I had been given to read. My God, I thought to myself, the universe had always 'been on my case' in the most intimate of ways. Six years ago it had used J as an instrument with which to speak to me and here I was, six long years later, only finally understanding its message!

The following morning, I caught the train back home to Ambleton, still as exhausted as ever, and with 'the penny dropping' slowly into my worn-out consciousness. 'Dying' to my controlling thinking function – my inner Beast or inner leader of the refugees – was what my stay at Willow Lodge had meant. However, what was so bizarre about all of this was that over the countless years of my odyssey, abandoning control had always been the lesson for me, and yet I had never really seen it with such clarity until now!

Despite all the 'beatings' I had endured over so many years, I had never realised just how entrenched and demanding that controlling thinking function in me was. The sheer depth of the lesson at Willow lodge had taken me completely by surprise, and even though its processing would require more than just a few days, I knew something irrevocable had happened to me there.

My new direction didn't seem at all clear to me - this rebirth had barely begun to take shape - but whatever the future had in store for me, I only hoped that it would all be for the better – A TRULY BETTER ME.

26

ME, YOU AND OUR SHADOW

**Love is the difficult realisation that something
other than oneself is real.**

Iris Murdoch

AFTER my decidedly COSMIC RITE OF INITIATION at the lodge,
I might have assumed that the lesson given to me there had finally
been learnt. But, if the shadow were as easy to tame as a domestic
pussycat, then our world, and we ourselves, would be very different.
Oh, no, no, no. The lesson from the lodge continued, and more than
another year was destined to pass before Everest's summit could be
scaled and ultimately conquered.

This time the main element of the shadow which I was being
asked to confront wasn't CONTROL as it had been at the retreat, but
another aspect all together. It was that ever faithful companion inside
each of us — good old, 'predictable 'angst-inducing FEAR.

The first eight months of 2011 saw me consumed by both
conscious and unconscious fears, with most of these centring around
serious problems with my publishing house. TREASURE had finally
emerged into the world two days after I had left Willow Lodge —
clearly a MANIFESTATION of my spiritual light - but on receiving
a copy of the book just before Christmas I had been shocked to
discover several major publishing errors in the text. And so it was that
for the first five months of 2011 I became engaged in a protracted
correspondence with my publisher in order to produce an error-free
SECOND version of the book.

During this period, the pressing pressure of FEAR became the
very heart of every facet of my motivation and actions. This meant

that under such emotionally-charged circumstances it was almost inevitable that I immediately fell back on using my ego mind's thinking function in a frantic attempt to *control* something which had clearly spun totally OUT OF CONTROL. To his immense credit my long-suffering publisher Dan Burns responded to my inner light, and not the darkness of my fearful shadow.

That response manifested in the form of his generous agreement to meet the extra financial expense of a reprint of TREASURE from the company's own funds. In so doing Dan, like Robin at Willow Lodge, turned his back on his inner Beast, and his 'beastly' world, to become another Prince in this story. With so much fear running around inside me during this time, my perception of events became highly distorted. One consequence of this was that the corrected version of my book seemed to take forever to come back to me for checking and approval.

However, it eventually did turn up when I opened my emails on February 11, 2011 - no ordinary day on our planet. Synchronistically, on February 11 the Egyptian people finally found their own inner light after confronting the shadow of the **material** half of their national soul because that afternoon the radio informed me that President Mubarak was announcing his resignation as head of the country.

The revolution in Egypt had broken out in January, surprising everyone around the world, but confirming my deepest and most radical intuitions. With the capitulation of the old regime, once again the words from the billboard at Waterloo Station returned to me.

"The stones spoke to me"
EGYPT
where it all begins.

It was this 'Arab Spring', and the huge victory in Egypt, which vindicated what I had always intuitively known regarding certain parts of the world having archetypal soul energy.*

(My optimism about the revolution in Egypt reflected my naivety. In fact the events there were just the beginning of that country's encounter with the truly awful depths of its national shadow, and also Mankind's universal shadow. Despite this, I remain optimistic for the long-term.)

This was an insight which had suddenly emerged for me on my first visit to Santiago de Compostela back in 2004 when I had been on my way to Madrid. Spirit has created, and is the source of every physical aspect of our planet, and so our beloved Earth, and we who live on her, inevitably manifest and 'speak' a very specific spiritual language –THE LANGUAGE OF ARCHETYPES.

And so, for me Egypt with her pyramids is a special land of archetypal soul energy, and those pyramids are the most iconic archetype of all the MANIFESTATIONS of the **material** half of our souls around the world.

The events of 2011 in Egypt were also most definitely a sign that the new *Age of Spirit* I have spoken about is coming into being, and equally tangible proof of the existence of the Pyramid of Redemption I talked about in chapter 23. The incredibly brave souls who died at the beginning of the uprising, and the others who risked death in Tahrir Square, were the 'youngsters' I mentioned earlier 'light enough' to climb to the top of that pyramid and break through into the light.

On February 17, 2011 I returned my manuscript to Dan, fully checked and corrected for the final time – unfortunately even at this eleventh hour there had still been mistakes within the text. Then I began the long-anticipated wait for the publication of the reprinted copy of TREASURE; the light for which I had journeyed so long in order to bring it into being was now only weeks away from entering our world.

***

Throughout that first half of 2011, despite all the fear I had been experiencing around my publishing debacle, I managed to remain uncompromisingly in a deep and impenetrable state of denial regarding this aspect of my shadow. But when the new copy of my odyssey finally popped through my letter box in the middle of May, I was given a colossal sign I simply couldn't ignore. Running from start to finish of this new version of the book was an unmistakable COSMIC SHADOW. Each time I had placed words in an *italic format*, they now appeared in an ugly **bold, black italic.**

Perhaps the most striking, and symbolically significant of all these words were those of the title of Paulo's fable. Yes, on every single occasion I had written them in the text, they now called out to the reader in this particularly 'shadowy' form: **The Alchemist. The Alchemist, The Alchemist.** The conclusion to all of this was inevitable:

Ironically, my book TREASURE now seemed to contain its very

OWN PERSONAL SHADOW.

It is important here NOT to enter into needless speculation about how this 'error' actually came about. What is important was my honest reaction to it. I hated what I was seeing, but after a very uncomfortable examination of conscience over a protracted period of nearly three months, I finally realised that it hadn't been an accident. The inescapable truth was that:

the shadow of my overwhelming fear had produced
the shadow in the book.

With the unconscious collaboration of my publishing house, I had unknowingly continued to climb to the summit of The Tree of the Knowledge of Good and Evil. However, the question which now began to surface in my mind was whether I had been doing this all alone?

Quite suddenly in August 2011 all the insights I had written about in Chapter 23 almost two years earlier came flooding back into my consciousness. The appearance of the *cosmic shadow* in TREASURE had begun to allow me to once again see a much BIGGER PICTURE

The ascent to the top of The Tree of the Knowledge of Good and Evil I had described in Chapter 23 had been about a journey to redeem the universal shadow of Mankind, and towards the end of August 2009, when this realisation had come to me, I had understood that EACH AND EVERY ONE OF US was finally reaching the end of a two-thousand-year climb to the top of the Eden tree. So, given this reality, it was inevitable and now glaringly obvious that what had happened with my publishing house had been a manifestation of this final ascent, and more importantly:

ITS UNIVERSALITY.

I had made the climb as part of a 'team' made up
of myself, and all the staff involved in the publication
of TREASURE at the publishing house.
But, how was it that I had not seen any of this before?

Year after year, I had been labouring under the illusion that all of my 'beatings' had been encounters with my PERSONAL shadow, when in fact, year after year I had been meeting the universal shadow of our species - albeit in a specific form within me as an individual. For the manifestation of the revised version of TREASURE, the spiritual realm had in fact chosen its archetypal city - New York - and also its key players in order for them to participate in a cosmic reckoning with that UNIVERSAL SHADOW.

The shadow inside TREASURE had manifested out of the
universal shadow my publishing house and I each shared
as fully 'paid up' members of the human race.

How could I know for sure that this sudden insight into the metaphysical and UNIVERSAL NATURE of my 'apparently personal publishing experience' was true? Well, my memory gave me the answer to that when I began to recall that the invisible realm had given me an earlier insight into the workings of our world back in 2003.

***

In January of that year an invasion of Iraq by the Americans and British had been imminent, and I had sat with my Argentine friend Marta in my tiny Andalusian apartment praying for peace and making anti-war banners. The day after the invasion was launched in March I had come down with a recurrence of glandular fever and Marta and I had argued, with the result that there had been a temporary parting of our ways.

I had not had glandular fever symptoms for more than seventeen years, and yet, at this very moment of a war starting in the outside world, my body had broken out into its own INTERNAL WAR. My white blood cells had furiously multiplied and begun to 'attack' a suspected 'enemy' lurking within me. This experience taught me perhaps the most important lesson of my odyssey and the deepest truth about our world. Yet, inexplicably its full significance would only come to me eight years later as a result of the appearance of the cosmic shadow in my book.

That truth was that no matter how anti the war in Iraq I had been on a conscious level, subconsciously I had contributed to its manifestation along with everybody else on our planet. Over more than four decades large parts of me had been a normal person, behaving like any other 'normal' person. This meant that I had engaged in my own angry battles with other people and myself during the course of everyday living, even though simultaneously I had also earnestly endeavoured to practise being a more spiritual human being.

My realisation back in 2003 was that the recurrence of glandular fever had been my body's perfect metaphor to describe what had been happening in the outside world. It allowed me to see that at this very moment in history, we human beings had ALL COLLECTIVELY been responsible for the outpouring of violence that had occurred in Iraq.

The WAR which had raged inside my body for two weeks had not just been my dark, warlike PERSONAL SHADOW still gripping me internally even after so many years of spiritual questing. It had been very much a manifestation of our universal shadow – the shadow shared by each and every human being in our world.

From that moment on in 2003, I had somehow vaguely, if unconsciously, understood this uncompromising truth about all of us, and knew that the moral high ground wasn't territory that I, or anyone else on planet Earth, could occupy with any degree of smugness or certainty. The 'villains' we so enthusiastically needed to create in order to explain traumatic events were simply DOING OUR OWN DIRTY WORK FOR US!

So, what was this universal shadow that I had now identified through my second encounter with a publishing meltdown? The answer came to me with little effort. There was quite obviously an

Unholy Trinity to which we were all connected, and it was therefore the complete antithesis of the Holy Trinity of the Spirit – the trinity of Hope, Faith and Love – I mentioned earlier. In stark contrast to these sublime states The Unholy Trinity comprised the three pillars of our ego mind and its indomitable thinking function:

POWER, CONTROL AND FEAR.

This insight wasn't inconsequential by any means because it suddenly allowed me to see with total clarity what the overall pattern of my odyssey had been. The pyramid-shaped 'iceberg' of my soul which I had been climbing for all these years had had two very distinct phases.

The first phase of the journey had been through the subconscious part of my soul, and had come to an end in 2003. In this section I had journeyed through the Dark Night of The Soul, and the universal shadow through it all had been DEATH. For me, death had manifested in the form of panic attacks, the impulse to self-harm, anxiety, and imminent symptoms of possible epileptic seizures. However, even though these were all my very highly individual manifestations, no matter how differently we each manifest the shadow of the material half of our soul, all are simply various expressions of the UNIVERSAL SHADOW of our species.

The second phase of my quest had begun on my arrival in Santiago de Compostela in 2004. Unknowingly I had left the subconscious, submerged part of my soul behind, and had begun my entry into the conscious area – in other words the ego mind. From then on, little had I realised that each of my 'beatings' over the next ten years would once again be my personal encounters with the universal shadow – but this time the ego mind's Unholy Trinity of POWER, CONTROL AND FEAR.

Understanding that I hadn't grasped this obvious fact regarding the true nature of my quest, the universe had decided to begin signalling this insight to me during my stay at Willow Lodge. At that stage, even though I had sensed a qualitative change in my odyssey, I continued to want to believe that the lesson I was being given was that I needed to die to MY OWN CONTROLLING THINKING FUNCTION.

However, now I could see that because this insight had taken place within the context of a shared experience with several other individuals, it was signalling to me that the invisible realm had actually been *screaming* to me that the CONTROL I had identified in myself was in fact A UNIVERSAL ASPECT of everyone's shadow. Equally, from the moment I had signed my publishing contract and started writing TREASURE, I had also been consumed with the FEAR element of the Unholy Trinity. This was most evident in my reaction to news I had read on the internet.

One of America's most successful film producers had acquired the rights to make a movie of The Alchemist, and nearly all of my fear had revolved around an obsession that I needed to get my story out BEFORE the movie appeared. I was almost paranoid that were my book to be published AFTER such a movie was made, then I would be labelled a trickster and charlatan, desperate to 'cash in' on the success of what I assumed would be a worldwide blockbuster.*

From the very start of my quest back in 1995 I had always known that my odyssey was a matter of deep transcendental importance. Nevertheless, over the last two years of journeying I cannot exaggerate just how consistently I had failed to grasp the meaning of the insights which had come to me in August 2009.

The fact was that humanity's shadow had constantly eluded me as I continuously made the erroneous assumption that my journey was confined to the fate of my own individual soul. Now, however, clarity had finally arrived, and with it the full understanding that my quest had been something much more 'cosmic' than I had ever imagined. Perhaps my status as an anonymous citizen of the planet would finally come to an end if I decided to contact the Guinness Book of Records to let them know that my publishing house and I had inadvertently set a new world record.

Was it within the realms of possibility that I had been the very first writer in the history of publishing to have brought out a book containing the UNIVERSAL SHADOW of our species? Hmm............ food for metaphysical thought

(In 2012 Paulo Coelho announced on his blog that plans to make the movie of his fable had been abandoned.)

27

THE DARKNESS BEFORE THE DAWN

**The journey from life to death
leads finally from death to life.**

HENRI NOUMEN

WITH the first eight months of 2011 showing me the truly universal nature of my shadow, it wasn't surprising that this universality was miserably confirmed throughout the world when 2011 proved to be an extremely bloody and dark year. The darkness had begun in December 2010 with an extraordinary act of martyrdom by a street vendor called Mohamed Bouazizi in Tunisia.

Mohamed set fire to himself, and with this cry of total despair, a relatively short revolution broke out in that country. This was quickly followed in January 2011 by the wind of revolution spreading to Egypt, and the fall of the Mubarak regime. Then Libya erupted and the West felt morally compelled to engage in military action in order to assist the rebel fighters there. Shortly after Libya, turmoil spread to the Gulf States in the Middle East and then Syria exploded into civil unrest, culminating in the Syrian government carrying out a war against its own people, which is still on-going as I write.

Lastly, as if nothing more could happen, the Fukoshima nuclear plant in Japan went into meltdown in March 2011 after an earthquake and tsunami in that country. I knew intuitively from all of this chaos that these events were manifestations of a very clear and unambiguous reality: Redemption Road was still being travelled by our human race.

Our collective and universal shadow was being met on a worldwide scale. The Japanese were directly paying the price for humanity's nuclear folly. In North Africa and the Middle East many people had lost their lives in peacefully bringing spiritual light to the shadow of the **material** half of our collective soul. And finally, others had chosen to use darkness to fight darkness, in the hope that the 'apparently' lesser evil of war would indeed prove to be just that. In this unremitting panorama of pain and darkness, my year also ended in the same mood. In the autumn of 2011 I was given a painful encounter with the final aspect of the Unholy Trinity – namely POWER.

My lessons seemed to follow an implacable logic in which no kind of soul rebirth would ever be possible until I had experienced the whole spectrum of our universal shadow. I have decided NOT TO GIVE AN ACCOUNT of this encounter with POWER as, apart from myself, it involved a considerable number of people, all of whom I know would much rather remain anonymous.

However, the fact that a large group of us was involved once more underscores the universal nature of this aspect of the shadow we all found ourselves meeting. This final stage ended around the last week of November, but did not 'let me off' quite as lightly as I had hoped. That was because when I woke up on December 1 2011 I was surprised with a nightmarish end to my quest. As I clambered out of my bed there seemed to be 'SHIT' EVERYWHERE! And I don't exaggerate:

IT WAS ABSOLUTELY EVERYWHERE!!!

Now, what on earth do I mean by that?

Well, the reality was that IT WAS ME– I was completely covered not in physical shit, but metaphorical shit. However, then again, it wasn't JUST ME, ALL ALONE. This was the universal shadow, or rather my individual and highly personal version of the universal shadow.

That morning I had an overwhelming feeling of being completely covered from head to toe with my own, and everybody else's diabolical shadow. Here was the excrement which Alejandro Jodorowsky had predicted nearly sixteen years earlier when he had told me that I would have to climb into a bath tub and cover my entire naked body with my own excrement and urine. I was now fifty three years old, and this 'stuff' represented a life-time's worth of the universal shadow of the **material** half of my soul. The universe's timing had been impeccable.

There I was, suddenly completely aware of it all and I mean absolutely ALL OF IT: fear, my controlling thinking function, sexual passions, paranoia, anger, rage, cowardice, envy, hatred the list went on and on and on. It was quite simply:

THE WHOLE COSMIC LOT!

Compelled to be totally honest with myself, I knew deep in my heart that what was happening to me was no mere accident. I had been chosen by some universal intelligence to experience this total awareness because all of these things were the shadow of each and every human being on our planet. Yes, I'm sorry dear friend to be so explicit with the bad news.

When I had sat opposite Alejandro Jodorowsky back in February 1996, listening incredulously to the psychomagical act he had been prescribing me, how could I possibly have known that just over fifteen-and-a-half years later I would be experiencing exactly what he had talked about? I therefore concluded that what I was feeling that December day was the ultimate proof for me that this incredible quest had really come to an end. HOW COULD IT NOT BE?

My immediate response to how I felt was to use everything I had learned up until this very moment, and so I set about creating a new home for myself. The language of Spirit demanded that the end of this journey should be marked by my soul assuming ownership of a brand new dwelling, and the outer manifest world faithfully confirmed my conclusion with very specific signs. In the block where I lived two apartments suddenly became empty in December, making a total of four ready and waiting for new occupants to begin their NEW LIVES!

However yet again, with total honesty and integrity I accepted the fact that the invisible realm hadn't magnanimously assigned me any one of those vacant apartments. It was true that they were signs, but because my soul rebirth was so INNER in nature, this meant that my NEW HOME would remain the same, but would entail me rearranging it into a completely new configuration. Rebirth would take place WITHIN the same four walls I had occupied for the last three years.

***

HERE COMES THE SUN

December passed in a blur of ill-health and exhaustion and by February 2012 I had come to terms with this dramatic ending to my journey. From the start this extraordinary odyssey had been my own individual contract with a powerful, supernatural invisible spiritual realm. Fate had long ago decided that anonymous, British-born Karen was the person best capable of consciously confronting and chronicling the final stages of humanity's Age of Redemption.

Of course, as I have already stated in previous chapters, I wasn't by any means the only person living out this moment in history. In one way or another WE ALL WERE, but I was to be the person chosen to write about it. That was part of the unfathomable mystery of life, and one needed to respect it, and maintain ones' sense of awe and wonder.

Nevertheless, despite all of this, what I did comprehend was that two months of feeling myself to be covered in the human race's excrement wasn't so very long, given the task I had been assigned and what had been at stake. And, as ever, in order to deepen my understanding of what I was experiencing I turned my attention INWARDS to my intuition, and also OUTWARDS to the signs the invisible realm continued to give me.

The biggest sign looming ahead of me in February was the sixteenth anniversary of my journey to Paris to see Alejandro Jodorowsky. As soon as this realisation had dawned on me, I felt I knew with absolute certainty that this anniversary signified the end of my quest. Exactly what would happen around February 27 was a complete unknown to me, but my insight gave me the confidence to throw myself into my intuitive promptings with a total faith and conviction that I was following the path the Divine had set out for me.

***

On February 20, 2012 my intuition grabbed hold of me in no uncertain terms. In July 2011 I had met a healer when I had attended a garden party for local New Age practitioners. Robert the healer had captured my interest chiefly because he had told me that he was learning to perform psychic surgery. With so many years of questing under my belt, my consciousness was starting to expand to encompass many new ideas.

After our meeting in July 2011, I had invited Robert to come to see me at my apartment to give me a healing, but the session hadn't seemed to go too well. Nevertheless, I knew that he was a member of a healing group which met locally, and somehow I sensed that sometime in the near future I was meant to go to the group. With the anniversary of my meeting with Alejandro Jodorowsky approaching, I picked up the phone on February 20 and made contact with Robert once again.

He greeted my call warmly and told me that he would be at the healing circle that Thursday, February 23. But, despite this, suddenly my life began to take a turn for the worse. Only just freed of the two month period wherein I had felt myself covered in humanity's universal shadow, in between our conversation on the 20th and Thursday my chronic fatigue unexpectedly intensified alarmingly. Not only that, but the feeling of being covered in metaphorical 'shit' seemed to return with a vengeance.

However, in spite of the panic this started to engender in me, deep in my soul I knew that all of this was synchronistic, and 'cosmically' tied to the anniversary of my journey to Paris.

On Thursday 23 I barely made it to the healing group. I walked into the room where everyone was congregated, unable to muster a smile or greeting of any kind. Robert recognised me and approached the doorway enfolding me in a huge bear hug I was utterly incapable of reciprocating. I sat down at a communal table, knowing precisely why I had dragged myself to the group.

This wasn't Paris, and Robert wasn't Alejandro Jodorowsky, but the invisible realm had decided that the hands-on healing I was about to receive would be the equivalent of the massage Alejandro had said I needed to receive once I had reached the decision to be reborn.

I would be asked to sit in the middle of the square, and there I had to endure the smell of my faeces and urine on every part of my body whilst the music of Ravel's Bolero played. This would go on for the whole length of Ravel's piece. At the end of the music, if and when I was ready, I would ask to be reborn. When I had made this decision, I could then step out of the square, and two masseurs would take me back to the bath where every bit of excrement needed to be washed off me.

Now clean, I would be massaged by the two masseurs until I gave birth to myself. As this newborn being, the masseurs would then dress me in clothes I had brought with me, which would be specifically sky blue and pale pink in colour. These were the colours traditionally worn by newborn babies: blue for boys and pink for girls.

Clothed in these colours, I could then go out into the street and find a machine that printed I.D. and business cards. Standing in front of the machine, without needing to think, I would intuitively grasp my new identity, and instantly know my new name and new profession. I had to then type this information into the machine so that within minutes I would be holding a card giving the details of my new identity.

TREASURE: A Soul Journey with the Invisible.

Chapter 6.

I knew that I had made that decision for soul rebirth on Monday 20 when I had picked up my phone in order to contact Robert, so when he finally called me over, I went to the massage table and lay down, trying to relax as best I could. No Ravel's Bolero had played in the days leading up to this moment, but after sixteen years of questing my razor-sharp intuition sensed THE BIGGER PICTURE.

Totally unaware of his role in what was about to happen, Robert laid his hands on my head and began the healing. Within a minute or so, tears began to flood from my eyes and I sobbed and convulsed on the table as the pain and grief of my journey began to leave me. I briefly apologized to Robert for making so much noise, and when I received assurances from him that the crying wasn't a problem, it seemed as if floodgates had opened up inside me as huge waves of grief began to pour from my soul.

At one point I felt another hand grasp mine, and I heard a female voice gently ask me if I was alright. In between my sobs I mumbled that I was O.K. and then my ever over-active mind spoke to me.

God, Karen,
that's the other 'masseur' — there are two of
them - just like Alejandro had predicted!
Alejandro had always said that there would be two 'masseurs
facilitating my rebirth, and now this lady and Robert
were facilitating that process sixteen years later!!!

After the healing session I gave Robert my heartfelt thanks and appreciation and then returned home feeling more or less the same as I had before. That evening I switched on the radio for company, and to my surprise — and yet not to my surprise — I 'accidentally' caught the middle of a programme where a young English man was climbing up the second tallest Redwood tree in California. Hmm......I thought to myself....well, what do you know. With total synchronicity, the universe is showing me someone else who has just reached the very top of their personal Everest!

A person who is symbolically climbing up to the very summit
of **The Tree of the Knowledge of Good and Evil!**

What a beautiful sign from the invisible realm to
let me know that rebirth had been achieved.

The 'cosmic timing' of our world was truly astonishing! Yes, all of this was truly mind-boggling, but as I savoured the precision with which I had been given this sign, I didn't realise that the complete and total rebirthing of my soul had not come to an end after my session with Robert. As the days after my hands-on-healing began to pass, the invisible realm started to show me that this encounter had been only the INITIATION OF A PROCESS — and this was very much what it was — which would take place over a period of five days.

Sure enough, when I awoke on Saturday 25 once again I still felt myself gripped by the feeling of being covered in Mankind's 'existential excrement'. I lay on my bed enduring it until my intuition prompted me to go into the shower and wash myself completely clean. Then on Monday, February 27 — the exact date when I had been with Alejandro Jodorowsky in 1996 — I found myself once again in Robert's presence, however, this time I was sitting in his home.

As he began the recitation of a short prayer, I knew without a shadow of a doubt that because of the synchronicity of the dates I was now about to receive the very last healing of my quest – the five day PROCESS was coming to its end.

***

Finally, to end this whole rite the invisible realm - acknowledging my total commitment to following my intuition and the signs I had struggled so hard to understand - rewarded my faith by gifting me with another truly TRANSCENDENTAL SIGN.

It was on the following day – February 28. That morning a greetings card with a small piece of paper tucked inside it dropped through my letter box. When I opened the card and unfolded the paper, my eyes alighted on a child's drawing. The card was from a neighbour's great-grand-daughter, and her great-grand-mother wanted to explain that two year old Constance had 'drawn' me a picture to thank me for the alphabet set I had given her the week before.

What I saw before me was the outline of a teddy bear's head drawn by an adult, with Constance's colourful scribbles all around and inside the teddy's head. My mind instantly went back to the winter of 2008: **'Aurora – Gift of Smiles'**.

That had been the plastic label which had hung around the neck of the teddy bear I had seen on a patient's bed when I had been working in Ambleton Hospital. Now, gazing at this sign from a small child, I knew with total certainty that the language of the invisible realm wasn't in the least bit arbitrary or random. If a teddy bear with the name AURORA had been a sign of soul rebirth four years earlier, then it was only logical that another teddy bear would announce AURORA'S final, glorious arrival.

Yet again, I had discovered that the language of SPIRIT was all in seemingly inconsequential details; details which needed patience, passion, perseverance and humility to uncover. And what could be more indicative of spiritual rebirth than the tender, joyous scribbles of a two year old child – AMAZING!!!

BOOK THREE:
THE INITIATION
(LABOUR PAINS)

**Before the advent of modern technology,
no woman ever knew if she
would survive childbirth.
It was an unavoidable risk:
A SACRIFICE OF SELF.**

ELISE BAXTER

28

THE JUDGEMENT

SECTION 1

**Every Dream Begins in the Heart and Ends with
its Dawning There Also**

ANON

AFTER February, the month of March 2012 saw me continuing in very poor health. However, given that I had just experienced a rebirth lasting five days, and that my gestation period had been seventeen years rather than nine months, in all honesty I couldn't have expected anything else. April arrived and with it came spring buds and shoots, and the hope that I would now well and truly be entering the new *Age of Spirit.*

But, once again the universe would surprise me, and this time it was to be in the form of a final cosmic reckoning – played out in two distinct stages over a period of just over two years.

The truth about spiritual journeying is that the higher the stakes, the more exacting and soul-searching is the last 'hurdle' to be overcome. I had thought that my summit had been reached after my rebirthing with Robert, but the first of several NEW TESTS arrived without warning - just when I imagined myself to be on the threshold of savouring the joy of journey's end.

***

The invisible realm decided to make things very obvious by choosing the perfect scenario for the first of these divinely ordained 'trials'. It took place inside a courtroom in Ambleton. In April 2012, along with a few other individuals, I spent three days supporting a close friend who had been accused of sexually assaulting a female acquaintance.

The rules of this challenge were clear-cut and unambiguous. All of us had to prove that the universal treasure of SPIRIT which each of us, collectively, but separately, had unearthed at the top of the Tree of the Knowledge of Good and Evil was something we were resolved to live from NO MATTER WHAT. SPIRIT needed to reign supreme, and it wouldn't be good enough simply *to believe* in that supremacy. We had to embrace it with EVERY MOLECULE OF OUR BEING.

We pilgrims could not assume the mantle of 'children of a new *Age of Spirit*' and yet still dip in and out of the old 'AGE OF THE EGO MIND' whenever it seemed the easier and more convenient option. This was Higher Power's summons to an ALL-OR-NOTHING commitment to an invisible truth, and fortunately, in court our little band of bruised and imperfect souls passed this grizzly and nerve-wracking test.

No matter how bad the odds had looked for my friend as he sweated it out in the dock — and I can assure you that those odds had looked pretty horrendous - none of us was prepared to betray the light of love and truth we had found at journey's end. Our man was innocent; EACH OF US KNEW THIS IN OUR HEARTS, and despite all the fiendish lies which had been concocted against him INNOCENT HE WAS FOUND!!!

For where your treasure is, there your heart will be also

Mathew 6:21
The New Testament: NIV version

With this heart-stopping challenge 'apparently' successfully met and completed, I naively imagined my troubles to be over. Surely, a few months of rest awaited me before the appearance of new signs regarding the dawning of the *Age of Spirit*. However, the invisible realm's spiritual clock continued on its 'merry way', dragging little old me and the whole of humanity forward with each of its cosmic heart beats.

Before I could even draw breath, at the beginning of May I suddenly found myself engaged in yet another bona-fide stage of this twenty eight month initiation into Mankind's brand new age. However, this time it would be my introduction to the modus operandi governing these final months of my odyssey.

It was the first week in May, and I had climbed to the top of the hill on which I lived to make a You Tube video at my local internet café. I had decided to call it: **COELHO'S THE ALCHEMIST – THE TRUE MEANING.** Half way through the filming process I suddenly realised what I was actually doing.

The Lumen Dei of the **mystical** half of my soul
was melding with the Lumen Naturae
of the **material** half of my soul,

and this quite spontaneously sparked another astonishing insight for me.

Although after seventeen long years I had finally achieved soul rebirth, when I had received hands-on-healing from Robert, and had thus uncovered the spiritual light within the **material** half of my soul, my discoveries over the years regarding The Alchemist had also led me to a more complex understanding. It was that this process of rebirth also precipitated a second release of spiritual light – the one I outlined in Chapter 18.

In that channelled account I showed that AFTER Paulo Coelho's shepherd boy had found his personal liberation, he had 'coincidentally' provided the METAPHYSICAL KEY by which the personification of the other half of his soul – the leader of the refugees – had also discovered his own light. And, now, after recording my You Tube video, I was seeing that those two sources of SPIRIT within the two halves of my soul were melding together just like the two liquids held by the angel in the TEMPERANCE card I had discovered back in the year 2000. In fact, it suddenly became more than obvious that the angel in the card represented the redeemed human soul:

AND THAT SOUL'S NAME WAS AURORA

and the liquids in the chalices were Paracelsus' two sources of Spirit – Lumen Dei and Lumen Naturae.

WHAM, KABAM!!!!!!!! Another incredible
COSMIC TRUTH
was staring right at me.

What was being created in this process of melding was not another rebirth of the soul, as it had been for seventeen long years during the redemption process, but a SECOND BIRTH within the soul. Sitting in the internet café making my You Tube recording, it seemed to me that there was to be one final stage to the process of ascending the Tree of the Knowledge of Good and Evil.

This would be the birth of the light
of
DIVINE LOVE.
A level of consciousness I have been calling
The Age of Spirit.

Once I had understood all of this, I instinctively knew that this melding was the new MODUS OPERANDI of the new *Age of Spirit,* but as ever, I hadn't arrived at this conclusion by accident. In fact, this intuitive 'knowing' had been with me since at least 2008.

***

For a long time I had somehow sensed that the ultimate goal of my quest was to be not just soul rebirth, but

THE UNIFICATION OF THE TWO HALVES OF MY SOUL.

The first clue had come when I had read about the meaning of The TEMPERANCE card in the book **THE GAME OF LIFE** by Ram back in the spring of 2000. Then **MY BIG FAT GREEK WEDDING**, which I had seen in the autumn of 2002, had clearly pointed to this MARRIAGE between the two parts of me.

However, there had been something else which had also allowed me to understand the ultimate purpose of my crazy odyssey, and that was the Catholic church's image of the Virgin as:

THE IMMACULATE CONCEPTION.

The Immaculate Conception was the name of the church I had visited in Campana back in March 2008, and to me this had been no mere 'accident' of fate. The symbolism was strikingly obvious. Very early on in my search I had concluded that the Virgin was one of many symbols of the feminine human soul within the **Soul of The**

World of Mankind, and so it was then no great leap of understanding to deduce that for me the Immaculate Conception referred to:

A non-sexual union
between the two halves of our human soul:

between the **mystical** and **material** halves
of ourselves.

In the doctrine of the Christian faith, the Virgin gives birth to an incarnation of the essence of SPIRIT — Divine Love — in the form of the Christ child through that non-sexual union between the **mystical** and **material** halves of her soul. Lumen Dei — the Holy Spirit within her — melds with her Lumen Naturae, and a new consciousness is born for humanity.

This is religious symbolism as pure metaphysics, but by now, after more than seventeen years of journeying, I was able to see that the metaphor of a non-sexual conception was part of so many apparently 'unconnected' worlds which were in fact expressions of one great unified whole. In that whole The Tarot's TEMPERANCE card I had discovered back in the year 2000 is to my mind

ALSO ANOTHER VERSION OF THHE IMMACULATE
CONCEPTION I HAVE JUST ELUCIDATED.

It is, therefore, one more way of conceptualising the spiritual dynamic governing our new *Age of Spirit*:

namely that of the union of the two distinct sources
of
Spirit within our souls.

In 2000 I had mistakenly thought that this Tarot card would give me answers to Redemption Road. But no, I had had to learn that the process of redemption needed to end *before* this new archetype - and a SECOND BIRTH within the human soul - could come into being.

The Tarot card's visual imagery was a beautiful depicton of the new MODUS OPERANDI governing the final two stages of initiation into our new *Age of Spirit* through which I was unwittingly passing. By graphically showing the process of fusion between the two halves of the now redeemed human soul, it signals something very transcendental in that union; what meta-physicians refer to as:

The Sacred Marriage between
HEAVEN AND EARTH.

That marriage is what gives rise to the SECOND BIRTH I have just mentioned – the birth of SPIRIT through the fusion of Paracelsus' Lumen Dei and Lumen Naturae.

As I left the internet cafe after finishing my You Tube video, I felt utterly certain that I had just completed my first conscious act of initiation into this new archetypal pattern. However, unknown to me, that initiation process, during which my soul would engage in the Sacred Marriage between its two halves OVER AND OVER AGAIN, would in fact go on for another 24-and-a-half months - right until the very end of my quest at the end of June 2014.

***

Before embarking on an account of some of the other 'trials' I endured during the first stage of this final initiation process, I wish dear reader to confront a few issues which may be on your mind. How did I find myself living out this bizarre and painful odyssey in the first place?

"From the beginning I had a sense of destiny, as though my life was assigned to me by fate and had to be fulfilled............, though I could never prove it to myself, it proved itself to me. I did not have the certainty, it had me."

With these words the twentieth century psychiatrist and alchemist C.G. Jung describes the invisible contracts which inhabit our souls, even before we are born.

This journey was my particular contract and destiny, and in all honesty, as Jung says, I never had any choice in the matter as to whether I would take it or not. Did that lessen the pain of it all?

No. As I sit writing these words to you, I am just slowly emerging from much of the trauma of what I have been through. That trauma has felt quite catastrophic at times, but equally, because life is so paradoxical and contradictory, at this very moment I still feel immensely grateful and glad for it all - perverse as this may seem.

Probably the highest price I have paid during these endless years of questing I wedded myself to has been the loneliness I have endured. The fact is that throughout the odyssey I had to go against the conventional 'wisdom' of the society to which all of us belong, and this necessitated me daring to believe in myself, despite the inevitable isolation which came with that belief. It also meant daring to believe that my inner voice had something unique and important to share.

I had to stick to my intuitive promptings which constantly told me that I knew something that was undeniably the truth - even if in the eyes of the world I looked like some kind of madwoman. And, to add to this, I have to also point out that although this lonely self-belief was the greatest source of trauma and suffering for me over the years, it was also THE ONLY WAY of making real and profound discoveries about myself and our shared HUMAN CONDITION.

It also paid off during this first stage of initiation when yet another test or 'trial' entered my life as I pushed relentlessly forward with only blind faith holding me together.

***

THE SHADOW OF LIFE.

Mavericks are by definition lonely explorers of the unknown, and in June 2012 I agreed to journey to a small-holding in southern Spain to look after some chickens and fruit trees. My idea was to spend 23 days alone in the depths of the Andalusian countryside, doing simple tasks, and thus finding the peace and tranquillity I needed in order to recover from the Chronic Fatigue which had plagued me for four-and-a-half long years.

Romantic, dreaming, 'shepherdess Karen', in her pastoral attire knew that as she watered the fruit trees, and fed the chickens, the two halves of her soul would be engaged in the Sacred Marriage between her Lumen Dei and Lumen Naturae. And in embracing this MODUS OPERANDI, she would be one step closer to the end of her initiation into the new *Age of Spirit*.

In fact the water which I would be using in that process was the perfect symbolic manifestation of MY INNER LIVING SPIRIT finally BEING BORN INSIDE ME, and 'irrigating' the now two united halves of my soul. Well, the small-holding proved to be all of that, but far more; a more I had never anticipated when I boarded the plane in England to fly to Malaga.

On my arrival, I was still in 'pastoral mode' and utterly ignorant of what lay in front of me. Instead of being warned about any upcoming 'trials', I was gratified to receive a huge positive sign when I noticed something rather special about the straw-bale house my hosts had built for themselves. It had five walls, and was basically the shape of an elongated pentagon. But, the sign which really spoke to me was located in the roof of the building.

It was a plastic skylight which allowed the bright Andalusian sunlight to flood the interior of the house, and it too was a pentagon. My thoughts immediately returned to my realisation several years earlier that my journey was about my soul becoming a five-pointed star, and sure enough, this skylight, supported by a central wooden post and five radiating beams, seemed to be quintessentially just that — A FIVE-POINTED STAR! But, despite this glorious STAR IN THE ROOF, and umpteen fruit trees laid out on manmade terraces, all speaking of the opportunity for the birth of spiritual light, things started to go very badly.

The 'trials' began on my first day alone on the farm. After seeing off my hosts as they began a journey to Malaga airport, I returned to the small holding in order to harvest garlic bulbs, and suddenly a dog appeared from nowhere, chasing the cockerel into the nearby cliffs, and then ripping the poor bird to shreds in the process. A few days later a canny fox turned up, and grabbed one of the chickens, giving it a severe mauling before my shouting chased it away. Undeterred, the fox knew exactly where breakfast was, and returned a few mornings later to kill another of the chickens.

And then, to add to these sinister omens, the moon started to become full in the night sky, illuminating the desolate landscape with its eerie light.

Here I was, a single woman alone in the wilds, and everyone in the local village around two kilometres away must have known it. The killings of the chickens and the moon had suddenly alerted my intuition to the real reason I had come to this remote location. My initiation into the new *Age of Spirit* was continuing, but this time it was asking me to be as brave as possible as I confronted the dark, shadow side of life on this planet.

Yes, my friend, not only does Mankind have
a universal shadow,
but Life itself
IS A MANIFESTATION OF LIGHT AND DARKNESS!

As the moon became fuller and fuller with each passing night towards the end of June, I became truly terrified for my own safety. I have never known a fear like it. I would lie in bed in a small wooden hut at the bottom of the small-holding, desperately praying that no one would use the bright moonlight to make their way down the path to where I lay. This was certainly not my over-active imagination at work. After all these years of questing, I was now old and wise enough to know that just as the dog and the fox possessed the instinct to kill, we human beings were also 'endowed' with this passion.

Therefore, the only logical conclusion I could come to was that any emotionally unstable, oddball male living in the village could strike me with impunity on any of these terrifyingly moonlit nights.

I was, to be perfectly blunt, quite simply
an appetising 'sitting duck'.

***

One night, just before the end of June, my terror became a reality. There had been a party in the village earlier on, and around 2am in the morning I heard drunken men on the path at the bottom of the gorge near to my wooden hut. My bowel suddenly began to turn its contents into liquid, and I quite literally stopped breathing for a few seconds. I lay rigid on my mattress in a state of abject terror.

I knew full well that the tiniest of sounds travelled with ease in this environment, and had I moved on my squeaky bed frame, or opened the hut door in an attempt to escape, these men would have heard me and known exactly where I was.

By what I can only assume was the grace of God, and fate, I was not attacked because after a few minutes I heard the men's voices move away into the distance. But as I rushed out of the hut to 'relieve myself' into the rubber bucket wedged behind it, I realised with total certainty that I had lived through one of the most horrific tests I would ever face on this quest.

A day-and-a-half later when I reluctantly hitched a lift to the local village cafe, I saw that the television news was reporting the disappearance of three small children from another small-holding in Andalusia; this one was in the north of the province. A week later, from the same television I learned that the children's dead bodies had been found – they had been murdered by their father. Yes, this initiation into the new *Age of Spirit* was proving to be a massive confrontation with:

The wild, untameable chaos within
this experience we call
LIFE.

As I had always suspected, in our physically incarnated
life here on planet Earth, SPIRIT exists within a duality:
and that duality is both Good and Evil.

After 23 days of this nightmare, I left the small-holding and made a brief visit to my parents, using this opportunity to climb up to the spot where *'my ruin'* had once stood. I was on a mission to collect another two stones from the site, just as I had done in March 2008. I had given those stones to Paulo Coelho when I had travelled to the Royal Dorchester Hotel in March 2009, and now I needed my very own, personal souvenir of this mysterious odyssey I had lived out.

When I reached the top of the hill, I could see that the site of *'my ruin'* was now buried under about a metre-and-a-half of trash. Only the crumbling wall of an adjacent terrace remained above the surface of the debris. Gently I lowered my feet onto the earth and plucked two stones from the wall. I closed my fingers around them, and breathed in deeply. They were the physical embodiment of the simplicity I had gone in search of, and I really didn't need anything else. These stones are now here before you, dear friend, in the palms of my hands in this image, and I sincerely hope that somehow they speak to you. For me they symbolise the eternal I had yearned for so deeply all those years ago when I used to lean back against the broken wall of '**my ruin**' longing for an encounter with my soul.

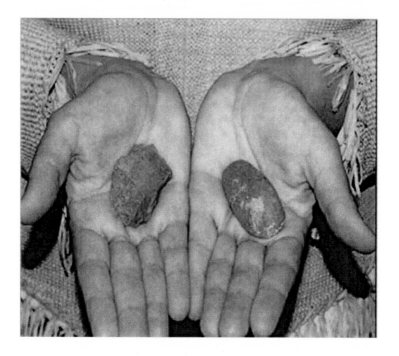

A few days later I returned to Ambleton, and once back in my apartment I found myself shaken and profoundly stirred up by everything I had experienced on the small-holding. Could things get any worse was the question which dominated my thoughts? My answer to that was a fairly confident no, but barely had I recovered from this unexpected 'trial' when another truly COSMIC event entered my life.

At the start of November 2012 I began to experience possibly the greatest of all my challenges.

THE JUDGEMENT

SECTION II

Over a period of a year I had developed a lump on my left arm. It had arrived quite suddenly one night when I had been looking after my friend's dog Bella in September 2011.It had stayed small and neat for about five months, but then, with no warning signs, it had started to change. It began to grow steadily throughout the spring and summer of 2012, and by September it was a bruised, purple hillock on my arm, measuring about three inches in diameter.

An ultrasound examination at the local hospital didn't shed any light on what it might be, and so an operation to remove the lump was scheduled for November 9 – a day after my father's birthday.

On November 2, I was busily trying to tidy my apartment in preparation for the operation, when I quite unexpectedly unearthed the photograph of the GIZA PYRAMIDS IN EGYPT which J had given me two years earlier. By now, it was half of its original size as I had cut off the ends of the image in order to use it for my You Tube video. Nevertheless, the three gigantic and emblematic pyramids built more than four thousand years ago dominated the centre of the photograph.

The picture had been making a random tour of my abode for the last eighteen months. I had tried hanging it on various walls, doors, and alcoves, but had never found a suitable 'home' for it. However, this time the timing was completely different. I knew that it was NO ACCIDENT that I had pulled out the photograph from inside a pile of books at this particular moment on my journey. The next day I stuck the pyramids proudly above my kitchen sink, and intuitively sensed that their long, peripatetic existence in my apartment had finally come to an end.

The operation was now only seven days away, and I found myself oscillating between a desire to postpone it, and another to simply get it over and done with. My doubts had arisen because I had experienced an extremely bad month of chronic fatigue, and was worried about the effects of a general anaesthetic on the brain fog I had been enduring every morning. Nevertheless, despite these feelings of uncertainty, I knew in my heart that the operation was part of the rite of initiation into the *Age of Spirit* which I had been living out for just over eight months.

Not only was the operation to be a cosmic point of transition into the new for me, but the lump on my arm was also symbolic of everything that had happened on my journey of redemption. Now that the new *Age of Spirit* was at hand, or so I imagined, the past would have to be metaphorically CUT OUT and discarded to make room for the next stage of my spiritual quest. Yes, it was all so obvious, but there was still a part of me that desperately wanted to postpone my appointment with fate.

The remaining days before I was due to go to the hospital passed in this uncomfortable state of ambivalence, but I had one thing which was proving to be of enormous consolation to me, and that was the photograph of the Giza Pyramids. Each time I stood in front of them, washing dishes, or washing my hands, they seemed to be trying to tell me something EXTREMELY IMPORTANT but I couldn't grasp what that *something was*.

Finally, on the morning of Wednesday November 7, the hidden message simply jumped out at me from the photograph. A calm, quiet voice inside me said the following:

**We are the marriage between
Heaven and Earth.**

We have been the Pyramids of Redemption for centuries, but now the planetary energy has changed. We have become the Pyramids of Life, just like the Tree of Life. Each time you look at us, you will see the Sacred Marriage between Heaven and Earth.

BETWEEN LUMEN DEI AND LUMEN NATURAE.

I gasped in wonder and awe as I stared once more at these magical pyramids. Never had anything been more obvious to me, and yet for years I HADN'T BEEN ABLE TO SEE ANY OF IT!

***

There was quite clearly a divine timing behind absolutely everything on our planet, and that 'timing' had deemed that the invisible realm would not be allowed to give me this insight until this precise moment on my quest. Until now, I had never been meant to see these monuments as manifestations and symbols of the Sacred Marriage between the two halves of the human soul.

The voice inside me was right; this new significance of the pyramids had only been given to me because the Earth's spiritual energy had changed. THE PISCEAN AGE was drawing to an end, and the dawn of the new *Age of Spirit* was upon us. With Mankind embarking on a new consciousness, everything in our world would now begin to take on fresh meanings.

THE PYRAMID OF LIFE.

A SYMBOL
OF
THE SACRED MARRIAGE BETWEEN HEAVEN AND EARTH.

Perhaps the Giza Pyramids had always been symbols of the Sacred Marriage between the **mystical** and the **material** in the human soul, but I didn't have to go onto the internet to find out. Rather, yet again I was being asked to trust the mystery of life as it unfolded second by second before me. That blind trust in a divine timing ordained by a universal intelligence would then show me everything I needed to know.

As soon as I had been given the insight into the Giza Pyramids hanging on my kitchen wall, it more or less confirmed my earlier understanding that the operation was most definitely a rite of passage into the next phase of my spiritual life, but more importantly, another Sacred Marriage between Heaven and Earth. **Mystical** old me with my Lumen Dei would meet the manifestation of the **material** half of my soul, in the form of the surgeon and his team.

This earthbound personification of my spirit – Lumen Naturae – would then meld with my Lumen Dei – the heavenly aspect of myself - and through the operation I would achieve the 'marriage' of the two halves of my soul, and a new light within me.

Being able to suddenly understand all these connections gave me the ultimate reassurance I needed that I should finally go ahead with the surgery. But, before I continue with this account, there is one more amazing detail I need to give you, dear reader, and it is deeply and cosmically connected to the new ending for The Alchemist which I miraculously 'channelled' back in April 2012 for Chapter 18.

This detail, or rather fact, dramatically pertains to my hospital experience seven months after that moment of channelling. On the morning of November 9, already kitted out in my surgical gown and awaiting a final word with the surgeon, I sat patiently on my hospital bed when suddenly I found myself face to face with a tall, dark stranger. He smiled warmly and introduced himself as the anaesthetist who would be working with the team.

"My name is Anwar," he said casually and in a friendly, confidence-inspiring manner.

ANWAR!!!!!! I couldn't believe what I was hearing, but then again, yes - I most definitely could!

"Your name means LIGHT in Arabic" I quickly informed him, as I beamed from ear to ear.

He looked surprised that I should have made this comment about his name, but recomposed himself in order to explain the type of anaesthesia he would be giving me. This anaesthetist could not possibly have known why I felt such unbridled enthusiasm for his name – a name I had chosen especially for the leader of the refugees in Chapter 18.

However, unlike the fictional Anwar, my real-life Anwar would not be giving me a 'beating', and then information regarding the true location of my treasure. Oh no, all that redemption work was now well and truly behind me. Real-life Anwar was no longer engaged in my soul rebirth, but in my SECOND BIRTH.

He was the REDEEMED MANIFESTATION of the other half of my soul - even if he had absolutely no awareness of that fact.

This 'Anwar of Light' and I would engage in the Sacred Marriage between Heaven and Earth, and what I imagined would be my final rite of initiation into the new *Age of Spirit*. As the gentleman concerned walked away, I marvelled at the incredible precision and beauty of the invisible realm's timing.

***

The operation proved to be a resounding success, and in many ways, more than fulfilled its promise of being the rite of initiation I so desperately needed. I awoke from the anaesthetic into the same old world I had left behind only less than two hours earlier, but now it had been completely MADE ANEW! The redeemed me, who had battled through more than seventeen years of encounters with the universal shadow, had somehow 'died' on the operating table, and someone new had suddenly opened her spiritual eyes to a startling awareness of the utter beauty and magic of life.

After this 'AWAKENING', as I came round from the anaesthetic I immediately jumped to the seemingly logical conclusion that even if the new *Age of Spirit* would require a few more decades of challenges before its full manifestation on our planet, at least for this lowly mortal – me:

My treasure, and **THE BIG DREAM,** of which I was only
another part amongst billions, had both become a reality.

However, as I fumbled forward on my unmapped path, I had
once more misread the signs. Although what I assumed to be the
definitive SECOND BIRTH of my soul, and its entry into the new *Age
of Spirit,* was truly amazing and extraordinary, it would turn out to
be just one of a SERIES OF SECOND BIRTHS within this twenty eight
month period of initiation I was undergoing.

It was thus that my euphoria after the operation was misplaced
and dramatically truncated before it had any time to take root. I
should have paid more heed to the omens regarding Life's shadow
which I had received in the summer of 2012 when I had been on the
small-holding in Andalusia. They had tried to alert me to the fact that
I was quite a long way off from the final end of my quest.

Unfortunately, the inevitable encounters with this OTHER SIDE OF
LIFE on planet Earth were set to continue, and confirmation of this
came two weeks after the operation when on one of my visits to
the hospital the surgeon glumly informed me that the lump he had
removed had been a cancer. In all probability I would be needing
chemotherapy very soon. Of course I was shocked at the news – very
shocked indeed - and experienced a few mornings when I awoke
thinking that the hospital must have got the wrong name and number
on its files. But, realistically, I most definitely wasn't surprised.

After so long on this path, I knew that my rite of initiation into the
Age of Spirit would not be something minor and inconsequential. The
cancer diagnosis was the inevitable emergence of one of the many
aspects of the SHADOW OF SPIRIT.

Yes, as I have already said, our spirits have a shadow –
the multifaceted **universal shadow** of Life itself.

The truth is that as long as we humans continue to incarnate into
a physical world and a physical form, there will always be a shadow.
And, ever brutally honest with myself, I knew that in the great scheme
of things, at this stage of my spiritual development the cancer was
MY PERSONAL MANIFESTATION OF THAT SHADOW. Yet again the

invisible realm had determined that I would need to confront my fear of death, *or even death itself,* before being granted my 'stripes' and a complete entry into the new age awaiting us all.

Twenty days after my diagnosis, on December 12, 2012, I received the news that the cancer was treatable. I had agonized for those twenty days in a no-man's-land of uncertainty as I underwent tests to see if it had spread to my brain. The surgeon had informed me that if this were the case, then I would be facing certain death. Luckily, it hadn't and I had been granted the chance to fight.

Even so, I now realised that a concrete limit had been placed on my life, and my mortality was not something I could continue to keep at a distance from myself. Henceforth it was an everyday reality. The shadow of DEATH which had come to LIVE UNDER THE SAME ROOF with me back in 1999, as I had performed the 'shamanic' ritual on the ground just below *'my ruin'* had kept its promise.

We were intimates — ME AND MY SHADOW. There was no separating us from one another on this journey we call LIFE.

Nevertheless, in spite of everything I was facing, the initial shock of the diagnosis did have some beneficial consequences. It served to protect me from going too deeply into the ramifications of my new circumstances, and besides I needed energy to face my first session of chemotherapy, and also the fraught business of revealing my diagnosis to family and friends. However, eventually nature's protective shield wore off, and an impenetrable darkness descended into my world.

It transpired that this darkness was to be a second, completely unforeseen encounter with the Dark Night of the Soul.

***

It began for me in the middle of January 2013, and was triggered by a bout of flu-like symptoms which went on for a gruelling 29 days. In that time my chemotherapy was cancelled four times, and a pit of utter despair opened up within my soul. Inside the confines of my studio apartment I found myself completely alone and 'abandoned' for periods of up to eight and nine days at a stretch. My isolation was so extreme during this period that I even descended into thoughts of suicide.

My neighbours largely ignored my existence, and my soul mate J, with his own health issues, and living as he did on the other side of town, was unable to make the complicated journey to visit me. Each day as I lay prostrate in my bed, counting the hours, I fell deeper and deeper into a pit of anger, rage, bitterness and despair over the state of my world, and the outer world in general. This Dark Night was giving me a first-hand experience of what remained of my personal inner darkness, but also what we as a species had made of our world at the very top of the Tree of the Knowledge of Good and Evil.

Our planet and its people were in a total mess. Isolation and cruel indifference seemed to be the order of the day. Families, communities, institutions, and whole nations had started to disintegrate, even though an illusion of well-being continued to prevail. People were pathologically alone and here I was, lying in the silence of my apartment, knowing that if I just so happened to die, my neighbours would only find my decomposing body because of the smell percolating from under the front door.

However, despite the horror of those four weeks of isolation and illness, they proved to be a very necessary experience for me. After 29 days I did finally recover my health and equilibrium, but I was also now much more intimately aware of the exact nature of the new agenda for myself and for our new age. More than ever it was about meeting a broken and agonizing world with:

THE LOVE OF OUR SPIRITS.

My first task in this endeavour would be to heal the last vestiges of my own finger-pointing anger, rage and bitterness towards that brokenness I had just been shown, and embrace the fact that I could no longer call myself a victim of either my past or my current reality. And for this:

I NEEDED TO FORGIVE EVERYTHING
AND EVERYONE IN MY LIFE.

However, right now, I am 'jumping' ahead of myself. The six months of my massive confrontation with death in the form of a cancer was showing me that the universal shadow was vital and inescapable for our spiritual growth.

It had been, and still was, the very material which had allowed me to grow and change and become conscious. And through that consciousness I had been able to learn that the good in my life was and is all the more good, wonderful and miraculous because I could now see it in relation to the bad or rotten aspects of my existence. I was now no longer a person gripped by inner forces of denial, but someone who had shown enough courage to face the whole of herself – both good and bad.

***

At the end of June 2013 I thought that I had arrived at the very end of my troubles, and was about to discover my inner transcendent capacity to heal my wounds and renew the very essence of who I was. But, yet again, I was wrong. All of that would be revealed to me almost a year later, in May 2014. Nevertheless, after my encounter with cancer – I really hate the use of the word battle - I was finally SHOWN THE LIGHT or in other words given the meaning of the mayhem I had experienced during this FIRST STAGE of my initiation into the *Age of Spirit*.

That REVELATION didn't take place immediately after the first part had come to an end but was given to me eight-and-a-half months later in March 2014 when I stood inside the very same bookshop in Salveira where I had been in 1995 holding a copy of Alejandro Jodorowsky's PSICOMAGIA – UNA TERAPIA PANICA. This LIGHT came in the form of the penultimate chapter in a Spanish book by Alejandro Jodorowsky called

YO: EL TAROT – ME: THE TAROT.

After buying the book on Monday March 10, I returned to my parent's house amongst the olive groves and in the evening quite randomly opened the text at an image from The Tarot, together with Alejandro's words. Suddenly, I instinctively knew that I was being told by the invisible realm that the sixteen months between March 2012 and the beginning of July 2013 had been my cosmic encounter with the penultimate Arcana of The Tarot – ARCANA 20

In the bosom of my parents' house that evening, just minutes away from the hill where **'my ruin'** had once stood, THE JUDGEMENT card's image gave me the missing piece of what had been happening to me.

**The God who comes down from Heaven is
the same as He who is within you.**

ALEJANDRO JODOROWSKY.

The card shows a young child emerging from a tomb, watched on by a woman and a man, who are also rising from their own individual tombs. An angel in the sky above the child's head blows a trumpet of triumph. My God, perched on the edge of my bed, I immediately understood what I was being shown. Here was the confirmation of my intuition. My spirit — symbolised by the child in the card - had emerged from the dark tomb of the universal shadow of Life. And this had only been possible because the **mystical** (female) and **material** (male) halves of my soul had constantly engaged in the Sacred Marriage or union between Heaven and Earth within me.

From that metaphysical 'union', repeated over and over again in the face of truly horrible 'trials', I had given birth to THE SPIRIT OF MY GOD SELF, and its triumph over the **UNIVERSAL SHADOW** of the physical world and my physical self.

Now, God, The Universe, Higher Power, or whatever one decides to call our Source, was not only WITHOUT in my outer world, but also WITHIN me - inside the very core of my soul. Wow, was all I could think!!!!

***

A few weeks after this serendipitous encounter with THE JUDGEMENT card, I went onto Wikipedia, and discovered the following words associated with this Arcana.

- *Judgement — Rebirth — Inner Calling — Absolution*
- *Restart — Accepting past mistakes/actions — Release*
- *Forgiveness — End of repression — Reconciliation — Renewal*
- *Decision — Salvation — New beginning — Hope — Redemption*

The implications of all of this were startlingly self-evident. From now on this meant that a constant, unstoppable dialogue between the Divine INSIDE me and OUTSIDE me was now possible. Sitting alone in my bedroom in March 2014 — the room which had accompanied me through so much doubt and confusion over so many years - I came to what I thought was a very obvious and natural conclusion:

the new Age of Spirit had finally arrived!!!

It was the NEW REALITY of my own individual world, and also the whole world in general, even if as yet we as a species hadn't quite reached the critical mass of individuals required for its final manifestation. This incredibly vulnerable 'sitting duck', who had endured so much fear, terror and chaos, over so many years was now beginning to feel like a decidedly very 'happy bunny'!

NEW LIFE

OUT OF DARKNESS,
YOU ARE BORN

OUT OF FLESH
YOUR SPIRIT COMES.

OUT OF THE TOMB
YOU RISE ANEW

OUT OF MATTER
HAS COME YOUR DAWN.

THE LIGHT OF LOVE
IN YOU IS BORN.

Karen Williams.

29

THE WORLD

JOURNEY'S END; JOURNEY'S BEGINNING

Life, the Human Soul, Mother Nature, and Mother Earth are all feminine in essence. When we can finally surrender to this truth, we shall find ourselves.

KAREN WILLIAMS

WELL, was that truly my NEW REALITY? Was SPIRIT finally the new dawn emerging inside me, and also close to breaking on the horizon of our amazing planet Earth? Reluctantly, I have to say no, and this is because there was just one more part to my twenty-eight month initiation left.

The 2014 revelation of THE JUDGEMENT card, and the insights which had come with it, had not been available to me at the end of June 2013. Although I had more than proved my metal over sixteen long months, there still remained just one, final major Arcana in the Tarot deck which I needed to confront. It was to give me the most extraordinary ending to my epic quest, and would also allow me to know true wonder and awe for what I had endured. That Arcana was, of course, number 21 - THE WORLD.

YES, THE WORLD, OUR WORLD.

So, where did my journey through this Arcana begin? As the trials of THE JUDGEMENT phase of my initiation into the *Age of Spirit* came to their end, the beginning of July 2013 saw my final series of tests emerge at the summit of my spiritual Everest. Without any immediate awareness of what lay ahead, I found myself metaphorically embarking on encounters with the whole panorama of what we 'experience and see' from the TOP OF OUR PHYSICAL WORLD. And, once more, I was only given the manifestation of this truth at the very end of that process.

***

It all started at the beginning of July 2013. Six days after finalising my radiotherapy I found myself sitting in the Intensive Care Unit of a major hospital hoping that a dear friend would awake from a coma. She had been involved in a terrible road traffic accident, and initially the diagnosis had been that my friend was brain-dead. However, the invisible realm gave me an unexpected sign on a train as I left her bedside to travel home on the first day of her ordeal.

It was an article in a newspaper I found next to the train seat I had apparently chosen quite at random. It concerned a woman who had been diagnosed as brain-dead. That 'diagnosis' had been spectacularly, and quite unexpectedly overturned when to every ones' shock she had spontaneously awoken as the life support machines had been disconnected. The next day I returned to my friend's bedside buoyed up with a new hope in my heart, but to say that I was confused and lost with regard to what was happening to me at this very moment is a huge understatement.

I did what all of us do in states of emergency; I simply *hung on* — but to what, I really can't say. Somehow I was beginning to vaguely sense that the universe was asking me to PUSH ON THROUGH DISASTER AFTER DISASTER with no explanation as to why I was being given these trials, nor any guarantee that I would survive them. Perhaps this is the ultimate test in life: that we are prepared to believe in the supremacy of light over darkness — NO MATTER WHAT! Thankfully, my friend survived her crisis.

In the middle of July I accompanied her from the I.C.U. in the hospital to a convalescence home, and spent the next two weeks making sure that she was settled and secure in her rehabilitation programme. Then, in the first week of August I turned my attention away from her needs and placed my focus on my own. I had supported my friend through her coma and the first two weeks of her rehabilitation at a time when I had been feeling very weak and unwell myself.

To be by her side only six days after the end of my radiotherapy had proved an enormous sacrifice for me, even though I had made that sacrifice more than willingly. Now it was my turn to recover from more than a year of unexpected and unpredictable 'catastrophes'.

One evening, after returning from the convalescence home, I spoke to another friend about my urgent need to simply 'escape' or 'get away', and within a day of my plea for help he had come across a Catholic retreat for me on the internet. So it was that off I went, deep into the depths of rural England, with my usual characteristic optimism and naive innocence. However, I was to abruptly discover that I would not be experiencing respite, but yet more of the UNIVERSAL SHADOW OF LIFE!

At the time, the invisible realm wasn't willing to give me any clues about what was happening, and I therefore had absolutely no understanding that in fact this was to be my second trial and encounter with THE WORLD Arcana.

***

For four days I choked on and suffered the ordeal of having to submit myself to the rules and dogma of orthodox Catholicism. Ensconced just a few miles away from the ominous shadow of a nuclear power plant, on my second night of so-called respite I packed my bags, and planned to leave as soon as daylight had broken. But, I didn't. After all these years, my spirit knew that there had been absolutely no accident as to where I had come, and what I was enduring.

Here, I realised was yet another encounter with the universal shadow. And, knowing how high the stakes of my spiritual quest were

I found myself accepting that I couldn't run away from it, even though my whole being was begging me to do so. This shadow had to be met with peace, and dare I say SACRIFICE. This last insight regarding sacrifice had come to me as a result of what I had gone through with my friend back in July in the I.C.U unit. Now, the universe seemed to be telling me that this quality was to be THE VERY HALLMARK of what I was being asked to do in this truly agonizing situation.

It was more than clear that even though I had redeemed the two halves of my soul back in February 2012, I was still experiencing the very top of the Tree of The Knowledge of Good and Evil in all its rigidity and controlling zeal, and my response would have to be one of love, forgiveness and peace. However, at that very moment little did I know that this manifestation of life's Unholy Trinity – namely orthodox Catholicism – was an expression of our:

WORLD'S SHADOW.

So, accepting the fate which this odyssey had assigned me, I successfully completed my mission of sacrifice and love at the retreat by withstanding the pain of my four day 'trial' there. There had been no possibility of any kind of recovery for me, but plenty of mini 'Hells on Earth' to get through, without finding myself erupting into my own individual shadow of rage and demonic fury.

When I had happily and innocently journeyed to the retreat I had never expected to be 'tested' yet again, and so returned to my apartment with an incomprehensible victory notched inside the inner recesses of my aching soul. Then barely recovered from this ordeal, I returned to supporting my friend who had been in a coma.

She continued with her long convalesce from the accident, and once again, despite my sincere, and heart-felt desire to stand by her at such a difficult time, I began to understand that I was yet again in the grip of being asked TO MAKE SACRIFICES. However, a completely unintended consequence of all of this was that as summer turned to autumn I started to experience a truly profound change in my sensibilities and understanding of the world around me.

In order to engage with THE WORLD Arcana, I had been completely unaware that the invisible realm had decided that I would have to allow my spirit to once more experience the collective shadow of our species – in other words the universal shadow.

But, this time, these encounters would be that of seeing directly the effect it has had on our physical world. This meant that I now became even more aware of the mess we were all in as a species. Where this had been obvious to me before, in the autumn of 2013 it seemed to hit me full on everywhere I went. The status quo of how we live and die at the beginning of this 21ˢᵗ Century jumped out at me from just about everywhere.

It came in some of just a few of the following observations: pollution from cars invariably carrying only one person in each of them as I sat waiting for buses. A seemingly exponential increase in homeless people begging on the streets, continuous talk of diseases and economic hardship on the T.V and in the other media - and then there was more. Sexual attacks abounding on children and young women, murders, war, hunger, poverty, and uprisings all over the planet from citizens realising that the 'system' we humans had created was no longer delivering any kind of justice, dignity and quality of life.

I heard friends saying it, and strangers were saying it too: 'The world's gone mad, the world's gone mad!' Of course, it hadn't, BUT IT MOST CERTAINLY FELT AS IF IT HAD! No, these horrors were not madness, but the manifestations of the old world order we so desperately need to leave behind. The *Age of Spirit* is demanding a NEW WORLD from us; a new world in our hearts and souls – one in which our **mystical** feminine souls will assume dominion.

***

The third most significant part of my journey through THE WORLD Arcana began on December 5, 2013, with the death of Nelson Mandela. Again, I had no awareness that this was what was happening to me, but subconsciously I understood that all of these events were highly significant. The day of Mandela's 'departure' wasn't just any old day either – it was also 'coincidentally' my friend Sila's BIRTHDAY.

That winter's afternoon I had just posted her some illustrations from the new edition of TREASURE, and then around a few minutes before ten at night I switched on my radio, only to be surprised by the voice of South Africa's President Jacob Zuma. He was announcing the passing away of one of the greatest human beings of the twentieth and twenty-first centuries. Suddenly, and without any kind of warning, a light flashed brightly inside my heart. It was the light of my spirit being abruptly and cosmically ignited inside my soul with this unexpected news.

With this, my intuition immediately informed me that Thursday, December 5 was not just my friend's birthday. The synchronicity of the universe had decided that the news I had just heard would herald a truly cosmic event. Consciously, and also subconsciously, this would be:

The World's Birthday
and only Nelson Mandela's death could
usher in this metaphysical moment.

Nelson Mandela — Madiba — had fulfilled a unique and extraordinary role in the spiritual life of Humanity. He had used twenty seven years in prison to defeat the physical world - both outside himself and within his soul. His SACRIFICE and suffering had revealed to him the true nature of the human heart, and he had wisely understood that there were NO MATERIAL ANSWERS TO HUMAN SUFFERING.

Nothing less than a FREE SPIRIT could rise above the horrors
of physical life here on planet Earth.

Only through forgiveness and reconciliation from a reborn spirit
could we move forward into the light.

Madiba had enjoyed a degree of happiness in his old age, but the last few years of his life had been characterised by yet another RETURN TO SACRIFICE. 'Thanks' to modern technology, he had found himself living far longer than he probably would have wanted, and had also had to endure being manipulated by the ANC leadership.

Near the very end of his great life, Jacob Zuma had posed with a very frail Madiba for the party's own self-serving motives in an opportunistic public relations photograph. It is apparently a reality of human life that our sacrifices are so often made within the bosom of our nearest and dearest 'families' - whether they be those of blood, ethnicity, social grouping, political affiliation or national identity. Nevertheless, one thing was blindingly obvious. Nelson Mandela's many, many sacrifices had been so transcendental, that he belonged not just to South Africa, but to all of us:

TO THE WHOLE WORLD.

And so, a week later, the whole world duly 'turned up' to say a heartfelt farewell to this extraordinary human being. But, once more, despite high hopes and noble ideals shared by all of us, the worst of Mankind, and what we have done with our planet, went on display.

Political corruption and infighting were embarrassingly captured by an omnipresent world media. Luckily however, that same media also managed to show truly moving expressions of love, awe, humility and gratitude for the astonishing life of this great man. Nevertheless, the overwhelming panorama beamed out to millions of television screens around the planet was that of the huge gulf between rich and poor, privileged and disenfranchised. The truth was that the summit of the Tree of The Knowledge of Good and Evil was more than painfully apparent.

Nelson Mandela's extraordinary life and death were now shining a spotlight on our universal shadow, and only he could have made sure that THE WHOLE WIDE WORLD WOULD BE IN ON THIS TOGETHER!!! This I knew was a massive global initiation into the *Age of Spirit* for all of us.

Our human family had come together in a spectacular
way to look into its own cosmic dirt.

MADIBA

Twenty seven years Madiba, twenty seven years.
Can we imagine five, ten or fifteen?
But yours were twenty seven long, long years.

In that eternity, you found the only way to peace:
to weep and then forgive;
to choke on pain and then start to breathe again.

Your suffering gave you time to understand the human heart,
and out of your ashes you were born again:
born to a greater light and truth.

That light has sparked once more around the world.
As you leave us, your long walk has set us free.

Free to leave our petty, childish selves behind
so that we may now walk the new road of Love;
the road your humble soul discovered
in the silence of a lonely prison cell.
Truly Nelson Mandela, your life has taught us well.

Father of a Nation, and beloved brother to us all
Madiba, I know your vision shall not fail.
None of us can forsake such courage lived out for all Mankind,
As long as we remember, you will not have lived in vain.

Karen Williams

***

It would have been a great relief to me to be told that my
odyssey had finally ended with the passing of Madiba, but then on
December 17, only a few days after this unprecedented farewell, an
amazing realisation came to me.

About three days earlier, my soul mate J had telephoned
me to tell me that he had just bought himself a huge map of the

world. Incredible, I thought to myself, that is something I have been wanting to get myself for a very long time. Then on December 17, I walked into a photographic shop to have a picture taken of me as a Christmas card for my parents. My energy was extremely low, and so I knew that I would be unable to make a trip to Andalusia to spend Christmas with them.

In order to get into the seasonal spirit, I looked desperately around the shop for any kind of Christmas decoration I could include in the photo. I saw nothing. Panicking, I quickly asked the assistant if she had any tinsel. Within seconds she pulled off a strand of gold tinsel from a small artificial Christmas tree. 'Perfect', I heard myself enthuse, and taking each end in either hand I wrapped it around my neck. Two minutes later I had a photo ready to send to my beloved parents, and also quite unintentionally a sign to interpret as soon as I returned home.

That evening I pulled out a copy of the photo and examined it. I hadn't realised that it was a sign when I had been busily wrapping the tinsel around my neck, but now it was astonishingly obvious. I had created a halo, or circle around me, and suddenly I realised that this was symbolic of something else which was circular or round:

THE WORLD.

Hmm, so that was why J had told me about
buying a map of the world I muttered to myself

These two events, together with Nelson Mandela's death, were giving me a very clear message: my initiation rite into the new *Age of Spirit* was coming to an end as a 'NEW WORLD' was being born within me and the rest of Humanity.

Yes, the world was changing, moving, evolving and being born again, but as it did so, I still had no idea that I was journeying through **THE WORLD** Arcana. However, what I had understood at this point was that since March 2012 I had been actively engaged in the Sacred Marriage between the **mystical** and **material** halves of my soul. I also knew that each time these two halves of my spirit joined together, a new spiritual awareness was being born within me:

THE LIGHT OF THE NEW AGE OF SPIRIT.

HAIR RETURNING AFTER CHEMOTHERAPY AND TINSEL WRAPPED AROUND MY NECK.

This process of the Sacred Marriage had also been performing another task on this odyssey — that of carrying me up yet one more metaphysical pyramid. This time it was not the Pyramid of Redemption which had been finally scaled in February 2012, and which had marked the rebirth of my soul. Now, since that moment of journey's end I had begun to climb THE PYRAMID OF DIVINE LOVE situated right at the very top of The Pyramid of Redemption.

Just like my Matroyshka doll I mentioned in Chapter 24, The Pyramid of Redemption seemed to have its very own mini-pyramid, or 'inner doll' situated at its summit. Scaling it meant that I was engaged in a deeply cosmic and sacred initiation of the dawn of the *Age of Spirit*, and the events before Christmas suggested to me that I was probably only weeks away from the summit of that pyramid.

***

At the beginning of January I bought myself a huge map of the world, and a few weeks later my intuition suddenly informed me that the end of my climb would once more coincide with a very 'cosmic' date in my personal calendar, just as it had done two years earlier in 2012.

For the second time it would be another anniversary of my visit to Paris to see Alejandro Jodorowsky - February 27 - only this time it would be the 18th anniversary of that epic and life-changing event. And then a quite unexpected flash of insight told me something else. I suddenly knew that the final assault of the mini-pyramid of Divine Love at the very summit of my personal Everest would consist of three parts; just as it had done back in February 2008. That had been the time when I had found my spiritual light in Ambleton hospital, and also with Imogen at the retreat — the first part - and had then journeyed back to Andalusia for my unconscious mind's encounter with my inner light in the church in Campana.

The third, and final stage of that process had been my return to Ambleton, and the insights I had achieved which had enabled me to put together the cosmic 'puzzle' I had been working on. It was therefore now more than self-evident that I would have to do exactly the same as I had six years earlier, but once again, without any kind of prior explanations.

My intuition never gave me any specific clues regarding its wishes for me; this journey had always been one of blind faith for this battered pilgrim. My questioning would have to wait because what had been demanded of me from the very beginning, and what was expected of me now was simply heart-felt obedience to the promptings I received, and nothing more.

However, what I did know from re-examining the process I had submitted myself to back in 2008 was that somehow I would GIVE BIRTH on a conscious level to the spiritual light of our new *Age of Spirit* here in Ambleton - in the same way as I had allowed my soul to be reborn in 2008. Then I would leave England to complete the second stage of this process by travelling to Andalusia and the church in Campana once again.

There, inside the hushed and holy space of the church, I would perform my unconscious mind's part of yet another Sacred Marriage between the two halves of my soul, and then on my return to Ambleton I would be able to complete a third SACRED MARRIAGE within the realms of my conscious mind in order to close the circle. I assumed that this third and final part of the process would be the very end of my rite of initiation, and I would finally be able to claim that:

The new Age of Spirit was at last with us!

***

And so it was that the invisible realm mysteriously arranged for all of this to happen. As soon as I had recovered from a six week bout of flu after Christmas, I responded to my mother's plea for help, and promised her that she could go and rest whilst I took over the task of looking after my 88 year old father for two weeks. However, before boarding a plane on Monday, February 24, and once again finding myself on Spanish soil for the 18th anniversary of my trip to Paris, I found myself completing the first conscious part of the three part finale.

On the Thursday before my flight to Spain I left a counselling session with my wonderful counsellor, and walked in the direction of the bus stop. As I did so, I noticed that the church on the corner of the street was open. Knowing that I would be going to Campana's church a few days later, I instantly understood that the universe had opened the doors of this church in order to allow me to bring the new light of the *Age of Spirit* into the realm of our collective consciousness.

Gratefully, and humbly I stepped into the building not knowing that I was about to perform a ritual which would in fact be a metaphysical act signifying the marriage between the two halves of my soul. As my eyes adjusted to the gloom inside the building, I spotted a circular pyramid-shaped candle stand at the side of the main aisle, and asked a gentleman cleaning the pews if I could light a candle. He went off, and then a lady returned carrying a candle lighter. She lit the very top candle at the apex of this pyramid which then allowed me to take a small candle from a tray, light its wick from the main candle at the very top, and then place it just below in one of many small holders.

Sixteen days later, I was doing exactly the same thing at the main altar of the church in Campana on International Women's Day.

More importantly, six long years later, and a mere twenty four hours after the day when I had gone to Campana's church in 2008, I had decided to share my experience with my dear friend Sila from Madrid. She had expressed a heartfelt desire to translate my book into Spanish, and I could think of nothing better than that the two of us would repeat the same journey I had taken back in 2008 to the altar of Campana's church.

However, as I have already said, this time our mission would not be to *find spiritual light*, but o give birth to the light of DIVINE LOVE. This would come about as a result of the union between the two sources of that same light – in other words the soul's Lumen Dei and Lumen Naturae.

And this would then represent the mystical Sacred
Marriage within the two separate halves of our souls.
The consequence of this act of alchemy would be the dawning
of the new *Age of Spirit*,

AND A NEW WORLD.

***

Well, thanks to my complete and utter faith in signs, the universe did not let me and my friend down. As we arrived at the altar, it was completely FLOODED WITH LIGHT!!!There was no huge cross with the figure of Jesus hanging from it, but instead a beautiful statue of the Virgin Mary.

She glowed in gold as the hidden electrical illumination transformed her and the surrounding sculptures into luminous, transcendental forms. And, even though this time, six years on, just as I had anticipated, there was no repetition of a physical sign lying on one of the altar steps, I now could see the sign I had not understood, nor had I been expected to understand, back in 2008.

It was of course the Virgin herself - one of the greatest feminine symbols of the human soul. She glimmered and shimmered, shouting out the victory of SPIRIT over Matter. She was:

THE IMMACULATE CONCEPTION,

Our transcendental Mother and a universal symbol of Humanity's Soul, and this was the church of the Immaculate Conception in Campana.

Here was the Christian symbol of THE UNIVERSAL MOTHER IN ALL OF US. But, she was also the maternal symbol I had talked about earlier – a symbol buried deep inside the collective unconscious of Mankind, and her name was also more than self-explanatory.

Through the union of the two halves of her soul, The Virgin was conceiving the spiritual light of our new age. She was just one of many symbols of the universal soul of Humanity; the feminine soul which had reached the top of the Tree of the Knowledge of Good and Evil, and had redeemed itself. This soul was now ready to embrace the immaculate reality of SPIRIT. Matter could no longer be our truth.

With this I am emphasising, and in a way shouting from the roof tops, that this journey has always been about the birth of our feminine souls. However, I am able to comfort any man reading this book by also highlighting a paradox within this reality. It is that although the human soul is in essence feminine, through the Sacred Marriage between Heaven and Earth within it, we have entered into a VIRGIN CONCEPTION AND BIRTH of the glorious MASCULINE SPIRIT of our new *Age of Spirit*.

Yes, there is no escaping the fact that Humanity is inextricably both male and female. Our souls are MOTHER TO OUR MASCULINE SPIRIT. JOB DONE I would have loved to declare with barely containable pride and joy! But, no, oh no - not quite.

***

As in 2008, I had to fly back to Ambleton, and return to the summit of my spiritual Everest and the mini-pyramid of DIVINE LOVE at that summit. Only this third stage, and this stage alone, would allow me to complete the cosmic ritual, and close the circle of this final rite in my initiation.

A few days after landing in England, I opened up Alejandro Jodorowsky's book YO; EL TAROT once more; the book I had found with Sila in the bookshop in Salveira. But this time I found myself at the page with the illustration and text for **THE WORLD** Arcana. And there, astonishingly and completely serendipitously, she was again – THE VIRGIN!

However, this time she wasn't clothed in silk and gold as she had been on the altar of Campana's church, but instead she was wearing her BIRTHDAY SUIT. Totally naked, she held a long scarf-like piece of material around her pristine body, much like the tinsel I had wrapped around my neck in December 2013. Her whole naked form was encased in a circular garland of laurel leaves, and the four symbols of the four quarters of the human soul occupied the four corners of the image.

With this sudden and unforeseen encounter, I immediately experienced the EUREKA MOMENT the invisible realm had been guarding safely for me, and all the events since July 2013 fell into their rightful places. THIS COSMIC ODYSSEY AND PUZZLE WERE COMPLETE.

On March 27, I once again left my weekly counselling session, and as I walked down the street the third and final part of the initiation process presented itself to me. Yet again I found that the church on the corner of the street was open, but this time I wasn't in the least surprised. I walked into the darkness of the building ready to perform the ritual the invisible realm expected of me. The same man I had seen there before boarding the plane to Spain back in February was busily engaged in cleaning the altar, and so for a second time I asked him if I could light a candle.

He obliged by lighting the large candle at the very apex of the round pyramid-shaped candle holder I had come to before. When he moved away to leave me alone I took four small candles from the metal tray located below the pyramid, lit them from the main candle and then placed them gently in the holders just below the apex of the pyramid. In February I had only lit one candle, but this time the pattern I made was a cross formation – NORTH, SOUTH, EAST AND WEST - to create my very own representation of **THE WORLD** Arcana I had seen in Alejandro Jodorowsky's book!!! At that moment, all the angels and stained-glass windows in the church seemed to glow with an unusually ethereal light.

On my way back home, from my seat next to one of the bus windows I spied a sign in a shop window. We were only three days away from Mother's Day, and the sign left me no choice but to get off the bus, and buy it to create one final transcendental image.

Clutching my new purchase, I walked up the road and back to the photographic shop where I had taken the Christmas snap for my parents. This time I asked the young assistant to help me create a manifestation of MY PERSONAL GIFT TO THE WORLD. Of course these weren't the words I used when I spoke to him. I couldn't in any way explain what I was *really hoping to do,* but together, in a final Sacred Marriage between Heaven and Earth we produced a brand new, contemporary version of THE WORLD Arcana.

A NEW WORLD ARCANA FOR
OUR NEW AGE OF SPIRIT

On Tuesday, April 1: NOT SUPRISINGLY APRIL FOOL'S DAY I returned to the photographic shop to collect a CD disc from the assistant. I had asked him to store the image in this way in order to allow me to bring it home and present it to you all. Creating this manifestation of the last Arcana of The Tarot convinced me that I had finally completed my initiation into the *Age of Spirit*.

By enduring the many tests, trials and painful insights regarding Life's shadow I felt that I had finally been able to show the universe that I had demonstrated the tenacity, true grit and courage needed to give birth to spiritual light. More than pushing through to this final birth, I had held on, and held on knowing that only this HOLDING ON TO TRUTH would be the answer to the reason for my life.

Yes, as I said at the beginning of this chapter, life, the human soul, Mother Nature, and Mother Earth are all feminine in essence. The Tree of the Knowledge of Good and Evil had been our conscious search for that feminine truth within us, through the masculine energy of knowledge, but now we can say a fond farewell to its dominance, and embrace the Tree of Life with its feminine energy of intuition.

After 25 months of anguish and sacrifice I now knew within the very deepest part of my soul that the *Age of Spirit* is all about accepting that we are no longer in control. LET GO AND LET GOD as the various Twelve-Step Programmes say. My lesson had been that everything we needed to know, be and have, would be given to us. All along the invisible realm's message had been telling us to trust our feminine soul, and without fail she would always show us the way.

Once I had collected the disc from the photographic shop on April 1, I then went to my local internet cafe to check emails. As I approached the counter where the assistant Marie stood, I saw something astonishing hanging around her neck. It was an enamel image of the Virgin Mary. My eyes grew larger, and larger, as I approached Marie and casually asked her which Virgin it was.

"It's the Virgin of Miracles," she answered.

THE VIRGIN OF MIRACLES, MY MIND REPEATED TO ITSELF. WHAT ON EARTH IS HAPPENING?

Even though I had assumed that my journey had ended, there would be one final cosmic twist to this quest, and I was given the answer to this question the very next day.

The very next morning I caught a local bus to explore some charity shops near my apartment, and whilst browsing aimlessly in one I found myself deciding to buy a mirror for my soul mate J. The mirror was a sign to let him know that spiritual light was finally in his life. However, although this was what I was engaged in, my mind was still thinking about the amazing **Virgin of Miracles** pendant Marie had been wearing.

As I fumbled inside my purse for money, beside me, resting against the sale's assistant's counter was a children's book. It was called TREASURE HUNT. My God, I thought to myself, another sign, but I still don't understand what Marie's Virgin was trying to tell me. Then, the miracle occurred. I looked up, and straight in front of me was a photograph of a newly-born baby boy wrapped in a blanket. It was a calendar of pictures of the new heir to the British throne — little Prince George.

A MALE NEW-BORN BABY KAREN,
THAT'S THE MIRACLE!!!

You are looking at a miraculous symbolic manifestation of SPIRIT.
This is the miracle you have worked for over 19 long years!
The Divine Love which is the immaculately conceived miracle
'birthed' from Humanity's redeemed Virgin Soul.

When I arrived home, I sat down and started to analyse all of these signs. Easter was just a few weeks away, and that religious festival was all about SACRIFICE AND REBIRTH. Then, I picked up Alejandro's book YO: EL TAROT for a third time. This time I turned to the front of the book, and was astonished by what I saw. Alejandro had written the following about the meaning of The Tarot:

I ALLOW MY PARTS TO SPEAK

BUT I AM MUCH MORE THAN THE SUM OF THOSE PARTS.

I AM THE ETERNAL SILENCE WHICH ANIMATES THEM,

THE PEACE OF THE ABYSS WITHOUT LIMITS,

THE UNFATHOMABLE *DIAMOND* WHICH
NESTS INSIDE YOUR SOUL.

Translation from the Spanish: Karen Williams.
My *own italic* for the word **diamond**.

Right at the very end of my odyssey, I had been
given this astonishing piece of information – the most
important piece of my cosmic jigsaw puzzle!

When my seemingly never-ending quest had brought me to England at the end of 2004, I had arrived at the insight that The Alchemist was in fact something called THE ROAD OF THE DIAMONDS. The priest Father Jordi in Paulo's book The Pilgrimage had talked to him about it at the beginning of his journey to Santiago de Compostela in 1986. And now, through Alejandro Jodorowsky, I was being given the manifestation of what I had suspected all along.

My odyssey had truly been THE ROAD OF THE DIAMONDS, but, Alejandro's words were suddenly signalling to me that this road which I had taken so blindly and courageously was also another 'road':

THE FOOL'S JOURNEY THROUGH THE 22
MAJOR ARCANAS OF THE TAROT!

This was the journey I had identified back in the year 2000 when I had read about it in the book **THE GAME OF LIFE.** However I had never pursued any of my insights regarding this journey because, in a sense, my obsession with The Alchemist had taken me away from that particular 'road'. Nevertheless, now the truth was patently obvious:

Paulo Coelho's The Alchemist and
The Tarot
were telling exactly the same story,

ONLY TOLD IN TWO DISTINCT AND ORIGINAL WAYS.

The Alchemist had been about the process of Redemption, which ends with Arcana 19 of The Tarot.

The Tarot then completes The Road of the Diamonds by taking us through an initiation process with the last two Arcanas:

20 and 21.

Had Paulo known all of this, he would most certainly have been able to include Arcanas 20 and 21 in his story-telling masterpiece, but he didn't. His hero Santiago never encounters the very last two major Arcanas of The Tarot, But, then again, perhaps, in the great scheme of things the universe had always known better, and had decided to call on me to live out and put together the final pieces of this cosmic puzzle.

***

Now, after this extraordinary revelation, further connections started to come to me. I suddenly knew that my journey hadn't finished, but would actually end a few weeks after Easter Sunday. There would be a final six weeks to this quest, with each three week group representing a recapitulation of the 21 main Arcanas of the Tarot for the two halves of my soul. This would be followed by one further three-in-one week, which would mean that this epic would finally draw to its close on May 20, 2014 — a day after my fifty-sixth birthday!

How did I know all of this? The simple answer, dear friend, is that this pattern had happened before on numerous occasions during my journeying. At the end of several mini rebirths of my soul during the final part of my seventeen year journey of redemption I had discovered the pattern of these two sets of three weeks, followed by one week. I had never made any association with a process of recapitulation through the 21 major Arcanas of The Tarot, but now it was more than obvious that this was what awaited me.

Easter I calculated would fall in the middle of this final seven week finale, and that too was no accident of fate. It was more than significant because it was the Christian church's celebration of Christ's defeat of the physical world, and more importantly it continued the theme of sacrifice which I had been living out since March 2012, and also July 2013 as I had worked my way through **THE WORLD** Arcana.

Christ is the archetypal God/Man who defeats the hubris and evil of our material world by SACRIFICING HIMSELF. He quite literally had to die in order to bring into being a NEW WORLD ORDER. Two thousand years ago when he performed this metaphysical act no one believed that SPIRIT was the supreme reality governing our lives here on planet Earth. In a way it was conceived as a remote 'world' BEYOND OUR MATERIAL WORLD. But, Christ knew that only his death, and subsequent resurrection from that physical death, would be proof that this wasn't true.

So too, two thousand years later Nelson Mandela had defeated our material world through his extraordinary sacrifices both in life and death, and thus 2014 would be the cosmic year when Humanity would live out the final part of **THE WORLD** Arcana, and so defeat the inherent evil of the world in which we live.

By saying this I am not trumpeting the supremacy of Christianity over any other faith - far from it! In fact, the modern 'epidemic' of Christian evangelism we are seeing at the beginning of this 21st Century, along with evangelism in other faiths, is something I find deeply disturbing. This is because it represents the antithesis of Divine Love, aiming to separate people from one another and create a-so-called spiritual elite – a chosen people of God. Clearly, my odyssey has shown that all of us belong to that elite – we are all children of the Deity.

I knew implicitly that these last seven weeks of my journey would be the absolute opposite of all that zealous, self-righteous fundamentalism. Instead, it would be a celebration of a NO to religion, and a YES to SPIRIT, and where we have arrived as a species. Humanity, despite all its contradictions, and appalling acts of Evil, is an image of Divinity. That Diamond is in each and every one of us and it's time has come! So, dear friend, I took my insights and waited for the invisible realm to reveal to me its plan for the very end of my quest.

Sure enough, just as I had anticipated, STUFF STARTED TO HAPPEN.

30

THERE ARE NO ACCIDENTS

**Round like a circle in a spiral, like a wheel within
a wheel
Never ending or beginning on an ever spinning reel**

THE WINDMILLS OF YOUR MIND: ALAN AND MARILYN BERGMAN

TODAY is Wednesday May 7, and I am at the beginning of the sixth week of my seven week finale. Each of the previous weeks has involved a huge sacrifice from me, followed by the birth of spiritual light within me. These sacrifices have been intensely personal and complicated, and so I will not go into them. However, one fact I will reveal is that The Virgin has reappeared in my life during this time.

On two consecutive Sundays I met my soul mate J at a local church. He had been attending a meditation group at another venue, but the meetings had been transferred to the hall belonging to this church.

"I'll meet you by the statue of the Virgin" he told me on the first Sunday.

I hadn't visited this statue for nine long years, and so only vaguely remembered that she was in the grounds of the church. That Sunday, I duly made my way to where she stood, and then once again a miracle happened. I stared at her stone form surrounded by flowers, and the words by her feet jumped out at me, saying a huge cosmic "HELLO."

THE
IMMACULATE CONCEPTION

I was completely speechless! None of these amazing encounters with signs and manifestations can be manufactured. They happen only because we follow them, believe in them and honour them with pure hearts in search of Divine Love.

Today, two weeks now remain in front of me, and yet another miracle has entered my life. A few days ago a dear new friend gave me a set of audiotapes. They contain the voice of a very special woman: Brandon Bays. I was well aware that she had written a book several years ago, but I had deliberately avoided it. The esoteric book shelves of bookshops are full of the smiling faces of authors all claiming to have the answer to our hunger for healing. This lady's face had been part of that irritating and annoying band of 'gurus' I had seen so many times whenever I had gone into a bookshop in search of direction.

But, now Ms Bays had come into my life as if *'by accident'*. Or had she? Desperate for healing after so many months of sacrifice during my encounters with THE WORLD Arcana, I swallowed my pride and played the first C.D. in the audiotape pack. After 40 minutes I was deep inside a truly amazing miracle. This incredibly brave woman had discovered a way of experiencing HER INNER DIAMOND!!!

She had learnt to travel through layers of emotional pain, and then finally fall into a black hole which led into a place of Divine Love, Light and the presence of her God Self. Brandon Bays used the word DIAMOND constantly throughout the reading of her book, and I knew instantly beyond any shadow of a doubt that my journey through the 22 Tarot Arcanas — Paulo Coelho's ROAD OF THE DIAMONDS — had led me to this woman and her healing technique.

My odyssey had been a long and painful process of redemption — the redeeming of the universal shadow of Mankind — and now I stood poised and ready to fall into Brandon's black hole to encounter the diamond light of my God Self.

So, dear friend, am I going to delay the publication of this book to tell you all what will happen in the next two weeks? The answer to that question is no. I know this week I am currently beginning will be week six of the grand finale of my odyssey. It will involve my sixth sacrifice in order to meet our world's universal shadow with love, peace and acceptance, and I hope, but also believe, that it will be my penultimate sacrifice.

As I sit here writing these words, I have absolutely no idea what that sacrifice will be, and what the subsequent manifestation of spiritual light will look like after it — although I suspect I could be seeing the Immaculate Conception statue for a third and final time.

From my astonishing encounter with the work of Brandon Bays, I have made a decision for my seventh and final week of this quest. All my understanding regarding the meaning of these recent signs which have come to me seems to be telling me to undergo Ms Bay's JOURNEY PROCESS during that seventh week. As I have already said, my birthday falls at the end of that week, and I can't think of any better way to celebrate it.

The universe must be only too well aware of my deepest desires because today I have managed to find a Journey Practitioner to take me through the process on May 19 — my birthday. In our miraculous world the SECOND BIRTH — spiritual birth — of my soul will synchronistically COINCIDE with the fifty-sixth anniversary of my physical birth. My long and arduous Diamond Road will have led me to the portal of:

My Inner Spiritual Diamond.

Am I implying with all of this that Brandon Bay's Journey Process is the one and only way for the human race to come into contact with its spiritual light? Most certainly and categorically not; this couldn't be further from the truth I wish to share. All I am really saying is that at the end of my own *Road of the Diamonds* the invisible realm has MANIFESTED the perfect next personal and unique direction in which I need to go.

Now, as I have just alluded, I will be ready to EXPERIENCE MY DIAMOND SELF, and like Brandon Bays, all I need to do is be willing to LET GO AND FALL INTO THE DARKNESS - a new darkness which will take me to MY NEW LIGHT.

THE DIVINE LIGHT EACH OF US SHARES WITHIN
THE VERY HEART OF OUR SOULS.

This really has been the most amazing journey!!!*

***

*In the end I was unable to go through the black hole on my birthday, realising that I would have to leave this experience for a full Journey Weekend Workshop. Nevertheless, the Journey Practitioner I saw allowed me to reconnect with my abandoned three year old Karen, and bring her back into the centre of my life.

My encounters with THE WORLD Arcana surprised me by continuing after May 19, right up until and slightly beyond the summer solstice, finally ending on Tuesday June 24. The sacrifices I made during those 'extra' five weeks are far too intimate and private to relate here, but I wasn't in the least bit phased to find my quest continuing until the longest days of the year — clearly a time of MAXIMUM ILLUMINATION!

In those five weeks, apart from more pain, a really magical end-of-journey miracle came to me. Once again my quest seemed to be a case of LIFE IMITATING ART as I found it coming to a close in almost exactly the same way as it had in Paulo Coelho's The Alchemist. But, instead of returning to where my ruin had once stood, I chose to pay one final visit to the church in Campana on Tuesday May 27, as part of a week's stay with my parents in order to celebrate my birthday.

To my utter astonishment, as I neared the building, something quite extraordinary met my eyes. On a narrow island of shrubbery separating the two lanes of a small road at the side of the church, and just beside the trunk and roots of a small tree, an archaeological team had begun to excavate the ground. They were in the process of uncovering the remains of a medieval Moorish dwelling.

As I approached the hole the team were working inside, and peered down into it, I didn't see any gold coins, cups, necklaces or rings as Santiago had in THE ALCHEMIST - although it was more than possible that some of these objects might be found at a later stage in the excavation process. However, what I did see with exceptional clarity was that none of my 'fairy tale stuff' really mattered anymore.

After nineteen long years of questing, deep inside me I had finally learnt the difference between fables and facts. My personal 'Once Upon a Time' had revealed the two sides to life on planet Earth - Light and Darkness - and I was now also being confronted with yet another amazing truth. Life was a constant process of the MANIFESTATION OF SPIRIT.

And so, unsurprisingly, just like Paulo Coelho's Santiago, right at the very end of my journey, I too was finding TREASURE manifested as the remains of human life buried close to the roots of a tree in a hole in the ground.

There before me were stones collected from the surrounding sierra nearly six hundred years earlier. They had been cemented together by hands which had once dreamt of building homes to protect, shelter, and nurture their cherished loved ones.

YES, THAT WAS OUR TREASURE, AND REMAINS OUR TREASURE.

**THE LIGHT OF DIVINE LOVE
WHICH BURNS ETERNALLY WITHIN
OUR
HUMAN SOULS.**

***

"We shall not cease from exploration

and the end to all our exploring

will be to arrive where we started

and know the place for the first

time."

T.S. Eliott

EPILOGUE: YOUR DIAMOND SOUL

WHAT you are is a human being.
WHO you are is diamond light.

KAREN WILLIAMS

ON Monday, March 10, 2014 I caught the bus down to Salveira to say my goodbyes to Sila. She had accompanied me to the church in Campana, and we had shared a very important part of my journey. On the very next day, March 11, back in 1996 I had received my first copy of The Alchemist from my friends Mayka and Susana in the Canary Islands. But this time, eighteen years later, I was going in search of a different book and author.

I was intent on finding a new volume by Alejandro Jodorowsky, and so decided to drag my friend Sila to the bookshop in Salveira where I had first found Alejandro's work PSICOMAGIA: UNA TERAPIA PANICA back in 1995. My intuition was telling me that one of his books would turn out to be a PHYSICAL MANIFESTATION of the spiritual light I had been searching for with my friend. As the two of us scanned a shelf with several works by Alejandro, a particular book seemed to be the obvious contender.

It was titled: **YO: EL TAROT,** and once I had purchased it Sila and I headed towards the beach to say our farewells. But, as fate would have it, we never arrived there. Moments into our walk, Sila stopped in front of the window of a jewellery shop. She needed to buy her niece a birthday present, and thought that a pair of earrings would be the ideal gift.

We entered the shop and met the owner. Her name was Fatima, from Morocco, and it turned out that she had designed all the pieces in the shop. Sila quickly found some earrings she liked and began to remove the diamond studs she was wearing in order to try on this new pair of earrings. As she did so, she posed me an unexpected question:

"Do you ever wear earrings, Karen?"

"Yes," I replied, "once in a while I wear some studs to stop the holes in my ears from closing up."

"Here," said Sila as she began to pierce my ears with the diamond studs she had just removed from her own ears, and with this seemingly utterly innocuous act I immediately erupted with an explosion of joy.

I had never ever explained to my friend that for many years now I had come to believe that The Alchemist was in fact something called THE ROAD OF THE DIAMONDS, and here she was, giving me her DIAMOND STUDS. In an astonishing turn of events I stood in Fatima's shop finding myself in the middle of a 'cosmic confirmation' of the theory to which my intuition had guided me all those long years ago.

***

Fatima was obviously surprised by my reaction to what my friend had just done, and quite spontaneously responded with an extraordinary act.

"Don't worry," she said, seeing that Sila now no longer had any studs to put in her ears once she had finished trying on the earrings she hoped to buy for her niece.

"Take these studs, I have plenty of them. You can have them for free." And, a second later, she handed my friend another pair of diamond studs; artificial ones of course, but diamonds none the less. Sila placed them in the holes in her ears, and finally, as my friend and I stood in the shop in a rapture of gratitude, she noticed that Fatima was also wearing diamond earrings.

"Yes, these are diamonds too," Fatima said when my friend drew our attention to them. "They are the first earrings I ever made, and they mean so much to me. I never take them off." My mouth fell open, and my mind was in complete turmoil.

Here we were, three women in an empty jewellery shop,
all wearing diamond earrings! How could this have
happened, and who on earth would believe me?

Perhaps, that is why this book has been written, and why this story most definitely needed to be told.

ONCE UPON A TIME THERE TRULY WAS
A ROAD OF THE DIAMONDS.

And even if there had only ever been one Santiago who had lived in Andalusia next to a magical ruin, many more Santiagos — and Anwars as well — have travelled that magical road.

Thank God for the reality of connection.

***

Finally, I would like to close with a poem written by an unknown nineteenth-century soldier. The poem has no title, but could easily be called TREASURE.

His words reflect exactly what I found my odyssey to be: a testimony to how the journey of life is a journey of AWAKENING. We travel through our lives thinking with our very clever heads that we 'know' what we are looking for. But, slowly and almost imperceptibly, just like Paulo Coelho's shepherd boy Santiago, an invisible realm begins to prepare us for the truth. Love — DIVINE LOVE - is that truth and the great mystery we have been asked to uncover.

IT IS OUR GREATEST TREASURE.

This quest has taught me that, whilst we search for Love, paradoxically it is love itself that travels with us and weaves the tapestry of coincidences, mysterious 'happenings' and signs which enable us to make the journey.

Back in 1987 Paulo Coelho decided to be true to his very own personal *once upon a time* buried deep inside the depths of his childlike heart. He followed that dream and it became The Alchemist. Then, quite independently, on another part of the planet, and at another moment in time, I decided to follow mine. The result has been this story TREASURE: a powerful testimony to the interconnectedness of all our hearts, minds and spirits.

That interconnectedness takes us all in many amazingly different directions, as each of us tries to find our own redemption and inner diamond. And, in the end, despite those apparent 'differences' between us, we come to know the absolute truth: THERE IS, AND ONLY EVER WILL BE, ONE TREASURE.

MAY THAT DIVINE LOVE BEYOND PRICE GUIDE YOU FOREVER.

I asked God for strength that I might achieve;
I was made weak that I might learn humbly to obey.

I asked for help that I might do greater things;
I was given infirmity that I might do better things.

I asked for riches that I might be happy;
I was given poverty that I might be wise.

I asked for power that I might have the praise of others;
I was given weakness that I might feel the need for God.

I asked for all things that I might enjoy life;
I was given life that I might enjoy all things.

I got nothing that I asked for— but everything I'd hoped for.

My unspoken prayers were answered.
I am among all men most richly blessed!

POSTSCRIPT

When Earth sings out the song of Divine Love,
a second dawn will come to us;
the dawn of peace, the dawn of Life.

ANON

THE BIG DREAM OR 'GOING GREEK'

All you need is Love

THE BEATLES

FINALLY, to end this epic tale I wish to answer the following question: what will our new *Age of Spirit* look like? What will it mean for us to live from **THE BIG DREAM** of Divine Love assigned to us eons ago by a universal intelligence? Well, you will be very surprised to know that we have already been given a picture of this NEW WORLD.

God, Spirit, Higher Power, the Universe or whatever term speaks to you personally hasn't decided to bamboozle us with a complex, highly esoteric version of this new reality. No, the Deity decided to do it through another fairy tale - the film I saw with my friend Sophie back in the autumn of 2002:

MY BIG FAT GREEK WEDDING.

The universal language of the Soul of the World has deemed that the symbolism of this new age for Mankind will be found in the spirit of Greece and her people. This small European country, which thousands of years ago gave birth to our modern Western civilisation, remains a central archetype in our collective unconscious. The film, whose main metaphor is 'all things Greek', could be considered the cosmic sequel to The Alchemist, and is a modern version of - you guessed it - Beauty and the Beast.

As I explained in Chapter Eleven, the unexpected serendipity that allowed me to see the film dubbed into Spanish in 2002 opened up for me its two meanings. On a superficial level it is the classic love story of boy meets girl and the triumph of true love over adversity. However, lurking in the 'HIDDEN' subtext is a very modern and transcendental version of Beauty and the Beast.

***

The film is set in the USA, which just so happens to be where we find the maximum expression in our contemporary world of the Tree of the Knowledge of Good and Evil. The hero of this tale is Ian Miller - a Beast with a difference because he is on the brink of a massive change of heart. At the start of the movie his world is that of a typical American W.A.S.P. It represents the controlling shadow of the **material** half of the human soul - the cold, rational, thinking-dominated culture of white, Anglo-Saxon, protestant America.

But, lovely, adorable Ian has already taken significant steps to leave his own inner beastliness behind, and embrace his inner prince. We know this because in the movie he is portrayed as a high school English teacher. Through this device, we are allowed to see Ian's poetic princely soul, but the story also makes it clear that other parts of our hero are still uncomfortably 'stuck' in his 'beastly' environment.

One day, into Ian's life walks Beauty, personified by the Greek American character of Toula Portokalos. At the beginning of MY BIG FAT GREEK WEDDING Toula is in a bit of a mess. She first meets Ian in her family's restaurant and our heroine doesn't need any time at all to see that her Beast is really a prince. However, Toula is bogged down in the unconscious shadow aspects of her greekness. Greece, and being Greek, is used throughout the movie as the transcendent symbol representing the **mystical** half of Mankind's soul. The 'light' inside Ian, with which Toula instantly falls in love, SPURS HER ON TO CONSCIOUSNESS.

She realises intuitively that she cannot sit back and wallow in the unconscious aspects of the **mystical** half of herself – Ian is her wake up call. This means that she must leave behind her comfortable, but imperfect unconscious condition in order to manifest her conscious identity. And so Toula transforms herself into a personification of Jung's CONSCIOUS MASTER FUNCTION OF INTUITION within the

mystical half of the soul when she signs up for a computer course, and in so doing, finds herself 'accidentally' meeting Ian for a second time.

This second encounter with her 'prince' is now the conscious manifestation in the outside world of the **material** half of her soul, and with this the stage is set for what the movie is really all about. At this point in the action Toula and Ian are ready to play out Part II of The Alchemist. They no longer have to meet in order to engage in a 'beating' between themselves. and the consequent redemption of their shared shadow. The story takes up the thread of The Alchemist AFTER redemption has been achieved.

Ian's second sighting of our Beauty leads to him falling in love with Toula, and this is when he understands that a new life awaits him. It is evidence of the moment in which he recognises that the light of Divine Love within the **material half** of his own soul — his inner Prince — is his one and only truth. By suddenly 'seeing' that Toula is the **mystical** complement of his own inner light - his Beauty - Ian no longer needs to hold onto any aspect of his beastly world.

Once this has happened Ian is ready to give up the remaining parts of the shadow's dominance of the **material** half of his soul and move from the Tree of the Knowledge of Good and Evil to the dominance of intuition or SPIRIT - in other words the **mystical** half of his soul. The movie beautifully portrays this shift to a new paradigm and a NEW WORLD for Ian when he accepts to be baptised in the Greek Orthodox Church and:

'Go Greek'.

In that instant at the high altar, as the water of baptism falls over his head, he chooses his new life - to be reborn to the new *Age of Spirit* and his true spiritual identity.

Ian's conversion to 'Greekness' symbolises his understanding that there is no more fruit to be eaten from the Tree of the Knowledge of Good and Evil. That path has taken him as far as he can ever go with it.

Ian and Toula marry in Aphrodite's Palace - more symbolism as Aphrodite was the Greek goddess of love - and end up making their new home right next door to Toula's parents' house. Our hero and heroine have left behind W.A.S.P America, and have moved into their 'Greek World'; a place where intuition reigns supreme.

***

The story is incredibly profound in that it shows us how neither the **material** half of the soul alone, nor the **mystical** half, has all the answers. In fact, the union between these two personifications of the two halves of the human spirit is what I discovered when trying to analyse the Temperance Tarot card back in the spring of 2000. Just as the Temperance card showed me that each half must break out of its isolation and seek to unite with the other if Divine Love – or **THE BIG DREAM** - is to be realised, now MY BIG FAT GREEK WEDDING was showing me the very same truth, but so much more besides.

Mystical Toula is prepared to enter the material incarnated reality of life to find her other half, and Ian is willing to abandon his 'beastly' world and move forward into a new way of being. Divine Love – our **BIG DREAM** - can now be accessed directly through intuition's dominance, and the fruit of the Tree of Life is waiting to be eaten by our new archetypal Adam and Eve. As I have already said, Ian and Toula are symbols of this archetypal pattern of our new age. In other words, the melding together of the spiritual light they both carry is once again a beautiful example of the Sacred Marriage between Heaven and Earth.

It is also the story of where Santiago and the leader of the refugees would have found themselves had there been a sequel to The Alchemist.

So there you have it, dear reader, the explanation of what we can look forward to once Redemption Road has finally been completed. My honest opinion is that I believe that as a species we have already reached the top of the Pyramid of Redemption, and the *Age of Spirit* is now on our doorstep. However, I also believe that there has to be a critical mass of individuals who have CONSCIOUSLY redeemed their shadows before the full initiation into the new order can take place. And as I hinted earlier, this may take a few more decades before that tipping point is reached.

Pierre Teilhard de Chardin was right - when we have mastered the physical world and all it glories Mankind will discover fire for the second time in its history, and in so doing harness the energies of Divine Love. That moment has come, albeit not completely, and we humans are now within sight of:

the beginning of Mankind's realisation of our

BIG DREAM.

The Tree of the Knowledge of Good and Evil has taken us as far as it can, and to expect to journey further with it would be sheer madness and folly.

The global financial crisis of 2008, global warming, epidemic levels of violence, drug addiction, sexual perversion, poverty and disease, all point to the historical moment in which we find ourselves. For those who hope that we can find solutions to our crises and still live in the same way, I have bad news. The old order cannot solve these problems pressing in on us, because despite all the marvels we have created and discovered as a species, it is the old way which has also created the problems we now face.

The times in which we are living are changing radically and seismically as we confront the greatest leap of faith presented to our species after two thousand years. Do we wish to continue to be creatures of shadow, or embrace our spiritual identity as creatures of light? We have grown out of the old home that served us so well, and despite any feelings of nostalgia for what once was, now a new dawn shines before us, and we have no choice but to turn to it and say YES.

**I will give you a new heart, and put a new spirit
within you.
Ezekiel 36: 26 (Old Testament) NIV VERSION**

***

As I said in Chapter 23, all of these insights began to flood into my consciousness as I embarked on the writing of the first edition of TREASURE in August 2009, and so sure was I of the truths I had uncovered that I took a bold step and DARED TO PREDICT THE FUTURE.

In December 2009 – and also April 2010 - just as I was 'penning' the last paragraphs of the first edition of TREASURE, I confidently projected myself forward into the summer of 2012, and wrote the following:

> As if to underline what I have just said, the universe will be marking the change of era with nothing less than the Olympic Games in London in the summer of 2012.
>
> Before the dawning of a new Age of Spirit can take place (signalled from the invisible realm as being symbolised by the spirit of Greece), our collective 'material Greece' must be met and redeemed. Another final, and definitive journey to the 'pyramids' must be made.
>
> Paradoxically, what will happen in London will have next to nothing to do with sport as such. This will be the Tree of the Knowledge of Good and Evil's final stand - if you are going to go out, it might as well be in style!* Millions of people will converge on a small island nation over a two-week period to celebrate excellence, sacrifice and achievement. But will that be what we see?
>
> Just over three hundred events and ten thousand five hundred competitors later, and with a gigantic carbon footprint etched onto our beloved planet Earth, perhaps we will understand that this modern Olympic movement has become a colossal juggernaut, and its flame now burns more in celebration of the shadow of the **material** half of our souls than anything else.
>
> What I predict is that in making a pilgrimage in search of this ancient Greek ideal rewritten in a modern form, we will all find ourselves taking a 'beating' at the end of it. In that moment of darkness,

a real 'end of an era' knowing will engulf us all, and then, just as it had for Santiago when he felt death close to him as he endured the beating at the end of his journey, our epiphany will come.

We will 'see the light', and with it experience the dawn of our SPIRIT - of who we really are. It is then that we will understand that a better way lies before us - the way of Divine Love, and we will know it in our hearts.*

In London in 2012, as we walk away from the waste and debris of the celebration of a very **'material Greece'**, we will have found the light of our 'spiritual Greece' and perhaps, just like Ian Miller, finally have come home. In **My Big Fat Greek Wedding**, Ian lets Toula know a new life has begun for him when, just after his baptism, he proudly announces, 'I'm Greek now!' It is my hope that, one day soon, we will all be able to say the same.

Hope sees the invisible, feels the intangible, and achieves the impossible.

HELEN KELLER

***(Now in 2016 I can see that this prediction finally bore fruit in the Rio de Janeiro Olympics. Why do I make this claim? Simply because the whole of the games took place under the outspread arms of the statue of Christ the Redeemer — one huge sign from the invisible realm that humanity has reached the very top of the Pyramid of Redemption, and now needs to change course.**

In April 2010, as I sat correcting the manuscript of the very first version of TREASURE, I became aware that events on the world stage had started to pre-empt my prediction concerning the London Olympic Games in 2012. Back then, in 2010, only six short years after its

own incredibly expensive Olympics, Greece was living the trauma of needing a rescue plan to save its whole economy from catastrophe.

This, of course, I interpreted at the time to be yet another sign that we were all caught in the material shadow of the Tree of the Knowledge of Good and Evil. The Greeks would be the first in the developed part of the western world to take the 'beating', as all of us would begin to face the end of this era of Redemption, but I knew instinctively that they most certainly wouldn't be the last.)

***

Now that August 2012 has been and gone, and also another Olympic Games in Rio, I, like everyone else, know full well that the sky didn't 'blacken' over London and thunder clap as the world sat glued to its television screens from Baltimore to Beijing witnessing the closing ceremony of the 2012 Olympic Games.

Contrary to my doom-laden predictions, the global carnival 'appeared' to have been a total triumph, and most people seemed to be as euphoric and 'high' about the whole affair as the athletes with their cherished, hard-won medals. There was quite simply a feeling that ALL WAS WELL IN OUR WORLD, and that FEELING was repeated once more in the Rio de Janeiro Games in 2016. But behind these 'global parties' REAL LIFE WENT ON AS USUAL

Greece remained in a precarious state, finding herself plunging into an economic abyss as she started to pay the price for being part of a Euro Club whose membership fee she never could afford in the first place. The world's oceans remained in jeopardy as they went on getting warmer, rain forests continued to fall, and millions of men, women and children still found themselves sleeping in rat-infested gutters and streets around the planet.

Worst of all, as the wealthy part of the world turned the athletic and physical glories of youth into a pinnacle of human endeavour and achievement, collectively humanity turned a blind eye to another set of youthful souls. These were the vulnerable, young, rudderless, and disenfranchised adults 'seduced' into participating in the mediaeval barbarity of Daesh or I.S.

There were also the young men of the Syrian army, brainwashed by State propaganda, who continued to obey orders and slaughter other youthful young men and women, innocent children and adults whilst our sporting jamboree rolled on its merry way.

The truth is that over the last twelve summers there has
been no Olympic dream for either the vast majority
of humanity, or our beloved Mother Earth.

It would be easy for many people to smirk at and also ridicule the apparently *exaggerated nature* of my 2009 and 2010 predictions. – especially as I erroneously saw the end of our Redemption Road taking place in London rather than in Rio. However, I know that in one respect I was visibly and very tangibly vindicated, and this vindication came in the form of the film director Danny Boyle's opening ceremony for the London games.

Mr Boyle and I are strangers to one another in our conscious lives, nevertheless deep within the collective unconscious of our species, he and I have been:

'singing from the same hymn sheet'.

In Chapter 23 I spoke of all of us reaching the very end of our journey up through The Tree of the Knowledge of Good and Evil. Well, quite unconsciously, but synchronistically, Danny Boyle 'spoke' of the very same thing in his ceremony – except that he chose to ignore all the evil aspects of that climb.

On the surface the Olympic opening ceremony in London was his recreation of the last three hundred years of Britain's 'glorious' history. He took the television viewing public from a pastoral land of farms and farmers, through the birth of the industrial revolution, and all the wonders that this produced, into our modern digital age of cyberspace and global communication. However, to me, this was self-evidently NOT JUST WHAT IT SEEMED – a celebration of the spirit of a nation – but also a clear manifestation of humanity's ascent through the last three hundred years of the summit of the Tree of the Knowledge of Good and Evil.

Of course Danny didn't know that this was what he had created, and as I have just said, he also had to leave out the truly 'horrible parts'. After all, social etiquette demands that one doesn't bring doom and gloom to a party. Nevertheless, if anyone wishes to contradict my take on the opening ceremony, then please do so; I doubt whether you will find a different explanation.

In August 2012 the end of an era which I predicted in Chapter 23 was there for all the world to see on their television screens and computer monitors. The **Soul of the World** had used a gigantic communication platform in order to give us its message, and because human beings are so very slow to respond to THE WRITING ON THE WALL, it did exactly the same at the Rio Olympic Games four years later.

Ask any Syrian, Iraqi, or Afghani refugee – or a favela-inhabiting Brazilian - if they had been part of these 'celebrations.'

If collectively, as a human family, we have any humanity left inside our hearts, then the gore and glory days of the Age of Redemption, which are now at last drawing to a close, must be seen clear-sightedly for what they have been. Naturally, we should continue to look back and celebrate with pride and nostalgia the greatest triumphs and successes of the Piscean Age – for not to do so would be completely inhumane – but we must now also bravely embrace the new *Age of Spirit,* and collectively CHOOSE to face our NEW DAWN.

We will from now on slowly be discovering the
second fire of Divine Love – a love written into our
hearts before we even knew who we were.

***

Finally, at this very endpoint I would like to thank you, dear reader, with all my heart and soul for taking this journey with me.

I know full well that it hasn't been easy - but 'needs must' as the saying goes. May we each embrace our new beginning with hearts, minds and spirits willing to trust in the mystery which stretches out before us. Life was, and is, that great mystery we came into many millions of years ago, and will remain so until the very end of time.

At its heart is the gentle beating pulse of Divine Love, and if we can be passionate, unconditional lovers of this truth, then we will be putting the Divine in the driving seat of our lives. With that, and only that, can we then start working towards all our transcendental dreams of peace, love and kindness, and with enough faith and perseverance, they will one day all come true.

Dream on, Mankind, dream on!

The time has come to proclaim to a nobler humanity, the freedom of the spirit...

F. W.J. VON SCHELLING

COINCIDENCES: TARIFA AND TANGIERS

MANKIND'S NEW WORLD AND THE BIG DREAM.

AS promised, I will now give the reason as to why in the story of The Alchemist Santiago journeys to Tarifa and then to Tangiers on his quest for treasure, and why, apparently COINCIDENTALLY I did the very same thing.

The explanation came to me in a friendship diary given to me by my neighbours Ruth and John when I first moved into my studio apartment in Ambleton. One of the entries for March recounts how the author, Francis Gay, has a friend called Joe who is a coin collector. One day Joe shows Francis a picture of an old Spanish coin that has the Pillars of Hercules engraved on it and the inscription: 'Ne Plus Ultra' - which translates as NO MORE BEYOND.

In antiquity, the Pillars of Hercules were two mountain peaks on either side of the entrance to the Strait of Gibraltar. The northern peak was the rock of Gibraltar, and the southern peak was a mountain on the North African mainland. They marked the boundary of the known world at that time. In 1492, Columbus travelled beyond this boundary by sailing across the Atlantic Ocean, and discovered the new world of the continent of America. After this, the Spanish coins were recast and Ne Plus Ultra changed to Plus Ultra — MORE BEYOND.

The Pillars of Hercules mark the inner entrance of the Strait of Gibraltar, and Tarifa and Tangiers mark the outer entrance of the Strait. Many months later I went onto Google Earth and saw the satellite picture of the strait, with Tarifa and Tangiers located on either side like sentinels standing guard over this gateway. I was immediately struck by how I seemed to be looking at the entrance to a birth canal with the womb-like Mediterranean Sea behind it. These two findings coalesced for me into one single flash of insight, and I suddenly realised that Tarifa and Tangiers, together with the rest of the Strait, were situated at a point of archetypal soul energy on our planet.

The Strait was effectively a birth canal
dividing two worlds from each other:
THE OLD AND THE NEW.

Santiago and I had gone in search of soul rebirth, and the hidden treasure of a NEW WORLD within ourselves. To find that new world, we had had to leave our old worlds behind, and so we both intuitively journeyed to the place that separates old from new — THIS ENIGMATIC STRAIT. Jung knew how the inner archetypes of our souls also exist in the world outside us, and it is the constant interaction of **inner** with **outer**, and vice versa, which is the metaphysical alchemy we are all engaged in.

This proves more clearly than ever that we and our planet are one. Whatever we do to her, we do to ourselves, and whatever we do to ourselves, we do to her. She is the amazing blue-green jewel both outside us and inside us. She is our heart and soul and faithfully, despite earthquakes, floods, and all manner of other natural disasters, she has taken us to the beginning of a new age. Now, it is time for us to embrace this new beginning with every fibre of our being. Love is calling: CALLING US HOME. If our planet Earth is truly Mother Earth, then let us become her children; children of the *Age of Spirit*. And like all mothers, I pray that She may feel justly proud of each and every one of us.

APPENDIX

A Summary of the Plot of Paulo Coelho's
THE ALCHEMIST

KAREN WILLIAMS.

SANTIAGO is a shepherd boy living in the region of Andalusia in southern Spain. He is young and full of dreams. He longs to be able to see and experience the world around him. His parents' lives and the life in his village seem to offer nothing to capture his enthusiasm and imagination.

One night, whilst sleeping inside the ruin of an abandoned church in the Andalusian countryside, Santiago has a powerful dream for a second time. It tells him that if he journeys to the pyramids of Egypt he will find his treasure there.

As he drives his flock of sheep over the countryside, he heads for a small coastal town called Tarifa. There he meets a stranger – a King – who tells him that he must have the courage to follow his personal destiny.

The King introduces Santiago to the concept of the Soul of the World, and tells the boy that this soul speaks to everyone through 'omens' or signs when a person is willing to open their heart to their deepest dreams.

And so with this, Santiago sells the King a tenth of his flock and takes a boat to Tangiers to begin his epic journey to the pyramids. In this small Moroccan town he works for a crystal merchant and finally acquires enough money to join a camel train crossing the desert.

Amongst the travellers making the same journey he meets an English man who tells him about alchemy and the ancient alchemists. The Englishman is also living out his own dream – a desire to find a real-life alchemist.

The desert journey is long and challenging, but begins to reveal signs from the Soul of the World to the young shepherd. Then, as if by chance, Santiago meets his soul mate Fatima at an oasis, and very shortly after that the alchemist the Englishman had talked about - just outside the oasis.

This man offers himself as a metaphysical guide to the boy so that he may accomplish his goal of finding his treasure at the pyramids of Egypt. However, just as the shepherd is within striking distance of that goal the alchemist leaves Santiago to complete the last part of his journey alone.

The young shepherd reaches the pyramids, and there, as he looks out on these extraordinary stone mountains, he begins to dig a hole in a large dune. He digs, and digs, finding nothing, and then is suddenly discovered by a band of refugees from the desert tribal wars.

They find gold on the shepherd, and immediately assume that he is digging for more gold. They force the boy to continue excavating the ground, but as daylight breaks, the dig reveals nothing. Contemptuous of this stranger, they beat him to within an inch of his life.

As Santiago feels his own physical death very close to him, he remembers the words of the alchemist, warning him that no money can save a person's life. In this moment, his epiphany comes, and he knows in an instant that his own precious life is his treasure.

He quickly confesses his dream to the gang, in the hope that they will free him. The leader of the refugees is the man who finally decides his fate. When he hears Santiago's dream, he laughs and tells the shepherd that 'coincidentally' on this very same dune, he too had a recurrent dream.

He dreamt of a treasure buried under the roots of a sycamore tree inside the ruin of an abandoned church in Andalusia, Spain. He then tells the boy that despite this, he was never so stupid as to travel hundreds of miles because of a recurrent dream. And with this the leader and the refugees abandon the blood-stained shepherd on the dune.

Weeks later, Santiago returns to the ruined church in Andalusia, and begins to dig under the roots of the sycamore tree inside the church. Sure enough, just as the leader of the refugees had said, he finds treasure - a chest of gold coins and precious jewels forgotten about long, long ago.

ABOUT THE AUTHOR

KAREN Williams was born in London to a Russian mother and English father in 1958. Karen believes that we are all born into our destinies, and hers knocked on her door at a very early age. Whilst Karen's classmates played games, she worried about the state of the world.

As she grew up this young misfit tried her best to fit into societal expectations.After leaving school she faithfully completed a degree in Psychology, but as soon as those studies had finished, her REAL LIFE began. The confusions, questions and pain that hadn't found answers in conventional life became the driving forces of her life.

Those questions led Karen to Andalusia, southern Spain in 1984, and ten years later cosmic forces met their young pilgrim and an extraordinary metaphysical journey began. That destiny was to be the living out of Paulo Coelho's allegory THE ALCHEMIST.

From 1995 till 2014 Karen lived out an incredible spiritual quest, in which she dared to step out of all conventional parameters, and follow my inner light. Her spirit was in search of itself - her inner TREASURE - and that search almost cost Karen her life. The toll on her health was huge, but despite the suffering she endured, it allowed her to demonstrate that we all carry the light of truth within us.

Society may wish to rob us of that truth, but if we are prepared to stake our lives on what we know inside our hearts, we will be the winners in the end.

You can find Karen on her facebook page: TREASURE: A Soul Journey with the Invisible.